MY DRUG DEALER

BROUGHT ME TO

GOD

MYDRUGDEALER BROUGHT ME TO GOD

I was my worst villain.
I was my worst victim.
I learned how to be my best hero!

BY RYAN JOSEPH ALLEN

ACADEMY
PRESS

For permission requests, write to the below address:
Ryan Joseph Allen
187 Pavilion Parkway #244
Newport, KY 41071

The opinions expressed by the Author are not necessarily those held by PYP Academy Press.

Ordering Information: Quantity sales and special discounts are available on quantity purchases by corporations, associations, and others. For details, contact the author at Ryan.allen@ lovemustwin.org.

Edited by: Ryan Joseph Allen
Cover design by: Nelly Murariu
Typeset by: Medlar Publishing Solutions Pvt Ltd., India

Printed in the United States of America.

ISBN: 978-1-951591-88-5 (hardcover)
ISBN: 978-1-951591-86-1 (paperback)
ISBN: 978-1-951591-87-8 (ebook)

Library of Congress Control Number: 2021912065

First edition, September 2021

The mission of the Publish Your Purpose Academy Press is to discover and publish authors who are striving to make a difference in the world. We give underrepresented voices power and a stage to share their stories, speak their truth, and impact their communities. Do you have a book idea you would like us to consider publishing? Please visit PublishYourPurposePress.com for more information.

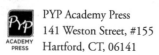 PYP Academy Press
141 Weston Street, #155
Hartford, CT, 06141

DEDICATION

To my version of GOD. An all-loving, all-caring, all-forgiving presence of light and love. Also known to me as Creator, Universal Energy, Gaia, Spirit, Oneness, Source, and Divine! Infinite gratitude to you and your everlasting support, guidance, and LOVE!

To my daughter, Harper, who stands by my side every day. Who encourages me to be strong, courageous, and kind in every moment. My reason for turning my life around. My greatest joy. I love you unconditionally!

To my mother, mom, and mommy! Who gave birth to me and has been my best teacher in life. Who thought your mom could also double as your bestie? My hero when I was a kiddo, today, and always!

To my twin flame, best friend, and companion in countless adventures. Who makes my life brighter, fuller and reminds me to love myself (when I often forget) simply by how much he loves me. I love you, Will—forever, for always, for eternity!

To my sweet, caring, and fun brothers, Brent and Cody! I'm always going to have your backs, and I'm honored to have such upstanding siblings who treat people with kindness and respect—momma must have done something right.

To all my amazing family and supportive friends: Ron, Shauna, Papaw (Grandpa Bill), Karen, Walt, Mamaw, Ed, Nanny, PawPaw, my cousins/aunts/uncles, Kim, Stacy, and countless other beautiful humans in my life!

To my teachers, co-workers, past lovers, old and new friends, and every amazing boss and crappy one along the way! You all helped form me into who I am today.

To my amazing manuscript strategist and friend, Fern Pessin, I simply could not have done this without you! I was divinely called to you and am so grateful I listened to that call!

To Love Must Win for helping me morph into the person I am today! For all the love you allowed me to pour into you that, in return, poured out into the lives and hearts of others! One of the most significant and best teachers, accomplishments, and honors!

To LOVE. You saved my life. You showed me how to not only truly love others, but more importantly, how to love myself!

CONTENTS

Foreword . . . . *xiii*

Preface . . . . *xv*

PART I   BECOMING RYAN 1

1   From Mom's Point of View 3

2   Ryan: Before I Was Born 9

3   Mom, Dad, and Me 15

4   Six Years Old—Chains 19

5   Be Careful What You Say 23

6   13 Years Old—A Cut for Help 27

7   The Birds and Bees 31

8   13 Going on Addict 35

9   Bad Influence 41

10   Free to Be Me 43

11   Mother Issues 53

12   Confrontation Reaps Turmoil 57

13   Living with Dad 67

14   The Pink Bath 79

15   The Airport. 85

16   A New Life 95

17   Here We Go Again 109

PART II   RYAN AWAKENING 113

18   To Heroin or Not to Heroin 115

19   Trippin' and Rippin' 119

20   Evanescence 123

21   Rebooting 127

22   Messages in the Dark. 139

23   School of Metaphysics 149

24   Joey 159

25   Education 163

PART III   THE ADDICTION TUG OF WAR 171

26   Recovery from Addiction. 173

PART IV   ADULT—RYAN 183

27   Perfectly Imperfect 185

28   Safe Haven 2015 189

29   LGBTQ+ Bible Study 193

30   Falling for a Married Man 199

31   Intention of Beliefs 207

PART V   THE WORK 217

32 Multi-faith 219

33 Pulse! 223

34 Dr. Allen, I Presume 233

35 Bestism 235

36 Five Connections, Five Love Languages 239

PART VI   NEXT GENERATION 245

37 Letter to the Reader from Harper (Age 10) 247

38 Is Hell Real? 249

Letter to Reader from Will *255*

Epilogue—Trauma Impact on Relationships *261*

Love Must Win *263*

Acknowledgments *269*

About the Author *273*

Hire Ryan to Speak *275*

About Love Must Win *277*

WORKBOOK 279

Healing Reflections, Exercises, and Affirmations
    for Self-Growth and Awareness *281*

REFLECTIONS & EXERCISES 285

Reflections *287*

Exercises *299*

FOREWORD

BY MOM/CATHY G

Probably every mother dreams of being valued and appreciated by their children. When Ryan asked me to write the foreword to this (his first) book, I couldn't breathe for a moment. I was so happy and excited that he had asked me to contribute. You see, Ryan and I have had our challenging times where we didn't speak to each other, especially when he lived with his father; we had little to no contact. Ryan and I spent far too much time and energy during his teenage years unknowingly fighting against each other. I diligently worked on my part and had moved to forgiveness within a short time, but like anyone working on a relationship with an addict, I didn't trust Ryan and needed proof that only time could reveal. When Ryan was ready, we both spent time together; some gracefully with ease and some in not so graceful ways, working to heal our relationship. Over an amazingly short period of time, less than a year, we arrived at a loving place of best friendship.

I know it will appear unbelievable when you read these pages, but if we can heal our relationship, there is tremendous hope for all parent-child relationships. We travel together and hope to work together in the future. We are each other's confidants and biggest supporters. The love I hold for my son is some of the strongest a person can hold for another. I'm writing this forward and chapter one because it is my story of hope to all parents and children.

It can be done! You can move from the worst of times in which there seems to be no hope to a deep-connected loving relationship. That's why this request from my son means everything to me.

For parents feeling challenged by the behaviors or attitude of their child, confused about what to do next, perhaps our story will illuminate a path. It is my hope that by reading my son's story, our story, all people will learn that no matter where you begin, you can achieve the life you aspire to, the love you desire, the peace you crave. I hope he can inspire and move you the way he inspires and moves me. I couldn't be prouder of him, me, and us. I love what we've cultivated and achieved!

The lesson Ryan wants to share, as he explained to me, is that we are all learning all the time, and no one is perfect. So, if you take your knowledge and "knowings" (as Ryan calls them) and share them honestly, then the people who need to see and hear them will benefit from your experiences and pain and absorb what they need to learn. And that's what he is doing here.

Ryan explained how generational trauma impacts each of us. I acted as a very young mother out of my own experiences. Ryan's father behaved following the model set by his own parents. Ryan first acted as a young father out of his distressful experiences, but his journey to spiritual awakening has brought him to father his maturing daughter in a healthy, beautiful way.

From Ryan's pain, he has emerged as a leader, coach, counselor, and motivator and has helped so many others find their path. Isn't that the most important thing, ultimately, what we do and how we contribute to the world?

PREFACE

My first thought of suicide was at the age of six. My last attempt, I was seventeen. My last thoughts about suicide I was twenty-three. God, church, family, and love impacted all the highs and lows of the first quarter-century of my life. The quest to be accepted, welcomed, and connected drove me to self-medicate, act out, and generally do things I now recognize were calls for help.

To be clear from the start, this book is my story, told from my perspective. It isn't anyone else's story, as I don't share other people's personal stories without permission. But I think you need to know a little bit of my mom's backstory in order to understand where I come from and what I experienced. You need to understand my dad's story and how becoming a father at a young age impacted him.

My parent's ultimate separation (physical and legal) along with the various stepparent and sibling relationships that entered my life definitely impacted how I saw myself fitting into the world. Moving from home to home and school to school, and the resulting constant flux of finding new friends (new cliques), influenced my habits and behaviors. The underlying and overtly expressed religious influence of my extended family and the church molded the foundation of my life.

The stories I share are from my own recollections. How I experienced each situation is fully my own version. I am quite positive that each person included throughout the following tales would most likely have a different perspective on exactly how things transpired. That is human. The person I've become with all my passions, successes, and faults is a result of my accumulated experiences. The content of this book begins with a memoir-style story of how I became me, including all the bumps, burdens, and eventually triumphs along the way. Additional stories from my life (and others who generously shared with me) impart lessons I learned and inspiration I received. I hope that you find connections to your own stories and have insights illuminated that help you live your best life.

Perhaps the examples from what I and others have gone through will offer starting points to initiate better communication with the people you love and care for one day. I've come to believe that people are put into our lives for a purpose. Circumstances and challenges are meant for us to resolve and/or overcome, which then allows us to have compassion and gives us the ability to help others in similar situations. Now on the other side of a rough beginning to my life, I feel I have more appreciation for every good thing that happens and a very optimistic view about new challenges that arise.

The lessons I learned on my journey have inspired me to reach out and help others in many ways. I went through my battles in my own bubble. I was confident that my connection to a universal force larger than myself would guide my way. As a result, I made many false starts and fell backward as often as I moved forward. In retrospect, had I turned to resources in my community, I might have avoided a lot of pain. When people share their burdens, trials, and challenges with me now, I do my best to introduce them to resources in the community to make their journey easier.

Throughout this book, and more extensively in the workbook at the end of this book, I've included pauses for reflection, a series of exercises, and positive affirmations for those who may need some support while in transition or looking for a way to guide others. You can skip these during your first read through and view them at the end, or you can take a pause as you move along with me on my journey to reflect on how what I've learned could provide insight into your current situation (or that of someone you care about) by working through the exercises in the workbook.

Communication, authenticity, and coming from a place of love can only help any relationship and, indeed, the human race.

MEET MY DRUG DEALER

I met Marie while we were both working as servers for a local restaurant. We clicked immediately. I was attracted to her colorful hair (her natural jet-black hair changed with artificial colors all the time), and her light brown eyes smiled at me. We were both high-energy, bright, bold people, and both efficient workers who were really friendly. She smiled almost as much as I did at work. She even complained that her dimpled cheeks hurt at the end of the day. It turned out that I lived in the same apartment complex as her mother.

I was going through a bad moment with my daughter's mother and realized that Marie was struggling too. We started talking a lot on breaks and after work. We got high together. Marie said I sounded like I was a crab in a bucket of crabs, and every time I climbed to the top of the pile, the other crabs would drag me down.

Marie's divorce proceedings had left her in a place where she was sleeping in her car. Her kids were divided and staying with various relatives week by week. I told her, "I have a couch. You should come stay with me!" She couldn't believe I offered, but she said okay and moved in.

It was a good arrangement because we boosted each other's spirits and kept each other on track. Marie needed to earn more money to get back to having her own apartment so she could be with her kids again and take care of them. She wound up selling some drugs (mostly pot) to our co-workers and friends for extra cash. She was my co-worker, friend, roommate, and drug dealer.

Most people think of drug dealers as dangerous, cold, calculating, unfeeling about anything but money and protecting their turf, as they're presented on the news, in police dramas, and in documentaries. And those drug dealers do exist, but a lot of time, dealers are just people trying to get by. They have strict codes of conduct where they wouldn't sell to strangers or kids or out on the street and so on. Marie was like that.

She would sometimes call herself "the pharmacist" because I think she knew that she was helping a lot of people self-medicate instead of being on antidepressants, anti-anxiety, or bipolar medicines. In my experience, and from my circle of acquaintances, marijuana can be really beneficial for these types of conditions.

Being on your feet for -twelve, -fourteen, or sixteen-hour shifts in the restaurant business is not easy. Being as courteous as possible to people who treated you rudely and made to feel like you're begging for money when you wait to see what the customer's tip will be can really put a strain on your emotional and physical well-being.

In addition to the typical waitstaff challenges, Marie also had customers tell her they didn't want her biracial skin to touch their food and other more personal affronts. She believed that everyone comes into our lives to teach us something, so she had a rather philosophical attitude about customers and co-workers, but we still both got high to help cope. I won't speak about that too much, but I will tell you about an amazing conversation Marie and I had.

BELIEVE

About a month sober from hard drugs, I couldn't get out of bed. I was buried under the covers, feeling miserable (sorry for myself probably), and definitely contemplating the idea of not going on anymore. Marie came in and jumped up and down on my bed like a little child, saying, "This is not how we're doing this!" She dragged me up, we got some liquor and some pot, and we started talking.

Whatever happened that day, I was buzzing; pretty high. But not high enough to not know what was going on. Marie and I were perched at the island that separated my living and dining room areas from the kitchen like we were standing at a bar downtown. I revealed that I wanted to change but didn't think I could. I was heading down the path to doing hard drugs again. I shared my feelings about not being accepted for who I was. There were tears.

The conversation moved to my sharing some weird spirituality-type moments that had happened since achieving sobriety. It was ironic that it took drinking and being high on pot for me to share this!

She told me she was a Christian, and though I'd known her for about nine months before that day, I had no idea that she identified as such. We started talking more about her beliefs.

"It's weird," she explained, "because I just love God, I love churches, and even though sometimes I don't love the message, I love church itself. I love

▼

the music, and I love the feeling, but every time I go in, I literally fall to my knees, and I can't move."

I was totally intrigued because I felt quite similar as a child. I said, "Well, why do you believe in God? How do you believe in God as I don't know if I even believe in God anymore?" She opened up and began to tell me a little bit of her life story.

Identifying as bisexual and being biracial, she had lots of conflict in the church with stigma. And yet, she still believes we're made for a certain purpose and that God wants us to just be ourselves. We are who we are for a reason.

She asked if I didn't believe in God because it says in the Bible that homosexuality is a sin? I agreed that maybe subconsciously, that was true. I disassociated with anything to do with God and the Bible because I wanted to disassociate with anything that made me feel more horrible than how I already felt.

Then she asked me what I felt in my heart. Her advice was, "Stop listening to your head. Stop listening to what you should do. It doesn't matter what your grandparents, mom, dad, aunts, and uncles told you, nor what society told you or what the church told you. Listen to what your heart tells you."

I had a *moment* of connecting with my heart, and an overwhelming sense of love entered into my whole being. I said, "I feel love. I used to love God. I don't now."

"No? What happened?"

"I don't know." I was looking around the room, thinking about why I didn't know, and up on the counter, on the wall near the microwave, was a placard that said, *Believe*. I was talking to Marie in my kitchen in March, but this *Faith*, *Hope*, and *Believe*-themed placard set had been put on display for the Christmas holiday season. I'd originally had all three hanging, but I left *Believe* out for some reason after putting the others away with the rest of the twinkly décor items. It was weird because I happened to look at it right when I was thinking about what was in my heart. I felt something in me move.

I told Marie and directed her to look right there at the *Believe* placard. I had an epiphany. "I think that's a sign," she agreed.

I said, "A sign from God? But I put that up there at Christmas."

"But why?" she dug further.

I told her, "I had a set of three, and I don't know why I left that one out."

She wanted to help me understand, "Why would you have left that one instead of all the other ones? *Hope* is just as much a thing to have out as is *Faith*. Why would you just leave *Believe* right in the middle over your microwave?"

"It wasn't deliberate," I defended.

"God had you leave it there so you could see it now and realize that this conversation is super important for your future," she determined. She made it seem magical, not accidental.

She said, "We can't control who we love. You'll find the right church or community to accept or love you for you. Listen to God. God's talking to you. God doesn't make mistakes! Surround yourself with the right people."

Once she was sure I was past my morning melancholy and negative thoughts, she gave me a huge hug, then went on her way.

I went to my bathroom. I shut the door and I leaned up against the wall with both hands on it and asked God to save my life, to change my life. I told him that I believed in him; that I believed in the power of his love. I said how I might not understand everything yet. That I didn't necessarily know about the Bible and what I believe or didn't believe but that I didn't care. I didn't care about that because I could worry about that later. What I had to worry about at the moment was how much I loved God. "I love you, and I need you, and I'm asking you to be in my life, and to guide me, and to save me. I need you to save me," I pleaded and prayed to God.

I knew I wasn't okay. I knew I wasn't good just because I stopped popping and snorting lines of pain pills. I knew I needed saving beyond just getting away from hard drugs. I needed God back in my life and in my heart.

I fell on my knees, and I said, "Thank you. I love you, God. I love you, God. I love you. Thank you!" I just started bawling because I had this overwhelming sense, probably for the first time in my life (maybe the only time), that I felt like everything was going to be all right.

Marie lived with me for about six months, which ultimately was a time that completely shifted my whole perspective around and brought me back to God. I can never thank her enough for that.

FAITH

The morning after my conversation with my drug dealer that reawakened my love for God, I woke up feeling on fire for once in my adult life. Things were going to be okay. I was okay. I got in the car and drove down the complex to Marie's mom's apartment. Marie has always had an angelic soul, and we had a very relevant conversation as I drove her to work.

The conversation was around faith. I told her that our conversation last night changed me and concluded with, "Now I believe in God." She said she could sense a shift in me. She wanted to know, *How can I have faith? What is faith?* Faith being the next step to believing in God. We talked about this concept of faith the whole ten to fifteen-minute drive to her workplace.

I gave her a tight hug and a kiss on the cheek on the curb before letting her head into the restaurant she waited tables at. I told her I loved her and I thanked her. She asked me, like a homework assignment, "Now that you've had your epiphany, now that you have belief, how are you going to build your faith?"

That was what I was thinking about as I pulled out from that parking lot and noticed the Kentucky custom license plate on the car in front of me that literally said *Faith*! There were over 1,500,000 registered cars in Kentucky at that time (I looked it up)! I won the lottery that day because I knew I had God's love. This was something that I did not just believe in. I had to start building my faith. God gave me that sign and it, still to this day, is one of the most illuminating moments in my life and one of the times I've felt most connected.

I saw *Faith* in front of me less than twelve hours after I was sitting on the floor of my bathroom telling God I believed in him and asking him to save my life. I meant it. I didn't say it for church. I didn't say it for my family. I didn't say it for my child. I didn't say it for anybody else except myself. I said it because I felt it, because I needed it, because I wanted it.

Years later, as I recorded my thoughts about this experience in my audio journal while walking on a beach in Punta Cana, Dominican Republic, a shooting star shot by in the sky. I hadn't seen one single shooting star the entire time I had been in the area. I fell on my knees, knowing that God had saved me and God's love was made for me. That's what that shooting star in the sky affirmed when it passed as I recorded this story.

These aren't things that you can simply create; you can't just chalk that up to a coincidence. When people ask me how I know I believe in God and I tell them it's a feeling in my heart, I also let them know that God gives me signs. I thank God for those signs every day because they help build my faith.

Marie told me later that I was ready to hear her message about God on that day. Had it been delivered any earlier, I may not have connected with it. Had it waited longer, I may have slipped back into hard drugs or maybe I wouldn't have chosen to keep on living.

My shooting star and that license plate were significant to me. I've learned in life that nothing is coincidental. Nothing. Everything meticulously happens for a reason. Every single thing.

PART I

BECOMING RYAN

1

FROM MOM'S POINT OF VIEW

The experiences I brought to raising children as a teenager were rather distressing. I told Ryan; I've had much trauma in my life. I was raised in a psychologically and physically abusive family, molested, raped, and went through pretty much anything vile that you can think of growing up. At seven years old, during one of my father's many suicide attempts, he threatened with a gun tucked in his pants to "take me with him because I was the only person that loved him." I thought, at that moment, my father was going to kill himself and me. This caused me to suffer from PTSD and pretty severe panic attacks into adulthood. My entire family's favorite uncle also molested me. So, two men, traditionally people who help establish our abilities to love and trust men, had created significant and, to a certain point, prevailing trauma in my life at an early age. I unknowingly walked through the world with pretty complex trauma and anxiety, unbeknownst to me until graduate school.

I survived it all. The wisdom I learned from all my experiences ultimately helps me understand and treat complex trauma and anxiety. My understanding is how especially childhood PTSD can imprint trauma in our brain patterning and triggering. But, in my early 20s, as much as I tried to work through my childhood, I lived easily triggered into responses. It took time for me to work through all my baggage and my children were along for the unpacking. Being able to look through our darkness and trauma is definitely where real healing happens.

My son Ryan has always demanded attention. He has so much energy! He also has the most vivid spirit. I've watched as he tried to wrangle the energy that coursed through him since he was a child.

Ryan was the child the parenting books didn't have answers for. I thought something was wrong with him or me. He would cry, scream, and have tantrums on the floor every time I set him down or he didn't get his way. The biggest regret I have is that I listened to all the doctors who told me that as long as my child was fed, diaper changed, and physically safe, I should just let him cry. Ryan would cry until he literally was turning blue and couldn't breathe. I tried to hold him as much as possible, but I eventually would let him cry for hours on end to go to sleep when it came to bedtime. I had tried rocking him until way into the night, and he still would not go to sleep, so I thought maybe the doctors were right, and I just needed to let him cry. What did my abandoning him to let him cry do to his psyche that left him feeling unaccepted for so much of his young life?

As a school-age child, Ryan was active, popular, outgoing, and insatiably curious. He loved being with the girls, and because he was adorable, they loved him. Ryan craved teachers' attention but, at times, seemed to be picked on at school by other children. So, without his knowledge, I went to the principals, teachers, and officials. I protected him and tried to make his school experience go as easily as possible. I didn't want to humiliate my son by showing up at school or in his classroom, so I acted behind the scenes and was the perfect class mother, parent/teacher association advocate, cookie/cupcake baker, etc. I spent my life trying to make up for anything I had done as a young parent that might not have been the best. I wanted my son to thrive, to be understood, and to feel safe.

When Ryan went to high school, I thought the girl friends he made were getting him in trouble, so I moved him to an all-boys school. I didn't know Ryan was gay. I didn't know that the Catholic school followed the doctrine that clobbered gay behaviors and that his questioning psyche would feel traumatized or that leaving a school where he was already popular would make things worse in his mind. This is still painful for me, knowing that I unintentionally made things more difficult for my child.

When I was a child, my parents took me to church. At a very young age, I stomped my feet and got very upset because I thought the message that day was awful and insisted that my God loved everyone and would not hurt anyone. With no guidance or pushing by me, Ryan loved the idea, music, and physical space of churches but questioned some of the ways the messages from the Bible were espoused by the people at the podium. And now, Ryan's daughter has those same questions. Ryan and I share a passion for God and spirituality and connection to the universe, nature. We share a goal to help others in whatever ways we can.

I am so proud and honored that Ryan co-founded the non-profit **Love Must Win**, and I now sit on the board. His energy and passion have provided our community with a safe space, supportive programs, educational events, and materials for all ages of LGBTQ+ people. The organization and his leadership are such a blessing, and he could only have learned all this and gained credibility by going through everything he's faced.

When Ryan and I work at community events and talk to people, it is clear that trauma and generational trauma significantly impact how we see the world and how much trauma plays into everyone's journey and story. During Ryan's teenage years, he triggered PTSD reactions in me by getting in my face and yelling, and most of the time, I did a good job responding correctly. The times I didn't, he undoubtedly remembers more vividly and molded his brain patterning and connection most significantly.

It honestly feels like it never happened. The odd thing is, when your life never has any hold on you, and it feels as if the memories must be someone else's life, you know you've made the event neutral, i.e., really overcome the event. It no longer has any real weight or pulls in your life. These events in this book are exactly that for me; to replay them almost feels as if I'm rehashing someone else's life. My sons are my best friends. We are all super connected and deeply love and support each other. We are the truest of a true family.

Ryan's honored to show you how you can overcome your past, your abuse, and heal beyond what you thought was possible in the pages of this book. I'm proud of my son Ryan, but I'm proud of our whole family for not only overcoming these events but making them no longer have a hold over our lives. We transcended and now show others how it's possible.

Also, I want to speak to all parents, particularly mothers (single or not), who find themselves trying to evolve their children into good human beings; just keeping them safe in today's world is a task easier said than done. Never when we hold that newborn in our arms could we ever think, let alone say, anything mean to them or, worse yet, hurt them physically. The thoughts of these things are simply horrific, and we'd like to burn anyone at the stake who would verbally, emotionally, or physically hurt our babies. But life happens, and in the raw reality of having a teenager who is endangering his own life and you're afraid will hurt you, what happens in these waters is much murkier. What would you do to save your child's life? Anything! Including throwing a bowl of chili at them because I would've thrown a thousand bowls of chili if my son would've been safe. It's easy to parent when you have the easiest of children in the most straightforward situations, but when you have a child hell-bent on destroying himself on drugs or risky or scary behaviors, what will you resort to? How can we act sane in an insane circumstance? Sometimes we do, but when we are emotionally depleted and physically tired, it can degrade fast. Then, once shame hits you, you just take your anger at yourself out on the teen you are trying to save.

Can you imagine admitting this? Well, I will own it. I'm human. Parents are human. Mothers who still caretake most for their kids are human. You checkout, they die. You yell, they die. You try to shower them with love when they are beating you up, and they still die. Life is complex, and we can only do it moment by moment, no matter how we are holding up in those moments.

We've all literally did what we thought would help in the moment—grasping onto anything to help our kids. We are human.

Forgiveness of yourself is key to transcending all the pain. You have to be your greatest support and hold yourself in the most loving way. You have to show up for yourself first.

Mothers have been villainized for why we have issues since Freud. It's time we stop mom bashing. Most moms I know love their kids beyond any other humans that exist on the planet, and yet they are responsible for their safety, education, what kind of person they grow up to be, what type of job they have, or if they go to college or not. It's overwhelming! We are not just responsible for their personalities and their ability to be successful but everything in between. We need society to give us a break because this is society's problem, not a mother's problem. I truly believe the adage "it takes a village to raise a child." But often, we've become so disconnected from ourselves and our families, let alone our neighbors and friends. Sometimes it's all about getting back to the basics and remembering that we rise together.

Ryan, after overcoming suicidal feelings, self-harm behaviors, and multiple addictions, has found love with a life partner, is a wonderful and fully engaged father, has become a beacon and leader in our community, and has found his path in life. He, at this writing, is finishing up a doctoral degree. I hope that in reading about Ryan's journey, you will find answers to some of your questions, and shooting stars will illuminate your sky.

2

RYAN: BEFORE I WAS BORN

My family story all began when my mother's sister's husband (my uncle) introduced my young, strikingly blonde-haired, blue-eyed mother (Cathy) to a timid older man who was drawn to her and treated her like his dreams had come true upon meeting her. Mom's suitor was a Navy man who trained on the job as a nuclear engineer. With a very high IQ, he was a quick learner who did very well. In his crisp uniform, his plain looks transformed into someone who was reliable, impressive, secure, and most attractive to a teenager.

While holding plans for attending college in New York City as the escape from her rough home life, Cathy's older, more experienced suitor showed her how much he liked her. She appreciated the attention.

He showered her with positive physical attention. When my mom got pregnant at sixteen years old, she dropped out of high school and got married because that's what you did in those days. My grandmother had to sign the marriage papers because my mother was too young to sign legal documents.

My mother gave birth to my brother Brent and, two years later, me. The reality of being with someone for practical reasons who was never home (dad was away at sea a lot), on top of the very not-fun responsibility of caring for babies, led to my parents divorcing when I was still a preschooler.

Most of my youthful father/son-type memories are of my first stepfather, Ron. Eight years after I was born, Ron and Cathy's son, my little brother Cody, was added to our family.

RECREATING FAMILY

To the outside world, my mother and I might look like a tightly bonded duo. The truth is, we had to go through a lot to get to where we are now. My mom was my best friend growing up. Wait. To clarify, she was *my* best friend but, in her mind, she was my parent, which meant she was there to provide for my well-being, coach and guide me, and love and nurture my brothers and me, which (despite my secret hopes) meant she didn't consider herself my friend.

I had this dependency on getting approval from my mother. I felt connected to her. I needed her to praise me. I needed her to accept me and had to have her express her love for me—CONSTANTLY. I developed those dependent behaviors because I didn't love and accept myself. I certainly didn't extend grace or love or kindness to myself. I was always hiding who I was.

My mother and older brother tell me stories now about how I rode a tricycle around the neighborhood, stopping to knock on doors to say hello wherever I saw signs of kids living there, looking for friends that would like me and want to spend time with me. I was always searching for a sense of belonging. I believe some instincts and needs are just born in us.

I don't know if you've ever hidden anything in your life for an extended amount of time. It feels like a dark, gloomy cloud casts a shadow over everything you do. The sunlight you crave is always concealed. You observe other people frolicking in the sun, and you yearn for that; reach for that. So, in the times when the cloud thins and light is able to shine through, you want as much of it as you can while still always dreading the inevitable rainstorm coming. For me, my cloud hid the truth that I'm gay. Even if, when younger, I couldn't put that label on it, it was clear to me that I was not like the other boys around me.

For others, their clouds may hide their authentic self or some secret they don't want other people to discover. I wanted to be accepted by everyone outside of myself because I was sure that would bring me joy. I hid my natural instincts and became a chameleon, able to change and become whatever the person/people in front of me wanted. That got me approval (at least in those moments).

I know now that all I needed was someone to give me permission to be me and to tell me that I was wonderful, just as I was. Through my work as an adult, I try to offer that permission and assurance to the people I meet through my writing, presentations, and programs offered through various organizations and coaching.

My mother gave me attention, but on her schedule, not mine. Once she gave me praise or spent time alone with me, I needed it more and more. It was my first addiction. I needed her validation because I couldn't get that within myself. That said, as much as we loved each other and had fun together, we also fought a lot because I was never settled and always wanted more of her.

My older brother tried to keep the peace between our family members, quieting the noisy arguments (he had movies and cartoons to watch after all), even as he was a co-conspirator with some of our wild plans and adventures. I have to say we both spent a lot of time cleaning things in the house to get out of being grounded or having a time-out. We had too much curiosity and energy, and that, no doubt, overwhelmed our mother.

When we were really young, and my father was in town, he spent most of his time with my brother. They had similar interests like sports, math, and science, whereas he didn't understand me and my artistic and dramatic interests. He tried to be a good dad by keeping us busy. He would take us out of the house and show us off as his boys when he introduced us to his cronies. I do remember being fascinated by the fantastic stories he would tell us about being on a submarine. I would repeat my dad's stories and adventures to my friends and extended family.

Later, Ron would play sports and video games with my brothers. I would try, but it just wasn't in my comfort zone. He was always there for us, attending school functions, in the stands at sports events, and just being an important part of our everyday lives. We moved into a nice house in a nice neighborhood and had concerned and caring parents taking care of us. Even now, I am still close with my stepfather.

In conversations with my mother to write this book, I learned that she gave birth to me with no pain medication. With tears in her eyes as she told me her story, I learned that doctors told her to let me cry and scream until I literally turned blue. This absolutely was traumatic to my mother. She regrets listening to others and wishes she followed her heart.

I now realize all the subliminal and chemical messages that were sent into my system: abandonment and neglect. How could that have been healthy for our bonding and relationship?

I was a difficult child (just ask my brother, Brent) who segued from a rebellious drug- and alcohol-addicted, self-mutilating teen into a depressed, angry, and lost adult.

My mother and I were separated (not by choice) in my teens, which forced us to re-evaluate the kind of relationship we wanted to have. I had to end my addictions and learn to love myself instead of expecting others to fill the void I felt. In order to live, ultimately, I needed to find a way to end my codependent relationships or convert them into healthy ones.

My mom and I came together over a shared interest in metaphysical and spiritual awakenings. When my mother stopped energetically carrying me, we reached another level in our ability to heal ourselves and our relationship.

I am aware that I am following in my mother's footsteps. I had a daughter without being married when I was quite young, and after moving beyond years of self-created traumas, I am now on the way to earning my doctoral degree. My mother brings healing and spiritual guidance into my life. I have studied religions and energy work. I founded a non-profit called *Love Must Win* and organize *Hearts & Hugs* programs around the country for people after traumatic events. My mother's story inspires me every day to do better and be better.

Ultimately, my mother never gave up on her dreams for higher education. She went back to school and got her GED, then went on to undergrad, and from there, she continued on to earn her master's degree. She did an ABD[1] for a doctorate.

---

[1] ABD: all but dissertation

Even when it was difficult and financially challenging, my mom worked hard and accomplished her goals. That's something she instilled in all of her children. I thought, *wow, look at this woman who had one child when she was seventeen and another when she was nineteen, was basically a single mother, and yet she accomplished so much in her life.* I am so proud of her!

My mother (a board member of the non-profit I helped found) and I enjoy working together and keep attaining new levels of communication to heal from our past. In many ways, my desire to tell my own story has helped me learn more about my mom's story.

As a parent, I can see that healing my relationships with adults in my life increases my understanding of how to be with my child. This will hopefully lead to healthy relationships between my child and her children. And so on.

3

MOM, DAD, AND ME

My older brother, Brent, told me that we lived pretty simply when we were very young, while mom was married to my birth father. My parents didn't have a lot of money. Dad was always away for work. There's a vague memory of having mattresses on the floor in the apartment where we first lived.

When my parents divorced, Mom was working full time. So, we lived at my grandparents' house, where Brent and I shared a room under a neon star ceiling.

Having birthdays a week apart by two years, Brent and I would always have a shared birthday party. When we were young, the guests were mostly family, so it was easy and less expensive to have one party for both of us. As we aged and cultivated our own friends, we would have two separate parties on the same day.

Having a party meant cleaning the house and inviting guests. Since Brent and I had to clean up for the parties (let's face it, we made the majority of the mess in the house), it was much preferred to economize on not just money but energy as well.

When mom met Ron and they married, we moved out of our grandparents' house into a new house. My first "real" birthday party (at a venue instead of our house) was the year I turned four. The party was scheduled to take place at a Jump Zone, which was an indoor play area (think McDonald's play area on crack). I was excited for my birthday and presents and whatever was going to happen, but I think the biggest thing I was excited about was to see my dad. I missed him a lot. I was a ball of energy waiting with great anticipation for my dad to come into town.

MISSING DAD

Missing my dad and waiting for him was a common theme throughout my childhood. My dad lived almost five hours away near Nashville, Tennessee, where his parents and siblings lived. I lived near Cincinnati, Ohio, where my mother's whole family lived. Brent and I would go see dad for Christmas, Easter, other holidays, and summer break, and he would come to us for our birthdays. When my father showed up for my fourth birthday, I couldn't wait to show him the venue and show off all my friends. I don't recall if there was tension between my parents, but the party was so much fun for my friends and me. I got to spend time with Dad at our new house after the party ended.

After my dad left the Navy, he started working in the printing business. He traveled the globe managing huge projects, installing machinery, and setting up operations for commercial printing enterprises. My time with him was restricted by his travel schedule. He never fought my mother for custody of his two boys. He eventually started a new family.

I was a really good listener. Brent called me "Harriette the Spy" (a popular book character). I would pay attention to everything going on around me, which meant I knew things I wasn't supposed to know. When I was in fourth grade, I knew my dad was supposed to be coming into town to pick us up to take us somewhere to do something. His plane got delayed and delayed and delayed again until it was ultimately canceled until the next day. It's probably normal for kids to go through; we all go through times when our expectations aren't met due to adults canceling or changing plans. I just remember feeling this agony that was beyond tolerable. I tortured myself further by going through picture albums that triggered memories of us all growing up. My brothers and me. My mom and me. And some pictures with my dad. No doubt that made the delays worse.

My father didn't know how I felt. It wasn't his fault that the plane was delayed or canceled, and, after all, I did still get to see him the next day. But by that point, the pain was in unrelenting anticipation. I had been excited and looking forward to his visit ever since I found out about it a few weeks before. Usually, his plans were pretty solid if he committed to something, so this particular situation wasn't the norm. At my young age, I didn't recognize his usual reliability; I was just distraught in the moment.

Can such simple everyday occurrences and family situations trigger a malaise that can lead to suicidal thoughts? In me, it pushed me further into the need to feel connected to family, friends, authority figures, God. Without connection, an open hole that needed to be filled appeared.

KEEPING SECRETS

"The Spy" title my brother gave me was very accurate; my nature pulls me to investigate. When something's off, I want to know why. At the early age of nine or so, I figured out about the affair my mother was having with her college professor. I kept this to myself for what felt like years.

At home, there were times that my mother would lie, and in turn, I'd have to lie to my stepdad, Ron. That would be the worst.

"Where's your Mom?" he'd ask.

"She said she's shopping," I'd answer (holding her lie for her). But she wasn't shopping. When she didn't come home with bags of newly purchased items, my mom and stepdad would fight.

I felt I needed to pick a side (which is what some people do when they have codependent behaviors, even if that person didn't ask you to), so I was on her side more than his. My mother never came to me and said, "Will you do this?" It was more that I felt obligated to make sure I protected her and made her life the easiest it could be. I had an allegiance to her. In a lot of ways, this was beautiful. It was all based on love. Around then was the beginning of where we started butting heads because from there, things only got worse.

It's obvious to me now that I felt resentment for having to protect my mother. I was searching for a connection, and holding her secrets felt like a private bond. When she didn't appreciate my efforts, the disappointment and feelings of abandonment were some of the many aspects that led to my eventual abuse of drugs and alcohol.

My mother did what she had to do to keep my brothers and me safe. She acted on what she knew from her history and what she learned from watching others and the media. I didn't like her restrictions because they infringed on my escapism, which would thus lead to us being in conflict. Sometimes things turned into really nasty exchanges. There was verbal abuse and threats on both sides. Hurt people tend to hurt other people. Even if you're cognizant of things around you, such as my mom (who became a therapist and had done a lot of work on herself), it's hard to stop repeating the cycle if you were also hurting.

In retrospect, the fatherhood that my dad showed me taught me how to be a better father to my daughter, if only in knowing what not to do. I'm sure he's a better dad to the children he had later in life.

We have to learn how to break those family trauma cycles. Sometimes we fail, and sometimes we do great, and either is okay.

4

SIX YEARS OLD—CHAINS

I was a seemingly happy, normal child who adored Christmas time. When I was six years old, roughly ten days before Christmas, I was on the futon in my room when I had my first thoughts of ending my life. It's odd because I don't know where the thought originated from, which engulfed me. It wasn't anything I'd seen in a movie or acted out in front of me. It's not something that I overheard. But I had a really solemn feeling that overwhelmed my mind, body, and spirit that I didn't need to be on Earth in my body any longer.

I was in the midst of doing arts and crafts, making a chain out of strips of paper. I cut colored paper strips, rolled them into circles, and used glue to connect the circles together to create a separate link for each day until Christmas. I was making this chain so we could count down to my favorite day of the year by peeling off a link of the chain every day until Christmas Eve.

As I did my crafts, I found myself thinking, *if I took the scissors and cut myself, I'd die. What would happen then?*

I thought about sitting at my funeral, watching this little boy (me at six years old) in a coffin. I don't know why this happened. I believe when we struggle with mental health, it sometimes starts at a really young age. While there had been traumas in my life and whatnot, there was nothing traumatic enough at that moment, near Christmas, to contemplate suicide at such a young age.

I'd been exposed to fighting and yelling like normal kids get exposed to in the home. Maybe the suicidal ideations and depressive thoughts were triggered by a fight my father and mother were having on the telephone, or my stepdad and mom were having with each other? Maybe it was residual post-divorce anxiety?

As an adult, I have spent much time working with people who struggle with the concept of happiness and feeling valued. I now believe that there's an energy that is transferred between people at birth, and how we're raised in the home is all something that we absorb. Then it gets passed on to the next generation. It's not something we are even aware of, which is possibly why I was considering death at such a young age. With all that my mother went through before I was even a thought, followed by a marriage that ended and the stress of putting a life back together as a single mother, it's possible that my brain chemistry made it so that I had a high susceptibility to depression.

Or maybe these thoughts were triggered by feeling different than other kids at a young age? I watched my brother playing video games, and I sat by while my other friends were participating in sports and playing outdoors, and I would think *I would prefer to do arts and crafts.* I recognized that I was different from some of my friends and family since I didn't see many artistic people around me. Not to say that kids don't like arts and crafts, but I just had a very special connection to creative energy with God. I actually liked going to church, whereas my siblings and neighborhood peers did not.

My older brother and I were playful but aggressive boys. My mother said we were always wrestling and destroying things around the house. Sometimes we even wrestled with her as she worked so hard to fit in as one of the "boys."

Brent and I weren't always destructive. We had great quiet times too. We read books to each other at bedtime. We'd make up our own stories.

Brent recalled that once, he locked me in a dark bathroom while I was in the bathtub. Our parents had to break the bathroom door, and thereafter, whenever my brother and I were together, we were always supervised by someone!

I thought we had a "normal" life, so how I reached the highs and lows of my depression and how I ultimately chose to cope with everything is still somewhat of a mystery.

5

BE CAREFUL WHAT YOU SAY

There was a church across the street from the house where I lived when I was in elementary school. A couple of my neighborhood friends started attending services, and I would go with them every now and again because my mother and brother didn't attend church. My grandparents, aunts, and uncles went to church regularly, but not near me. I chose to go to church because I felt a special connection to God since I had my first cognitive thoughts.

I was in the middle of third grade when a leader at church asked, "Has anybody had a suicidal thought?" I raised my hand and admitted *yes, I had that thought before*. About half the other kids in that room also raised their hands. I wasn't alone. I wondered (even at that young age), *what were their stories? What happened to them? Why did they think this?* I question now, why did these questions pop up in me? Was I feeling helpless? Abandoned? Lost? In need of guidance?

I always thought my mom didn't like my neighbor friend, John. When we were discussing it more recently, she said she thought of him and his sisters like extended family but at the same time didn't think they were good influences on me. John was older, and when we would get together to play, mom would always think it was a better option to be at our house where she could supervise.

For some reason, my friend John's dad intuitively picked up on something with my mother (maybe something John saw or heard at my house) and questioned me about it. I confided in him about her affair and how I felt about it. I must have been just ready to burst, needing someone to talk to about the ordeal. This father figure, without my consent, shared my secret with his whole family! I felt betrayed.

Once John's whole family knew, I made them swear they wouldn't tell anybody else, feeling that it was no one's business except my family. But honestly, once they knew, it gave me a place to blow off steam and discuss my feelings about my mother's infidelity.

Finding a safe space, having a place to go to unburden, likely saved me from activating negative, self-harming behaviors. Having an adult with whom I felt comfortable talking was a gift. Without God putting that resource there for me, would I have gone down the path of the suicidal thoughts that were wafting around in my brain? Would I have gotten angry at my mother for something inconsequential and taken it out on her through my behaviors or back-talk? I'm so thankful for them in my life at that time.

Mrs. Smith, my third-grade teacher, was not the kindest lady by any means. I saw how mean she was to other people. She had grabbed a student by the arm, leaving a nasty bruise. She yelled and screamed and touched kids in ways that now would be called corporal punishment; this was not okay. Even my mom got into it with Mrs. Smith a couple of times. One day, after the church talked about suicide, Mrs. Smith told the whole class that a kid threatened to kill someone.

"This is how life works—you think something, you say something, and then you do something. If you think you're going to kill someone, and you say you're going to kill someone, then you might actually kill someone," said Mrs. Smith. I don't think she was implying that this little boy was going to kill somebody, at least not in elementary school, but I think what she was getting at was actually really important. She was saying to be careful what you say.

This phrase—think something, say something, do something—is like the church asking you to "ask, believe, receive." "Think, say, do" would actually be more like "believe, ask, receive," I suppose. These three pieces are connected and correlate back to what I was thinking with the kids in that church room talking about suicide. I thought these thoughts, then I said these thoughts out loud, and ultimately there was a progression to act on these thoughts, even if that was years later.

It's important to listen and *hear* what people are saying because when they start talking about what they've been thinking, the next step is to take action. Whether it's about self-mutilation, suicide, violence (against others especially), intentions to harm (that lead to terrorist- or school shooting-type incidents), or anything else, it is up to all of us to pay attention.

Funding for programs and qualified personnel to help people (especially the young) interpret their thoughts or fears and manage insecurities and stress will go a long way toward preventing the kind of negative, self-hurting, and community-harming behaviors we see in the news. John's father "listened" to me and made my burden easier to carry.

While Mrs. Smith didn't seem to have an affinity for children in general, she really liked me for some reason. I vied for attention from her. I yearned for her love. I needed her to like me and accept me, and I needed her to want me to be her number one student. Do you see the pattern here? It was always (for me) about acceptance and love from outsiders—almost a competition I needed to win. I had to be more loved than anyone else in my class or in my family, to be honest.

I was rewarded in my codependence with Mrs. Smith. On the last day of class for the school year, Mrs. Smith got me a little arts and crafts set and put it in my backpack. She told me not to tell any of the other kids. I watched her a lot when I wasn't doing my schoolwork. She didn't put stuff in any-one else's bag. She didn't talk to any other kids. It was just me. I knew that I was special to her for some reason and that only made my codependency stronger.

I took her gift home and found a little note that said something like, "Ryan, you're very special. Stay that way." Did her positive attention help delay my eventual suicidal attempts, drug use, self-mutilation? Perhaps. Did her abuse of other children cause them to act on their negative self-talk? We don't know. So, be careful what you think and say because it will lead to action, and listen because you never know when your kindness can make that huge difference.

6

13 YEARS OLD—A CUT FOR HELP

The first time I ever self-harmed was in eighth grade when I was twelve, perhaps thirteen. Believe it or not, it was the trendy thing to do at the time. Self-mutilation—who would think that's a trendy thing to do? Well, it was. Sixth, fifth, fourth, third grade, even younger kids were doing it. It was all around me.

Brent called me Mr. Popular because I always had a group of girls around me. He was shy and introverted, while I was outgoing, always craving attention. I had a girlfriend at the time who cut herself. I saw that all our friends who sat with us at lunch did it also. Some of them did it way worse than others. I don't know how their parents, a counselor, or a teacher didn't see it. Maybe they did, and maybe these kids were getting help and just didn't tell the rest of us.

Cutting is a weird thing to do in front of other people, but one day on the bus ride home from school, I broke one of those see-through acrylic pens and started cutting my wrists with the jagged edge. Not enough to draw tons of blood, but I felt a release of endorphins from the pain. This release was weird at first, but I then understood. *No wonder these kids do this. No wonder my friends are doing this. No wonder my girlfriend's doing this.* That's how it started.

As bad as it was to watch some of my friends become hospitalized or start counseling, I struggled with self-mutilation until I was almost out of my teens. It wasn't every day or week. It was probably a total of ten to fifteen times between the ages of thirteen and nineteen. Some of those times were way worse than others. After I cut, I felt ashamed that I did it. But there was also this part of me that wanted someone to see that I needed help. I wanted someone to say they cared about me. I wanted someone to notice when I was hurting or see the scars that visibly expressed my suffering. Since I guess I couldn't express how I was feeling in words, I thought if I showed them how much I was hurting, maybe they would understand. No one saw or said anything, though.

There's a misconception about self-mutilation that people only do it for attention. Some do hurt themselves as a cry for help. Some hurt themselves for the physical rush and release that comes with and after the pain. There's an element of control that appeals to people who feel like they have no control over anything else in their lives. But some do it because they're suicidal and do want their life to end; they cut as part of completing a suicide. Though for me, I believe it was a combination of all those things.

Completing vs. Committing Suicide

Suicide, as an action taken, is illegal in many places and thus takes on a negative energy and connotation. People in the social and emotional support fields have cultivated a new language to express the taking of one's life by choice. *Completing* suicide is a more politically correct, humane way to say ending one's own life.

We don't want to demonize or villainize people who complete a suicide. Someone who struggles with mental illness is not a villain. They are hurt. They are in pain. Like an animal caught in a snap trap that will chew its own leg off to be free, people in pain get to a point where they can't deal with whatever trauma is going on in their life or head. They choose to cut themselves free from the pain.

I've been in that spot. I always want to make sure I'm respectful of those who didn't get to the place I eventually reached where I'm truly grateful that I was given a second chance at life. I'm looking for ways to provide support when I see people who haven't found a way to love themselves yet.

I was fighting a battle inside of me. I was unsure of who I was because I couldn't define my differences in a way that was acceptable to others. Being gay or bisexual or pansexual (basically just being different) during a very unaccepting time, in an unwelcoming community that obviously didn't support LGBTQ+ students created internal conflict. Boys denigrated and insulted each other by calling someone "faggot" or "gay" or "girlie." My brothers and I talk now, as adults, about regretting using these words as insults lobbed at each other.

Despite tossing around slang gay words as insults, I had crushes on some boys. I would fantasize that one of them would push me into the bathroom and have his way with me because I didn't know how else I was ever going to move from my feelings and curiosity into action. I looked at men in underwear advertisements and watched movies and television shows where men took off their shirts and found myself drawn to them. My friends didn't notice the same things I did. They didn't notice the men; they'd tease each other about the women. They'd look at the same ads but look at the bras on women, bikini photo shoots, the *Sports Illustrated* swimsuit edition. I didn't look at *Sports Illustrated* for the women. I didn't look at *National Geographic* magazines for the topless women the way my peers and brothers did. It was like I was living in the "opposite" world. Can you imagine how confusing that is for someone? Does that help you understand why I felt the need to hide what I was thinking?

My cutting was not just "oh, I want attention." I was desperate for someone (anyone) to pay attention to me, to help me. I needed someone to help me help myself. I needed someone to guide me and show me unconditional love. To tell me that I was okay being who I was, no matter who that was.

7

THE BIRDS AND BEES

Growing up, my family talked openly about sexuality. My mom and stepdad would always say, "Oh, if you boys ever end up being gay, that's okay. Your life would be different for you, but you're okay; you're good." But this was said to all of us, as a family. Not one-on-one, where someone might feel free to ask questions or share feelings, especially when your older brother was prone to insulting you by declaring you as gay.

My parent's assurances did not negate everything I heard in church or saw on signs around the community. It did not change the teasing of boys in school and my neighborhood or even in my home with my brothers. As adults, we assume we can put a generic statement like this out there and that gives someone permission to come and tell us something that has been haunting them. In reality, it does not.

Conversely, pulling someone aside and asking, "Are you gay?" could send someone into a negative spiral in another way. A girl might ask herself, *do I look too butch?* A boy might wonder, *do they think I'm too feminine?* A trying-to-be-helping adult might spur additional questions such as, *why are you asking me that? What am I doing that makes you think I'm gay?* So, we were in the I-can't-win-no-matter-what-I-say cycle, which led to the generic all-inclusive statements above that my mom and stepdad offered to us at various times.

I always had girlfriends because that's what you did at my age and in my circle of friends. So, my parents may have had a huge question mark about me. Maybe he's just feminine? Maybe he's artistic? Maybe he just doesn't fall into those typical gender norms that society tells us we have to fall into? They told me this later on in life, but all of these things contributed to my cutting back then.

So, what should I do, **you're probably asking?** Of course, there's no simple, one-size-fits-all answer. Family history, family dynamics, community mores, traditions, and religious dogma all come into play which renders each situation unique. However, in a general sense, just like the famous birds and bees (aka "sex talk") that parents should have with their children at some point, we know that many are too uncomfortable even to venture there. So, how can we expect people to feel comfortable speaking about something that seems to be going against what friends and media are primarily saying is "normal?"

My good friend Fern told me that when she was ten years old, her mother took her (alone, no siblings) for a walk, in the rain, down a very large hill, sharing an umbrella. During the walk down the hill from their cottage, Fern's mother told her about becoming a woman—starting her menstrual cycle, where babies come from, and how important love was. On the way back up the hill, her mother answered Fern's questions. When they got back to the summer cottage, Fern received a box with a starter kit for getting her first period, a book with pictures of babies in utero for all different kinds of animals as well as humans, and a bunch of brochures and flyers about where to get more information (pre-internet days). From that point on, Fern said she felt much more comfortable about asking her mother all kinds of questions about her body and sex, being a woman, dating, and so on. It was the creation of the one-on-one bond that Fern felt was more important than the content of what was shared that made having potentially uncomfortable conversations less traumatic.

In my own experience, I think that if I was asked about having relationships and then given the birds and bees chat along with something like:

> *I am here to talk to you about sex and love, how babies are created, and all that. I am in a heterosexual relationship and feel comfortable talking about my experiences in that world, but if you have questions about sex between same-sex partners or if there's something else you're curious about, I have some people we can speak to together, or you can see on your own. I just want you to know I love you and want to support you with whatever will make you happy and help you find love when you're ready.*

It may have made my decision to speak openly less stressful.

If my parents had offered a brochure with information about things like a suicide hotline, sexuality, drugs, alcohol, etc., and said something like:

> *We know that there are lots of things going on at your age that might be overwhelming or confusing. Rather than just searching the internet, here are some local resources you might find helpful if it is too weird for you to talk to me or us. Hang on to this in case any of your friends might need some answers. Of course, you can always come talk to me or us, and if we don't know, I/we will find the answers for you. I/We love you and only want to support you the best way we can.*

8

13 GOING ON ADDICT

When I was thirteen, I hung out with my older friend John, and I wanted to impress him. I started to sneak alcohol from my parents' liquor cabinet around seventh grade. I noticed my parents had a bottle of Bacardi, and being a clever kid, I came up with a rather sophisticated plan. I knew that after I drank an ounce or two of the rum, my parents (who hardly ever drank) wouldn't be able to tell the difference if I replaced the clear rum with water. They mixed their rum into margaritas or orange juice anyway. I started to drink every now and again. I would make myself a rum and Coke, and a rum and orange juice for John. Sometimes I'd even use a dry erase marker to mark the bottle while we were drinking to make sure it was filled to the exact same spot because I knew my mom was pretty aware.

I was smart about filling the bottle up, but I never thought about the fact that each time I drank and replaced the liquor with water, the bottle held a more and more watered-down version of rum. I didn't notice the difference in the taste at the time either. Joke's on me!

I was very cautious about being caught. I'd rinse out the cups and put everything we used back where it belonged. I didn't want to get in trouble, so it's clear I knew I was doing something against the rules. I'm sure you can see clearly that my drinking was another call for help. Notice me! *If you were here and paying attention, I wouldn't be able to do this stuff!*

Even though my mother knew John was a bad influence on me and she watched me when I was around him, she still somehow thought being friends with a boy was better than the girls I hung around with. So, when we were in eighth grade, with my mom's permission, John and I went out of town together to visit some of his family.

I knew we were going to spend time with his sister. While mom felt reassured that adults would be present to supervise us, John told me that his sister's fiancé would buy us alcohol if we wanted any. I always had money saved up from Christmas and birthdays and chores. I saved so I could buy $100 worth of alcohol. That's a lot of alcohol for a kid! I brought a bunch of cash with me, and I brought some alcohol packed in water bottles on the trip. I asked the fiancé to go to the store with my cash and buy more alcohol when we arrived. I got drunk every single night and one time, in the middle of the day.

John and I were out at some type of college-aged party. Those eighteen to twenty-four-year-olds didn't stop me as an eighth-grader from getting black-out-drunk. Who does that? I don't even remember how we got back to John's family.

At a dinner with John's family, I just got up to get a wine cooler from the fridge. John's mom asked, "What are you doing?" Boldly, with confidence, as I removed the cap and took a huge gulp, I said normally as could be, "I'm just having a wine cooler. What's your deal?" She didn't stop me. She wasn't happy with it, but she let it happen. I remember getting drunk again that night, and then I went home Sunday morning.

On Sunday, when I got home, my mom was out of town. My stepdad was elsewhere, playing soccer, I think. I was ready to drink again. With only my brother home and off somewhere distracting himself, I was by myself, and so I started drinking around 6:00 in the evening. I was plugging and chugging and doing straight shots of whatever I had with me leftover from the fiancé's purchases, chasing it with wine coolers and malt beverages.

Alcohol loosens lips, and I, for some reason, thought it was time to spontaneously share with my fourteen-year-old brother the knowledge that our mom had been having an affair for several years. This really upset him, and Brent punched the floor. Better than the wall (or me), I suppose. His hand swelled up, as did his anger. Seeing Brent getting upset only made me start drinking more. I hadn't intended to make him feel bad. I asked him if he wanted a drink. He said, "No, I'm not drinking." Instead, he went into his video game world and disappeared. He could ignore everything going on in the real world when he put on those headsets and picked up the joystick.

When my mom and stepdad came home, I felt compelled to confront them and blurted out everything I had bottled up inside me. I advised them that they needed to get divorced or go to couple's therapy or both. "But," I instructed, "you have to do something because you're not happy, and it's annoying having to be around you all when you're not happy." Obviously, they could see that I'd been drinking. They saw my brother's swollen hand. They knew that we knew what was going on with them. No more secrets. They told me to go to bed and promised (threatened) to take care of this the following day.

Well, being upset, I didn't know what to do with all my feelings. After I was sure my parents had fallen asleep, I got out of bed and went over to my friend Kat's house and slept with her in her bed for a while. She nudged me out of bed before her parents were about to wake up. She told me to go sleep on the deck. I went outside and went back to sleep on the lounge chair.

Because Kat happened to be on the same bus line as me, I got on the school bus with her that day. I just told the driver that I missed the bus at my stop and had run over to Kat's stop. He let me on (I can be so charming), and I went to school. My parents never even noticed I wasn't home all night.

That was a Monday morning, which meant student council meetings. I was the Vice President of our student body. I went into the meeting and was talking with the adult coordinator. I can't remember her name, but she was our art teacher and one of the loveliest human beings I've ever met. I told her I needed some aspirin, and she asked why. I said that I had a hangover. She got me aspirin somehow. I don't know if it was hers or another teacher's.

I don't know if she believed me or not about the hangover. This was back in the days when giving students medication wasn't such a big deal. Now, I think if kids bring aspirin to school, they can get in trouble. She didn't really say anything, but she gave me that "mom" look. I knew I was in the wrong.

Well, come to find out that when my mom hadn't seen me at home that morning for breakfast, I guess she wanted to check on me to make sure I was okay (and make sure I wasn't hungover after my drunken explosion). So, she came to school and pulled me out of class. My mother took me straight to the hospital and made me get drug tested.

My alcohol level was still pretty high. I recall stopping on the side of the road on the way home from the drug test and dry heaving. My mother had to take off work that day. She stopped and got herself lunch and ask me if I wanted anything. The smell of any food was making my stomach swirl, so I made her pull over again so I could dry heave some more. No doubt I was super dehydrated. I had nothing in my stomach to throw up. While dry heaving, I had a revelatory moment, *why would I ever want to feel this way ever again? I don't want to drink ever again,* I resolved.

I had brought home the alcohol from my time with John and made sure to hide some away in my room. I put some in obvious places because I knew my mom would find the big bottles, but I transferred a lot of alcohol out of the labeled bottles into water bottles and then hid those water bottles in other places throughout my room. My parents were smart. But I always felt I was smarter. They found some of my alcohol stashes, but they didn't find most of them. I still had alcohol, and I remember feeling triumphant because I beat the system.

I was grounded for a month, and my parents made me go to a drug counselor because they assumed alcohol went with drugs. I went to one meeting, even though I had never done drugs. I told the counselor that I didn't know why my parents made me come because I had only had a drink a few times and had one night of binge drinking. (It was actually one whole crazy weekend.) The counselor told me that he didn't think I needed to come back to another meeting. My mother didn't force the issue when I got home, so I didn't question it. Recently, I learned that my mother was more worried about me hanging around with other drug addicts at the group meetings than the potential counseling I might have received.

In retrospect, if I had gone to more meetings, and if the counselor had asked more probing questions about my home life and why I was drinking, or if I would have been referred to a pre-drug/alcohol program, would I have ever gotten into drugs? Would I have been "scared straight" hearing what others went through or seeing the consequences? Would I have learned enough about myself and developed coping skills to avoid the drug episodes of my future at that point?

No one asked or checked for scars from self-mutilation, which would have demonstrated a need for counseling and intervention, one would think. If there's one issue (like drugs or drinking), I suggest that it makes sense to look deeper and check for other signs of mental and physical health issues.

One of the unintentional side effects of my visit to the drug counselor was that I started thinking that if my parents already thought I was involved with drugs, then I might as well do them. That started my brain going in a whole other direction. I would look in the mirror and see only darkness inside of me. I would see that dark cloud from childhood still circling above my head, keeping the authentic me in the shadows. I couldn't really see or love myself. I found another way to get back at my parents.

My parents did everything they could logically do. They searched my room. They grounded me. I had to apologize to all my teachers. I had to write letters. My parents did everything to the best of their ability and knowledge to try and keep me safe and teach me a lesson while still making it clear that they loved me.

And still, by summer, I forgot all about having been grounded and forgot about dry heaving on the side of the road. I also forgot about the drug counselor visit, and I started drinking again. I would drink at my friends' houses, and I would get them drunk. I would go to my grandma's house, where they always had open alcohol. I repeated my refill-the-alcohol-bottle-with-water trick. I didn't really care what I drank. It could have been gin or vodka, tequila, rum, scotch, bourbon. I just wanted alcohol. I just wanted to get messed up. I didn't even taste the difference in any kind of alcohol, except some of them tasted worse than others.

9

BAD INFLUENCE

For all of my eighth-grade year through to the summer of my freshman high school year, I had a neighborhood friend who went to a different middle school than me. However, we knew we would be going to the same high school. Cara accepted me in fourth and fifth grade when I didn't have many friends. We may have been different in many ways, but we bonded over searching for a connection. She and I were spending lots of time together. We were going down similar paths not only regarding sexuality questions but also with religion, with being different, and eventually with drugs and alcohol.

My mom knew Cara was probably a bad influence, but she couldn't really keep me away from her. When people think of drug addicts, they think of emaciated, lifeless, strung-out, near-dead addicts, not the functional addicts who look just like their own kids. They don't think of the regular kid-next-door who is selling some weed because he has extra or the girlfriend whose parents or grandparents are on a lot of drugs for various ailments and won't miss a pill or two or three. I was happy, smiling, effervescent Ryan with a babyface, chubby cheeks, a huge grin, blue eyes, and so funny! Why would anyone think I was depressed or that I'd take drugs or smoke weed?

The first time I ever smoked weed was with Cara and Brent's gamer friend, Alan. We would get high in Alan's car, go back inside to drink some 191 proof Everclear grain alcohol, and then get high again and finish at Taco Bell. All I remember from those evenings was laughing the whole time and having such a feeling of invincibility.

I was free and could just be myself. I hadn't come out to anybody at that time. I hadn't even truly admitted that I was gay to myself yet, but my behavior was probably enough for people to have guessed. I didn't need to wear a rainbow flag.

When I was high and drinking, I could say and do anything I wanted without feelings attached. As far as everyone else was concerned, I was gay in a fun way, not gay in a he-likes-boys way.

A few months later, on a night I was supposed to be along for whatever adventure was planned, Alan was in a car accident. He was on drugs (probably harder drugs than just weed), and he died. I'd only hung out with him a couple of times, but I had been packing for a family vacation, leaving the next morning, and had begged off partying that night. I am sure this was an example of God providing intuition and protecting me from what could have been my last night alive.

Brent had spent a lot of time playing video games with Alan. Brent never knew that I knew Alan because my brother didn't really do the druggie stuff and didn't know about Alan's druggie friends, of which I was one. Brent later shared that he never smoked with Alan because the repercussions at home would have been too severe. Looking back, I was probably hoping to get some attention and, if not, I could disconnect and have some fun. I would be more fun than Brent to Alan, and Alan would like me better. I win.

I think when we're in the midst of something, we don't see the big picture, and a lot of times, we don't even realize that we're doing something that's wrong or that could get us hurt because we're caught up in the actual moment of doing it. I was in that place. Alan's accident should have been a wake-up call to the dangers of drinking/drugging and driving. When you're young and inexperienced, you tend to believe you're immortal. Nothing can bring you down until something does, and then the dots start to connect, and you begin to recognize consequences. But does that stop you? It didn't stop me.

10

FREE TO BE ME

I became addicted to alcohol and drugs and found the getting high experiences amazing when I first started. I was suddenly free to be myself. My mannerisms didn't matter to anyone else because I was just stoned. I didn't have to conceal anything about myself. I would laugh and giggle, be silly, and find myself lost in my own little party.

Despite all the merriment, when you're in the middle of active addiction, it brings you into a darkness. When you're an addict, it takes control over you. That's the difference between myself and a person who can have a few cocktails here and there, enjoy a bottle of wine over dinner, or smoke a joint under the stars, and then not smoke or drink again for another month. The thing about drugs and alcohol for me is that they took over my life. I couldn't wait until the next time I could smoke or drink, sneak out of the house, or rebel against my parents. I wanted to go against my religious judgmental extended family, against society, and do what I knew I wasn't supposed to do because it made me feel free. I could only be myself in those moments; that's how it all began.

Between highs, I had a great longing until I could smoke again. I loved the sensations of marijuana/weed in my mind and body. Even to this day, I can still close my eyes and relive the intensity of the smoke moving through my lungs and nostrils. The way my brain relaxed and all the anxiety and stress I was usually walking around with would leave my body, allowing me to feel free of constraints. I've learned how to be free in many other ways now, but pot probably saved my life by allowing me to self-medicate what was likely a bipolar disorder and/or clinical depression. It's sad that I felt I needed an intoxicant to help me feel safe and that it was okay to be me.

THE LETTER

At fifteen years old, I was sitting in my bedroom after some particularly rough days, considering again if it was my time to go. I didn't want to have to deal with anything anymore. I was *so* tired of pretending and acting like I belonged when I really didn't feel that I was accepted at all. I was determined to leave this world.

Even in my despair, once I was secure in the rightness of the decision for myself, I started thinking about all the people my suicide would hurt. I'm a sensitive guy and didn't want anyone to think I did this because of them. I didn't want to find relief from my own torturous life, only to leave my family and friends to live with the guilt. So, I sat down at my computer and started typing a letter. I wanted the people I cared about to know that my choice was not their fault and that they could not have done anything to save or stop me. I wrote about how I was struggling with demons that had nothing to do with them.

Ultimately, my ten-page letter began with a general statement about how I loved everyone and how sorry I was to leave them with this hurt. I wrote about struggling with feeling like I was just different and didn't feel that I belonged, that I felt left out even when I was included. I never felt like myself and never thought that I was good enough. I never felt whole or complete. I didn't mention anything about being gay or that I liked boys/men or that perhaps I was bisexual, or any details that would have clarified some questions my family may have had about the challenges I faced. The reality was that I never felt truly loved, and I didn't, by any means, love myself.

I started typing a separate personalized message for each person in my life. When I got to my best friend Megan and started writing her note, I found myself wailing! I hadn't cried until this point. I kept strong and was determined to finish this project. I typed, "I'm done. I can't do this anymore." I told Megan that I loved her, that she was my best friend, and at moments she seemed to be the only person who mattered to me.

When I got to this part, I stopped. I stared at the screen in front of me. I couldn't go through with it when I thought of how Megan would feel reading my letter. I was ashamed of even just writing that letter and having those thoughts. I saved it on my computer in a secret file I had stashed away with some gay porn or something. I hid it away from others, but I kept it because I wanted to be reminded that through writing that letter, I recognized that people did love me, and I loved them. Looking back, I find it bizarre how, at one of the darkest moments in my life, I was able to create a moment of love.

The next day was unusual. Instead of feeling doom and gloom at my morning wake-up after writing this ten-page letter, I felt renewed. It was almost like the cry I had at the end released everything, and the letter-writing was a cathartic learning experience where I realized that there were people who loved me.

COMING OUT FOR THE FIRST TIME

The first time I came out, I came out to my friend Megan. I had met Megan because she was Kat's neighbor. Kat and I used to sit on the bus and ride to school together. When I met Kat in seventh grade, she was just a dorky kid like me. By eighth grade, she was a popular cheerleader, and we sat together in the back of the bus, in the "cool" seats. As a cheerleader, she became a bully toward girls who were overweight or larger sized, which included Megan. And yet Kat was the friend I ran to when I was having difficulties at home. Eventually, Megan took over that friend role.

Kat had been my date for the freshman homecoming dance, and I wanted more than a friendship. But Kat could occasionally be a really nasty person, so we didn't date.

After her, I had many very brief flirtations of relationships. Were we friends or more was always the question in all of them, probably because of my unrecognized sexual ambiguity. I came across as just another screwed-up boy who didn't know what he wanted!

Kat and Megan lived in a rough neighborhood where people had to be tougher. There were more drugs and alcohol there than in my neighborhood. These girls were street smart. They were, to some people, probably considered "mean girls," but they were both nice to me. Since the mean girls were sweeter to me than others, I loved feeling worthy of the kinder treatment. Ultimately the meanness took over, and Megan and Kat could not be friends any longer, which put me in the middle.

By the way, my mother disliked both of these female friends. She actually disliked most of the girls I was hanging out with in general. She thought the girls were "trouble." She hated that I was involved in gossiping and being mean (by association) to others. On the other hand, my older brother was amazed at how all the girls loved me. In his eyes, I was Mr. Popular. Boys liked me because I had access to the popular girls. It was a complicated time, but really, what young person doesn't go through self-discovery this way? I believe we all try on different people and personalities, groups of friends, and interests until we find where we fit.

Megan and I connected on an intellectual level at first. I liked her so much and wanted to be with her all the time. Our relationship was complicated because we started out as more than friends but very quickly settled into being best friends. We didn't have sex (until once or twice in college), but we were affectionate with each other—holding hands, snuggling while watching television or movies, etc.

I was in the middle of my freshmen year of high school when I remember sneaking out to my mom's car with the cordless phone so no one could hear what I was saying. The day was chilly but not so cold that the car was uncomfortable. It was starting to get dark. My mother was making dinner in the kitchen. In the days of landlines, if someone picked up the phone in the house, I would be able to hear it. Cell phones were around but cost too much to use often.

I told Megan, "I have to share something with you. You've probably picked up on it or know about it or thought about it before, but I need to share with you that I like guys and girls."

She said, "What do you mean?"

I said, "I like gay porn, and I like the idea of being with a guy."

"Have you ever been with a guy?"

"Oh my gosh, no. I'm scared to even think about that." I told her about the time I created a fake AIM (AOL instant messenger) account, which got me into a chat room to talk to gay men, but it felt weird and creepy. I used AIM and AOL for porn or to chat with people I knew I would never meet.

She wanted to know how long I'd known I was gay. I told her that I'd always known I was different. Ever since I had cognitive thoughts, I always felt different, that I didn't fit in, that I wasn't "normal." I said how I didn't like the same things other boys liked or the same things my brother or friends liked. I told her that I would sometimes find my friends and my brother's friends "cute." That I didn't know what that really meant, I just had weird, different thoughts and didn't know how to process them.

Megan had grown up enveloped in the Catholic faith. Her family went to church. She attended a pretty prestigious co-ed Catholic school. I had gone to some of her school dances and met some of her friends. I liked all that. I respected her faith. Megan said, "I love you. I always will love you, but the church says it's not right in God's eyes."

That was such a significant moment for me. It was her reality but very harsh for me to hear. She wanted to be authentic. She told me she loved me, but she shared what she really thought too, and I didn't know how to process the idea that maybe God wouldn't love me. Coming out in effect pushed me further away from God, religion, and my spirituality.

In that moment, Megan did not have any ill intentions. A lot of times, when people say or do things that we find harmful, they do not mean to be hurtful. They say what they've been taught and what's in their mind versus what's in their heart.

I felt so relieved to get that weight off my shoulders. I'd finally shared my secret. A feeling of lightness encompassed me. But then a new weight came on my shoulders in knowing that yet another religion, another group of people, thought I was wrong. I was already going to Hell, according to my Baptist family. Now all of Megan's Catholic school friends, teachers, and families would also think I should go to Hell. They might accept me, but their God didn't. Their God thought that I was full of sin.

Walking back into the house after the conversation with Megan, I felt in my heart that something wasn't right. I knew I trusted Megan and trusted in her faith. I took her word at the moment. I thus added another layer of self-deception and self-hatred to what I was already carrying around. I asked her to keep my secret. She agreed. We were drawn closer together.

I know that we as humans don't intentionally go about life trying to hurt people or thinking negatively about people. That comes from what we've been taught by family, friends, religious leaders, and society. These negative thoughts are not necessarily thoughts that are rooted in love or from our hearts. It's what other people and institutions impose and instill in us.

Oftentimes I still have to look into the mirror and look into my heart when a situation arises where I feel myself holding a preconceived, predetermined idea about a person, situation, or thing. I need to search my heart to find what I really think about something until it is correct. When I feel it's right in my heart, that's when I know how to act. Megan and I remained friends.

EMBRACING THE FIEND

I started high school at fourteen years old. High school added a whole bunch of new stress to my life. There were new people to meet who weren't all on my former bus route to school. I had to try to blend in with a whole group of people from other parts of town and different backgrounds. I had to learn and follow new teachers, classes, rules, and a very different schedule. The dark cloud that hung over me was more like a tropical storm with lightning and thunder at this point.

I remember finding pain medicine in the family medicine cabinet and just taking it to see if it would help with all my anxiety. I swallowed a couple and was feeling a little out of it. I was high, and I wasn't too impressed with it, but hey, it was a free high. *Let's go for it.* I would take a pill every now and again.

One night, probably toward the end of my freshman year, I got super drunk, came home from wherever I had been, and snuck back into my house after being out partying. I was lonely in a room full of people who were my supposed friends. I was lonely in a house full of people who were my family. Drinking to the point of peeing myself and throwing up with alcohol poisoning was becoming a more regular thing. Perhaps, I was not actively trying to kill myself but resigning myself to whatever came my way.

Instead of bed that night, I went to the medicine cabinet, crushed up an assortment of pills together, arranged the mix in two lines, and inhaled them up my nose the way I saw the people in movies and TV do it. I was sobbing in the bathroom with the vent fan running to cover the sound of my cries as, for the first time, I snorted. I mixed pain pills with anxiety pills and downers. Two of each kind. I took this cocktail of prescription drugs. My health ed teacher said mixing prescription drugs could kill you when he warned us away from drugs. I'm not sure of my intention at the moment, but I regularly wanted to leave Earth to find oblivion, wherever and however it took.

After the first line, I felt like I could be sick. No problem—take more! I did another line. Then I vomited up whatever was inside me. My body had rejected my attempt to disconnect from reality. I tried to clean up the mess, but I was not exactly seeing or thinking clearly.

Still tripping, I flipped on the light and looked in the mirror. At first, I was overwhelmingly sad and upset, and then, like flipping the wall switch, I suddenly flipped moods and got really hyper.

I went out to our pool, which wasn't open for the summer yet, so there was a pool cover on it. I began dancing naked on the pool cover. Luckily, it didn't collapse and I didn't drown (because that was a real possibility). That's why you're not supposed to stand or crawl on canvas pool covers. I knew that rule. Once again, I was tempting fate and challenging God.

This was the first time that I had snorted pain pills, which was the beginning of my hard drug journey. I somehow stumbled back inside and away from the pool, and the next morning my mother found the mess in the bathroom and knew what I had done. She knew she had a problem on her hands;

I was in trouble. Maybe she had so much going on in her own life, but she didn't push me into therapy or drug programs or take me to a counselor. I think she thought (since she was a therapist) she could work with me and take care of my problems privately.

My mother recently shared that she worked with troubled youth all day long, and she did not recognize any of the signs of a potential addict in me. She saw me as happy and busy, active at school, with good grades. I was doing the things I was supposed to be doing. I "seemed" well adjusted, if just a little hyper and needy at times. I had friends, even if my mother didn't like them. She and Ron began to worry after the pool dance night. They began to look a little more closely at who I was with and what I was doing.

My mother had been diagnosing all of her kids for years. We must have ADHD[2], or we were bipolar and depressed. Maybe we were suffering from anxiety. She always had a holistic way of managing whatever she diagnosed.

Drugs and alcohol seemed the only things I could find to help me disconnect from my day-to-day pain, but it didn't satisfy that deep-down reason I needed to seek relief. Snorting this cocktail could have killed me, mixing uppers with downers on top of my blood alcohol content being so ultra-high. I know I hadn't blacked out because I was aware of what was going on, and I have memories of that night.

Pain pills made me feel invincible. They gave me a sense of solemnity and nothingness. Sometimes I would take anti-anxiety medicine. I loved Adderall because it would make me intensely focused or sometimes really hyper, depending on how much I took and whether I mixed it with alcohol or marijuana.

I craved the feeling of losing control. I was infatuated with the idea of being able to escape from reality. I loved self-medicating away my anxiety, fears, and all my worries. Somehow, in the midst of the high and blur, my true self would be revealed, and I could live in that space for a while.

In reality, I wasn't myself at all. I was being controlled by the drugs. Throughout the next several years, from the time I was fourteen and started using pain pills until the time I stopped when I was twenty-three, I just took them whenever and wherever I could find them. I would rarely ever buy

---

[2] ADHD: attention deficit hyperactivity disorder

them until I was using them every day after Harper was born. Sometimes, I traded weed for them. I stole them a lot from friends and family members. I would also persuade my friends and girlfriends to steal them from their family members.

When I took pills, I would enjoy the continuous release of the medicine into my body. When I started crushing and snorting the pills, the reaction was immediate, a short-term but bigger rush. Snorting them all at once would also make me feel itchy. That meant it was working! Most people would say, "That's awful. Why would you want to be itchy?" I knew that if I was itchy, I was not in control, and that made me feel free. It wasn't a scratchable itch. I called it the fiend itch. Being itchy was the signal to stop ingesting because any more would cause me to throw up. I never wanted to throw up the good stuff!

The pills gave me psychological freedom from my thoughts. Being high helped me not worry about everything going on. Being high helped with my anxiety.

SEWING SHEARS

I was fifteen (about two months after my suicide letter-writing) and was still with my girlfriend Lucy, but we were having problems again. I thought I was in love with her. We had started dating my freshman year. Lucy replaced my mother in my quest for attention. I needed to feel connected all the time. I would talk to Lucy incessantly, reread her notes when she wasn't with me, and I was convinced that she was the only reason I was alive. When we broke up, I couldn't stop crying because, once again, I was being left, abandoned, and obviously, I wasn't good enough.

I was sitting in the corner of my dim bedroom with a pair of sewing shears. This polished, lustrous, metal scissor tool was heavy in my hand. Rather large and frightening at about twelve inches long, the shears had become my go-to option for self-mutilating. I was holding the scissors, ruminating, and crying. *Why wouldn't she love me? Why couldn't I just be better? What could I have done to make things better?* Come on! Guess what? We all think similar things when a relationship ends, but I sat there with the open shears gripped in my hand, the blade pressed against my arm.

Could this also have been connected to having those same feelings about my parents? Why didn't they love me? Why didn't they want to be around me?

I didn't move the shears. In my mind, I was working up to, "this time was the time." My inner drama queen was making a speech to a non-existent audience. This is the time I go, and I wasn't even going to write a make-them-all-feel-better letter. I was done. I was done with this world! As tears blurred my vision and dripped off my nose onto the arm draped across my lap, the self-mutilating weapon fell out of my hands. I just dropped it, let it clatter to the floor, and cried even harder.

How was it that my family didn't hear me or didn't seem to know because I was bawling in my basement bedroom for hours? I finally lifted myself up off the floor, picked up the bloodless (this time) scissors, and went upstairs to an uneventful dinner with my family. They didn't say anything. Nobody asked about my red eyes. I didn't tell them anything. I didn't ask for help. Family dinner went on as if everything was fine.

11

MOTHER ISSUES

There were times in life when I know that my mother tried her best but fell short of treating me as I wanted to be treated. I'd intentionally push her buttons to see how far she would go, just to see what reaction I could get, which led to things between us becoming deeply distressing and disturbing a few times. I would especially hit triggers if the conversation we were having at the time wasn't generating my most desired response.

I used getting-the-last-word challenge mind games to push her. If I could have the last word, I would win. I had an unhealthy need for not just validation, acceptance, and love but a need to win arguments. I also needed to do what I wanted to, and I expected her to support me because I supported her and kept her secrets. It was all a big cycle. If you mapped it out, you'd see the Catch-22 circle.

I challenged my mother psychologically and emotionally as I stood up to her. I was tall and a big guy and probably scared her when I would yell and taunt her. Your kids aren't supposed to challenge you about how you choose to parent. They're not supposed to stand up to you because you're the authority figure trying to make sure they're safe. Years later, my mother admitted that I terrified her, but at the time, my tiny mother stood up to me like a huge mama bear.

Mostly, the things that led to our fights were just normal parent/kid things. I want to go to this dance. I was invited to a party where no parents would be present. I didn't do well on a project or test. I wanted to skip an activity. I wanted to go out twice in one weekend (maybe a friend's get-together and then a football game the next night), which was against the family rule; you could only go out once a weekend. That rule was created because our two parents had to transport three boys back and forth, and money was needed for each outing and all those logistical things. Simple challenges to what I wanted/needed would stir up these huge fights.

Mom said that the other two boys thought I was her favorite because of all the attention she gave me. I thought she loved the boys because they were "good" and not always getting into trouble. Every time she talked to me, she usually punished me for something, or it felt like that anyway. My mom would say that she loves all her boys equally, but I was just so demanding, and she wanted to protect my brothers.

What my mom didn't get (and what I wasn't consciously aware of) was that I needed connection. When I wasn't connecting with people who affirmed me and seemed to care about me, it impacted my mental health. If I couldn't connect at home, then I needed to be out with my friends. Solitude led to self-destructive drinking, pills, cutting, and other negative habits.

When someone is desperately in need of being affirmed and accepted, they can create negative or attention-seeking compensating behaviors when that need is left unfulfilled. That is what I did to my mom. I created situations where I would get the attention I desired and needed. I also got the acceptance I craved within the love of my friends. The parental punishment system of isolation and restriction (aka grounding) at that time in my life was extremely damaging to me. I know that's the purpose of a punishment, but it was beyond discipline for me. It was torture.

I don't think anyone can understand how harsh it was for me unless you've been withheld from something or someone that you love for an extended period. Maybe it's similar to how spouses feel when wives or husbands leave to go out of the country for six months for military service, an out-of-country/offshore business project, someone is held hostage or is in prison, etc.

I also always felt that my mother singled me out. She was harder on me than my brothers, most likely because my siblings kept to themselves and didn't challenge her as much as I did. They were computer guys, gamers and spent all their time lost in screens. They were very non-threatening. They were low maintenance. I can see that now, but living it in the moment, none of us were aware of what these triggers were for me.

I didn't get what I wanted and, like many teenagers, started to feel resentment and hatred toward my mother. I despised who she was and how she was caring for me. Her form of care wasn't the way that I wanted. Nor did I know how to express my needs properly. I didn't understand where my feelings were coming from at their core. She did the best that she knew how at the time. That's all any parent can do, really.

12

Healing Affirmation:
I am abundant in healthy relationships with those around me,
including parent/parental figures, kids, siblings, other family, and friends.
I am fostering beautiful relationships now that will blossom into
healthy relationships in the future!

CONFRONTATION REAPS TURMOIL

Sometime after my drunken verbal explosion all over my mother and step-father about my mother's affair, my mother and stepfather divorced. Soon after, my mother and her secret affair professor went public about their relationship, and he became a fixture around our home. Suddenly, he started to get involved in how my siblings and I were raised. Then, in the middle of my sophomore year of high school, after frequent arguments with my mother and her boyfriend, they made a decision that would impact my life quite detrimentally.

One morning, I woke like any other day, and as I was eating breakfast, my mom announced, "I'm taking you to school today." I thought that was really weird, but okay. We listened to music in the car, not saying much.

When I realized we had passed right by my school, I asked, "Hey, what's going on?"

She answered, "I'm taking you to your new school, and if you fight me on it, you're not going to get your driver's license. You're not going to get your car."

"What? Why?" I asked, perplexed. I was totally confused and had no idea where we were heading.

My mother explained that I was going down a bad road and I needed to change schools. Just like that! She and her boyfriend had decided that I needed a change to pull my behavior more in line with what they deemed was acceptable. They decided that I needed to go to an all-boys Catholic school!

I wanted to jump out of the car and run off. I admit I wanted to lash out at my mother. But my brain was quickly calculating my options and obstacles.

My mother had the advantage. She knew that for the full year before, I'd been working part-time jobs and saving up to buy a car. I had thousands of dollars tucked away because I wanted and needed freedom. I knew that a car would allow me to get away from my family. I could learn and grow better on my own. I felt confined with this new man in her life, having input on how I was supposed to behave, feel, think, etc. I really believed that my mother and I would get along better once I was free and able to leave the house, be out from under the constant aura of judgment.

Obviously, I also knew that having my own wheels would make it easier to access drugs and alcohol and be with friends I chose. Yes, that was a piece of it, if I'm being honest with myself. But the main piece was making sure I had that acceptance, love, and kindness from other people, and being grounded in my room was not fulfilling these basic needs. Taking away my option to have a car, to get my driver's license, that was too many points to her side of the challenge. I kept still. I sucked it up.

I went to the new school because I didn't really have much of a choice. My birth parents didn't understand me. The stepparents who were in and out of my life didn't get me. None of these people could understand how intense going to an all-boys Catholic school had to be for me. I didn't tell them I was gay. They didn't ask.

Right before I'd started at Catholic school, I'd come out to only two close friends, Megan and Kat. I made a pact with myself that no one else could ever know about my being gay. You just can't be gay and Catholic! I wasn't raised Catholic. I was raised in a mix of Protestant denominations. But I knew deep in my soul, and through my relationship with Catholic Megan and her family, that this school was not going to be accepting or affirming of my sexuality. I didn't know why I was the way I was, but *I am who I am*, I thought, and my true nature needed to stay hidden.

As I am writing this book, my mother and I have begun talking about my life, and I've been asking her what it was like for her. I learned that she did not send me to an all-boys school simply because I was misbehaving. She had noticed a link between the rollercoasters I was on with the girls I dated and my emotional well-being. My mother knew I tried to sell pain pills to come up with the money to take a girl to a dance. That girl told on me, and I was grounded for two months. My mother made a link between my drug and alcohol usage and the kind of girls I had befriended. She knew that I was getting pills from the girls in my life. It made perfect sense to her to remove girls from the equation to save me from myself.

No one is to blame here except for the lack of communication. If I told my truth about my sexuality, I wouldn't have needed to have relationships with girls that never felt right. If my mother would have told me what she noticed and shared why she was thinking of sending me to an all-boys school, maybe I would have told her the truth about being gay and why an all-boys school would be even harsher than a drug rehab program for me.

ALL BOYS, ALL THE TIME

When I got home after that first day in my new school, I confronted my mother and asked her *how long I would have to stay in this prison?* She told me that if I was really good, got decent grades, and stayed out of trouble, she and my father thought that the following fall I would be able to go back to my high school; that I would be able to get my driver's license and a car.

Great! I knew the terms. I made a plan. I made sure I was really good at my classwork. I got to know my teachers. I tried to fit in at school. I had my job to keep earning money for my car, gas, insurance, etc. I thought I could make it to the end of the year, and then I would have my life back.

Once I got settled in at the new school, figuring out the culture there, I saw that the boys at this new school all teased each other about being gay and acting gay, which sometimes included me. For some reason, they actually picked on me less often about being gay than they did on other kids. Maybe because they thought I really was gay? This place was far more disturbing than a co-ed school.

At Catholic school, in particular, there's this big stigma around being gay. I didn't know of any out gay kids in the school. Doctrine, church, teachers, and the Bible are in agreement; if you're Catholic, you can't be gay. This created a whole new layer of hiding who I was. Going to school was torturous because I couldn't bond with anyone. It was hard to be around all that teenage testosterone. I was surrounded by boys all the time, and some of them I found quite attractive. What was I supposed to do with that?

I did run into Brad. I had known Brad from middle school, where he was a great basketball player. Brad also attended this same Christian school, although he no longer played sports (except motocross). He had started at the Catholic high school his freshman year, so he was in the know about how to get around, who everyone was, and he knew all the teachers. He was a really great friend who stood up for me and helped guide me. He was such a nice, sweet guy. I was thankful to have him because I don't know how I would have made it through without him.

I would sit through daily religion classes where the teachers said being gay is a sin all the time. Where I had to hear that same rhetoric I heard growing up from extended family members, from society, from TV, from every other place besides my nuclear family. Listening to this only instilled in me more confirmation that I could not share my true self.

If my family was aware of how much it broke my heart and spirit to have to go to a school like that, they didn't indicate it to me. I would like to think they wouldn't have made me go there if they knew, but I don't know that for a fact. I also have to take some ownership in not having told them what was going on with me. I wanted them just somehow to know. I wanted them to intuit that I was different and needed guidance. But I was a teenage boy, and if they had asked, would I have admitted anything? I don't know.

BIRTHDAY TROUBLE

Though it sounds like maybe I became an angel in my Catholic high school, no, it was not true. There were times I did drink and do drugs. Getting super high on my birthday during my sophomore year and literally going to school on only three hours of sleep was not staying out of trouble. I slept through every single one of my classes the next day. I don't know how or why the school didn't call my parents and tell them, but they didn't.

Mrs. Ruth, one of my teachers, brought cookies every day for people who had birthdays. She gave me a full toothy smile as she handed me my birthday cookie, and like the blue Cookie Monster on Sesame Street, I devoured that cookie and all the crumbs in seconds because I was still high and had the munchies. I didn't even care that she looked aghast at the demolition I did to her gift.

I knew if I got caught for anything controversial, my parents would not let me go back to my co-ed high school, where I had a group of friends. My public high school friends weren't necessarily what my parents would have labeled "good people," but those friends supported me. I felt approval there, which was always important for me. I was able to let people get a sense of the real me while still hiding this huge piece of my core identity. *They actually liked me, for me*, I thought, but later realized it was only as long as I hid the way I talked and walked and who I was as a person.

I did not hide that I like arts and crafts. I did not hide that I'm funny. There are other aspects to our essence—other than our sexuality and mannerisms—that I was able to share. Being in a school across town prevented me from enjoying the company of this group that had accepted me.

Fast forward to the end of my sophomore year. My parents didn't find out about my Cookie Monster day, so I was well-behaved in their eyes; I had followed my mother's rules by doing well in school, and I kept my job. So, it was a real jolt to my system when, at the end of the school year, when I asked what I needed to do to get re-registered at public school, my mom told me, "You're not going back to public school. You're going to spend another year at the Catholic high school."

I was stunned. I stood there staring at her. Waiting for her to say, "Ha ha, just kidding." But she said nothing. She turned away and made herself busy to avoid having any further confrontation with me.

I left the room, simmering, confused, and headed for the bathroom. I locked the door, sat on the floor, and started hyperventilating. I had never known what hyperventilating was until I experienced it at that moment (and, thankfully, I've never experienced it again since then). My chest was heaving as I tried to catch my breath with tears pouring down my face and puddling on the floor in front of me. In the midst of a full-blown panic attack that was partially fury at my mother and partially freaking out because I did not want to stay in religious prison, my distress translated into hatred for my mom.

I don't know how long I wouldn't talk to my family. I don't remember how I hid my real feelings from them. The feelings I had the day I found out about their deception and betrayal did not dissipate at all. Those feelings simmered under the surface as I used my solo time to plot how to get my life back under control.

I spoke to my brother and asked him if he thought my mother's decision was fair. He said, "You and mom are crazy with each other! You've got to chill. You're making it hard on everyone!"

PAIN RISES TO THE SURFACE

Later that summer, between sophomore and junior year of high school, I was expected to join my siblings on a family vacation out of town as we drove my brother and all his stuff to his college dorm in Florida. My mother was really stressed out and sad because her oldest was leaving the nest and decided this might be the last chance for us all to spend family time together.

I picked up on my mom not doing well, but I also was not doing well, which my parents didn't really pick up on. My parents thought I was upset because I wasn't around my friends. They didn't see the much deeper, darker parts of what was haunting me. Would they have made different decisions if they knew?

My mom is not a villain. She's a beautiful, beautiful woman. She's always been my hero ever since I was a little kid. In fact, in fourth grade, we got an assignment to create a personal story book where we were to make separate pages on our favorite color, our favorite food, and choose our hero. I selected my mom as my hero. I loved her so much. Even in this angsty teenage time of my life where I had built this hatred toward her, I still loved her more than I could ever put into words.

I have since learned that the flip side of love is not hate, it is indifference. Hate requires as much passion as love. I still had love for my mother, but I had anger and hatred around the actions she took and the behaviors she directed toward me. I was being ignored when I was well-behaved. I received attention and became the focus of my mother's energy when I acted contrary to her wishes. So, to get the passion directed toward me again, I chose to instigate it in whatever form that took.

I had been waiting to battle my mother, to stand up and fight because I lost the battle over school selection. I felt my mother was weak, and my time to attack would come. It sounds awful now. It makes me sound like such a horrible person, but I was hurt and going through puberty. I felt like I needed to stand up for myself.

One night, while we were on this mandated family vacation, I was talking to Megan on my mother's cell phone, venting all my complaints. My mother came into the room and wanted me to get off the phone and go to bed. I didn't know that my mother's new husband was watching the minutes on the phone plan, and I was going over, transitioning into a very expensive call. I kept ignoring my mother's signals to hang up, and the more she got in my face to get off the phone, the more I turned away and ignored her. I kept walking away from her. I couldn't fight against the school situation, but I could fight about being on the phone. I couldn't see my friends, but I could talk to Megan. This is what I was assessing in my mind.

It was hard because I loved the person I was battling. I wish I could coach that young me now to help him realize what he needed and how to ask for it and then give him healthier strategies for managing his complex emotions.

However, without proper tools, on that day, when my mother tried to take the phone away from me, I kept pulling my arm away and twisting around, and we fell on the bed together. We wound up in a wrestling match similar to when I was a kid. She kept trying to grab the phone, and her long fingernail scratched me. I dropped the phone. I attacked my mother verbally. I went at her with my words. Megan was still listening on the other end. Finally, my mother picked up the phone, disconnected the call, left the room, and acted as nothing had happened. That's how I processed the day. My mother had a completely different experience.

Recently, I found out that my mother would lock her bedroom door at night because she was afraid of me. I towered over her. She was tough on me to make herself seem bigger in my eyes. That was her way of keeping me from feeling like I was in charge. She used her mental skills to keep me in check. My brothers just kept out of the way. They didn't defend our mother or me. My world was Ryan-centric. I was all about survival.

After a restless night, I woke the next morning with dark circles around my eyes and noticed a bruise on my arm. It was a small discoloration; not that painful, if I'm being honest. My mother was a slight, 115-pound woman, and at that point, I was a 175-pound teenager.

I funneled all my residual anger about the school, the phone call interruption, and the loss of control of my life into punching myself in the arm repetitively to make that tiny bruise much bigger. I wanted the bruise to tell the story of how I felt inside. It was like cutting—the pain released something in me. When I got home, I told a couple of my friends about my "abusive" mother and showed them the evidence. I basked in the attention and sympathy I craved.

On a deeper level, I wasn't really sure what I wanted to do. I felt I needed to get out of the situation with my mother controlling me. I was truly thinking, *I'm not going to survive.* I knew I had to win this battle with her about my school, or I was going to die. I was already self-mutilating at the time. I'd had suicidal thoughts and actions. When you live for an extended amount of time in the fight or flight mode, constantly waiting to be attacked or having to run, your body chemistry changes.

I had started getting into drugs to release the constant tension, which led to harder drugs and pills. If I kept on, my gut told me I was going to overdose. I was going to cut myself deeply and bleed out one day. I was going to jump off a bridge. My life was in jeopardy, and I don't believe my mother knew. I embellished my wounds on purpose so that I could maybe get out of the situation. I didn't want to hurt her physically. I just didn't want my mother running my life and making my decisions for me any longer. She did not know what was best for me. She did not know my truth.

Megan came to find out what happened. She didn't get to talk to me after she "heard" the fight through the phone. When she saw the bruise, she said, "You have to get out of this. We have to call the police. We have to do something with this; it can't go on." She was distraught for me. I was in a numbed-out state, but I didn't want to involve the police. Megan went into action and started taking pictures for me to have documentation.

I half-heartedly said, "No, no, no, we can't do this. We can't do this." I knew I had created the darker, larger bruise. I decided I wasn't going to do anything at the moment because I didn't know what to do. I did love my mom so much, and deep down, I didn't want to hurt her. So, I told Megan I didn't want to do anything. Not then.

Later, I was talking on AIM to one of Megan's friends who had just turned eighteen but was still a senior in high school, I believe. She said Megan showed her the pictures. "Look," she admitted, "I showed the photos to my boyfriend. He's a police officer. I just can't stand by and let this happen!" And you know, I didn't try to stop her because, at that point, I didn't know if I even could. It wasn't about winning an argument anymore. It wasn't about being right or wrong. I literally knew I wasn't going to survive. Any help I could get, I took.

After the follow-up by the police officer, officials became involved. Child Protective Services temporarily took me away, and I lived with my friend Brad and his family for about a month until the hearing. I used the time to come up with a plan for the next steps. I thought I was getting out from under my mother's thumb, and there would be some relief. I could breathe long breaths again. I wanted to be emancipated. I did the research to see if that was possible.

Unexpectedly, my long-distance dad got involved, and suddenly *every-thing* changed. Dad said he wanted me to come live with him in Nashville, Tennessee. My grandma, I believe, urged him to do it because she said I shouldn't have to live with friends or alone; I shouldn't impose myself on strangers. I should be able to live with my dad, with family.

Living with my father was something I had always wanted since I was little. I really don't think he would have taken no for an answer. I think my grandma would have applied additional pressure until I was ensconced in my father's house with his wife and their young children. This was an unexpected benefit that made me feel hopeful.

I felt that my dad didn't love me when I was young. I thought that I wasn't accepted by him and, as I grew up, that I didn't have his support. In the court hearing, I accepted the judge's ruling that I should live with my father. I was just so relieved I wasn't going to have to go to Catholic high school anymore. I took my father up on his generous offer with dreams dancing in my head of finally having my dad love, accept, and support me. This was going to be interesting. I had such high hopes for my junior year.

13

Healing Affirmation:
I forgive those who have hurt me and kept me from living
my authentic life now or in the past!

LIVING WITH DAD

I moved in with my father the year I headed into my junior year of high school. I treasured playing pool with him the night I arrived. Two men sharing an activity together. I hoped it would be the beginning of many shared times like that. But we did that just once when I first got there.

During my first week in their house, I had dinner with my dad, his wife, and my siblings twice, and that was about it for the whole remaining year and a half that I lived there. I mostly was on my own, fending for myself, as my dad's family went on about their routine without me. I was just a fly on the wall; there, but not there.

During rare whole-family-in-one-room times, it was usually at gatherings that included the larger family, hosted by my grandma. She and PawPaw (my grandfather) were the uniting factor for all of us to be together as a group. Cousins and other relatives were always present.

My father instigated (by his leaving me to care for myself) a repeat of the childhood letdown feelings of *Why am I not good enough? Why doesn't he want to spend time with me? Why doesn't anyone ask to spend time with me?* Someone else, coming from a different mindset, might have been pleased that his father wanted him to come live in the same house, and because he was independent enough, mature enough, and able to fend for himself, that young person would feel confident of having his father's respect. I didn't take it that way. I felt abandoned.

I knew my father was busy. He worked, traveled for business, and had a wife and two other kids who lived under the same roof. I needed reassurance to know that I was still important (or am I not important?). I didn't get that from him, I really got no feedback at all, so I just surmised that "no one thinks I'm important." The more time my father spent with his new family, the further exacerbated my feelings of isolation and lack of importance became.

NASHVILLE, TENNESSEE

I lived in a triangle of communities in the Nashville area. My father's 2,500-square-foot, white, colonial house, embraced by a wraparound porch complete with the traditional rocking chairs, was protected, like all the neighbors' carbon copy homes, by a picket fence and manicured lawns. We were in Springfield, about thirty minutes from Nashville, which was thirty minutes to White House, which was thirty minutes from Springfield. My grandparents lived within that grid.

Yet again, I found myself in a place where I was hiding who I was. Every single day, I was surrounded by conservative Christian evangelicals in a society that was even harsher than the Catholic school that I had tried to escape. My father's family was a big believer in the Bible way of life and Christian observance.

I lived my suburban life tucked away in the bonus room above the garage, just trying to figure out if and where I would ever fit in. I went from the basement of my mother's house to the attic-type space above the garage at my father's. I was in a country-chic home in a Stepford Wives-type community that couldn't be less like me. I couldn't help feeling that I really wasn't meant to be included in the day-to-day life of either family.

Several Christian congregations formed a circle around the house, so there was another judging congregation no matter where I turned. Southern Church of Christ. Southern Baptist. We had our choice of southern anything. Pentecostal, Presbyterian. The only church I knew that was accepting there was the Episcopalians, which was an eclectic small congregation located in downtown Nashville.

Growing up, absorbing signals from family, I was always trying to figure out how to be the "right kind" of Christian. When I was about nine or ten (still going to church with Aunt Jewel), I sat with my Tennessee grandfather (PawPaw) in his home, watching as he added content to his own religion book. It had a photo of him on the cover and important verses and content for him to refer to pasted and stuck inside. My grandfather told me that all these people who went to Aunt Jewel's Baptist church were going to Hell because they were not real Christians. What he meant is that they were not the same as he was.

"But they are still Christian," I'd argue. "They still think Jesus Christ died for their sins," and I asked, "What about Aunt Jewel who baptized me? What about her?"

Grandpa answered, "Oh, well, you better get baptized in the Church of Christ, or it doesn't count. You had better talk to her too about getting baptized the right way now because it's not going to matter unless you get baptized right." I remember walking away and thinking, "Wow. How wrong are they?" I knew in my heart that God loved everyone, no matter where (or if) they went to church.

When I sat in any church of any denomination, I felt the congregation and leaders were condemning me because it's their belief that gay people go to Hell. The rural Nashville area, in general, was just too restrictive and punishing for my non-Christian beliefs and lifestyle. Nashville was certainly not a place where you could just openly be yourself if you were anything out of the norm.

Because of the religious emphasis and the need to remain in the closet, even though I was hyper-aware of my identity at the time, being in Tennessee solidified my addictive behaviors. Self-harming escapist behaviors became an everyday thing as this was how I self-medicated to the degree that I actually believed I was happier.

I eventually made friends who I invited to my private space to share music, liquor, and drugs with me. I used my physical and emotional distance from my stepfamily to spend time with new friends who provided the illusion of family.

White House, Tennessee, is where I went to high school. There was only one out gay kid in our public school, and no one really bullied him because he was super flamboyant and in special ed. I got the impression that the students felt bad for him; they were not going to make fun of him too much. People made stabs and poked fun behind his back, but it wasn't a humiliation type of abuse. I'm sure he still felt the sting of their derision. While it was nice to see there was another kid like me, he was also different from me in other ways that made it hard for me to connect or relate to him.

One time, on the bus to school, someone was making fun of me for being gay, and my new friend Fred said to that person, "Dude, Ryan's straighter than any of you! He gets more pussy than all of us combined!" It was really funny because that wasn't true. I don't know how that rumor started, but there may, to be honest about it, have been some stories I elaborated on about my previous relationships with Kat, Lucy, and Megan. Perhaps, I embellished about the female friends I was making in Tennessee, as well, because that's what you do when you're trying to hide who you are, and you want to fit in with "the guys."

That time on the bus has stuck with me because of just how much it was not true. I'm not straight. It makes me sad that I couldn't let my new friends know me because I was too scared that they wouldn't accept me or love me or be my friends anymore. How many other people have secrets they don't share because they fear not being accepted or liked?

Fred and I are still friends on social media, by the way. I reached out to him when I got sober, and we chatted. I came out to him, and he's been super cool and chill. I haven't seen him face-to-face since I was younger because I haven't been back to visit Nashville very much except to go to funerals.

CONSEQUENCES—MORE FIRST TIMES

The guy friends I made in Tennessee weren't people I easily identified with at all. One was the quarterback for the school, another was a lead soccer player, and one was a super funny musician. Yet, I visited their homes, and they accepted and stuck up for me if I had issues at school. I liked the cool kids in school, and they all seemed to like me. But the reality was that they didn't really know who I was. To them, I was brazen and entertaining. I would often start a water balloon fight in the cafeteria or do other outrageous things that made people laugh. I was an instigator and a leader, but not for good. It's never been a question in my mind that I was fun. But I was always breaking the rules and guiding these friends in the wrong direction.

I definitely was able to put on a facade. I perfected societally acceptable gender normative male behaviors. (*Maybe I should have tried acting?*) To keep people from knowing I was gay, I had to learn how to walk and sit more masculinely and talk using fewer hand gestures. I had to learn how to eat and dress more macho. Once I got my license, I had to learn to drive more masculinely. I had to suppress my every natural mannerism and anything that was instinctive to me.

I learned to listen to certain kinds of music. I became knowledgeable about how to treat women. Everything about me was relearned so people wouldn't know who I really was. All this because the church and my neighbors and the media all said the true me was evil and bad.

One of my new friends/family members was Robin. She was a year older than me. She was part of the in-crowd that seemed to adopt me at my new high school. About a month after I moved to Tennessee, Robin felt there were some things I should really see, being new to the area, so she and I skipped school to go to the Opryland Hotel to get away for a day and explore. Getting in trouble at school with Robin led my teacher to contact my parents directly and Robin's parents as well. For some reason, the teacher didn't notify the principal.

When the teacher called my dad, he was, as usual, out of town because his business is out of town. My father called me and said, "Ryan, if you're going to act like this and you're going to cause problems with me, I'll send you right back home." What!? The thing was that I couldn't go back home because CPS had taken me away from my mom because they thought my mother and I had gotten physical. I didn't have the choice to go back. It was one of the hardest things to hear from a parent, ever. *I'll just send you back home* proved to me how my father viewed me. I was not home at his house. I felt that I was just an object to him. Something that could get moved around from place to place as was convenient. No different than a piece of furniture that no longer matched the other pieces in the room.

Robin and I eventually paired up. In my quest to be accepted, having a girlfriend was a way to avoid suspicion of my true nature. Like Kat from my previous co-ed high school, Robin had a very pep-squad energy that just made her shine. I felt happy when I was around her. She was my best friend and, ultimately, quasi girlfriend while I lived in Tennessee. Robin and I hung out a lot, smoking weed and drinking. She stole her parent's pain pills for me, and we'd get stoned together. Usually, it was me getting more wasted than her. I was a bad influence, no doubt.

I don't know much about sports, but I went to my new school's homecoming game with Robin. We had friends on the field, so we celebrated with them after they won the game. I got super drunk that night. When the festivities ended, Robin and I went back to my segregated space in my father's house.

I think we kind of fell onto my bed in a haze from all the drinking and partying, and she pretty much just took control. Alcohol definitely reduces inhibitions, and Robin was one to get what she wanted. For my part, at the moment, I wasn't blacked out, but I can't say that I was fully aware of the experience. I was just there, and as they describe near-death experiences, I floated above and just let the moment happen as I observed myself losing my virginity. Sadly, I don't have any romantic memories of this significant milestone in my life.

I don't recall talking to her about homecoming night or what it meant for "us." I don't know if Robin knew I was a virgin when she did what she did, or perhaps Robin thought she was giving me a gift. I'm not sure.

Eventually (after coming out to Megan and Kat in Kentucky), and after Robin and I broke up, I told Robin I was different. Even though it was my third time coming out, it was still hard. I cried, and she cried. Robin was much more accepting than anyone else I'd come out to in the past. She let me know it was okay. "God made you that way, and it's cool. I'm sad because I was in love with you." She couldn't 100 percentbe supportive because she loved me in that high school love dramatic way. Regardless, it was nice to have someone there in Tennessee who knew my secret.

Robin and I maintained a friends-with-benefits kind of relationship, after homecoming night, for the remainder of my time in Tennessee. I enjoyed my physical time with Robin even though I still found myself attracted to males. And it was nice to have a friend who didn't threaten to use it against me. When we fought, or she was angry at me, Megan had often threatened to use my secret against me.

Robin went off to college when I started my senior year of high school. We drifted apart eventually.

FREEDOM ON WHEELS

Though mostly my father left me to my own devices, with little apparent concern for my day-to-day comfort, wishes, or thoughts, he always provided what I needed to live. The one extra thing he did was teach me to drive soon after I moved into his home. Granted, having me drive would mean less bothersome pesky requests for a ride from my stepmother, and my extra car in the household would allow me to use it to taxi around my half-siblings.

With a driver's license, I could get to work, and having a job meant not asking for cash or necessities from the family. For whatever reason, my dad decided to offer this to me, and since it was to my advantage, I did not get picky about how it was delivered.

Back when I came of the right age, my mother took me to get my learner's permit when I was in Kentucky. She was a nervous wreck when it came time to allow me to drive. In Tennessee, my father took me to practice driving in the school parking lot and supermarket lots when the stores were closed. I had only been driving a few times with my mother, but I spent plenty of time in cars with older friends who I observed driving often enough to be pretty familiar with the basics. My father and I didn't have to go out together too many times. Legally, in Tennessee, I needed to have the learner's permit for only six months (not a year) and put in fifty hours of an assortment of driving experiences (day, night, parking, roadways, etc.), and my father had to sign off that I had done the work.

Our conversations in the car during lessons were no more personal than if I had gone to a professional driving school. There was no laughter, no reminiscing by my dad about when he learned to drive, no real feeling of father/son bonding. The whole process was quite mechanical where I felt the energy of let's-just-get-this-over-with rising like a vapor around my dad. No complaints. I was taking another step to independence and was okay with letting my childhood fantasies about a warm relationship with my father fall onto the road behind me.

I got my license when I was sixteen years old with absolutely no fanfare, no celebration. I called my friends and smoked a blunt by myself.

I used the money I had saved to buy a used car. It was my first major purchase. My father came with me. I had selected a used green Ford V8 Thunderbird that was really fast. I loved feeling the speed of that car in my control. My dad never said he was proud of me for buying my own car, nor did he want to go for a ride with me. What could have been a special memory became a task to check off his to-do list.

On the first day I got my new wheels, I drove to Robin's house, which was in the next town over, to show off my purchase. We celebrated by getting stoned in her bedroom closet using a homemade soda can pipe after sealing the door frame with towels and opening the outside window.

WORK & WHEELS

Once I had wheels, I started working as a server at a place in Springfield called The Catfish House. They have always been known for their hush puppies and all-you-can-eat catfish dinners. Amidst dark wood walls and furniture, big families, office parties, and milestone celebrations gathered together, laughing and celebrating at the brown paper-covered tables, you have to be on your toes. I learned how to smile my way through just about anything and reaped the rewards of good tips.

In the emptiness of my dad always being busy with other things, working was a good way to fill time, be away from the lonely house, earn money, and the place where I met Cecilia. Cecilia was such a delightful and upbeat person at work. She exuded light, and it wasn't just her luminous dark brown hair that made her look like she had a halo surrounding her. She had what I came to recognize as a beautiful soul. We started smoking weed together at work, and eventually, all the time. I would buy it from her friends, and we would smoke when we were together, and then I began to smoke by myself.

Cecilia got me into a rough group of people who were older than me. I made friends with Robert and Zeke and some of their friends. This group was filled with potheads. They did drugs and drank alcohol, and I spent my time partying. I turned to drugs as my main outlet to avoid thinking depressing thoughts and self-value questions. I smoked and drank and popped pills and all that stuff. The pills were sporadic, but I would smoke weed on my way to school and was getting high every single day. I would still drink every now and again, but I could never stop drinking once I started. My drinking binges ended with me passed out somewhere, peeing on myself, possibly throwing up, often not remembering how I got to where I woke up.

Somehow, I still earned good grades and maintained a job. When I wasn't at school or working or doing homework, I was doing drugs and partying.

INTENTION

I had made the room above the garage into a makeshift apartment. I ultimately wound up liking the distance it gave me from the rest of the family. I needed privacy. I had my own locked door, with a separate entrance through the side of the garage. Inside I set up a big-screen TV and a futon couch/guest bed. The privacy made it an ideal place to invite people over. My friends and I were smoking weed up there when my stepmom's sister, visiting from Wales, wandered in and caught us.

My dad, as usual, was out of town, but he let the kids I'd invited who were already there continue to spend the night as planned. When I got home from school (or maybe it was work) the next day, he was waiting for me and told me I was grounded indefinitely! I didn't like the ambiguity, so I pushed him to provide a time frame. He grounded me for a month.

I obeyed my father because I didn't want him to be angry. I had already been kicked out of my mother's home. Where would I go if I couldn't stay with my father? What would he do if something else I did disappointed him?

I made it through that whole month without smoking any pot whatsoever because I wasn't around my friends. I wanted to prove to myself that I could do it. Plus, I needed to play it safe and make sure I didn't get in any additional trouble. I just went to school and work and came home. I felt healthier and thought, *Well, maybe I have no problem with drugs or alcohol.*

I won't smoke at all. The problem was that when you're depressed and anxious, and you remove the one thing that stabilizes you, the symptoms of your underlying issues rise to the surface.

I wasn't able to see my friend Megan for that whole month. She would drive the three-and-a-half hours from college at the University of Kentucky to visit me some weekends. Not seeing her was really the hardest part of my punishment because, despite some of the toxic aspects of our relationship, we were so close. I shared everything with her. I connected with her in a deep and meaningful way that I couldn't find with my family. During the whole time I was grounded, I had no one and no place to vent my feelings and frustrations.

Naturally, as soon as I was released from being grounded at the end of the month, I was smoking weed again the very first day I was free. I was *not* strong enough to give it up on my own at that time. I needed to get stable. I went back to hanging out with my cool friends and partying because that's just what we did. I was able to find relief from my depression.

I kept going over the revelation that my father threatening to send me "home" meant that he didn't consider this house as my home too. It was always meant to be a temporary situation as if I was a visiting stranger. In my soul, I could feel that I wasn't part of the family he had built in Tennessee. My being with him was punishment. Punishment for him or me, I never knew. I struggled with it for a long time. I think that was one of the things that pushed me further into drugs and alcohol because I felt I had no communication whatsoever with my mom, and then my dad didn't want to spend time with me. Then, add on that he'd ship me back "home" if I wasn't not living up to his standards. What the hell?

To make matters worse, my stepmom, Nancy, and I had a really weird relationship. She and my mother didn't get along. There was some jealousy there. I think Nancy wanted me to like her more than my own mother. So, when Nancy tried to console me and talk to me empathetically after my dad got angry at me or grounded me, she would fight with my dad about it, later on, standing up for me. My dad would call me and say I was causing problems in his marriage. It was a whole dysfunctional cycle, and I wanted to be detached from them. I didn't feel like I had any parents nor a safe place to call home.

Luckily, I had my father's parents, Grandma Irene and PawPaw, and my other grandmother, Mamaw Patsy, and Papaw (Grandpa Bill), on my mother's side. So, I didn't alienate my grandparents, only my parents. I always had grandparents to go to and talk to, and they loved me and always supported me and never turned their back on me. And that was good.

14

Healing Affirmation:
I am releasing secrets or secretive vibes around me.
I don't need to hide who I AM.
I am proud of who I am and where I am going in life!

THE PINK BATH

I got really drunk with my friend Megan around Christmas time the first year I moved to Tennessee. I was seventeen. Megan had come to visit. We had gotten a hold of some alcohol. I don't remember what it was; rum or something. My go-to is Bacardi rum. We drank the whole bottle. Then I went into my dad's stash and drank some of his Beefeater's gin straight out of the bottle. (Side note: Ever since then, even looking at gin makes me want to gag!) Megan was passing out and needed to go to sleep.

I decided to listen to music that reminded me that I wasn't alone. Once again, I grabbed the shiny sewing shears and sat in the chair in my room. In some ways, you would think the sad music would have been reassuring, but it wasn't. It made me feel like I was in a darker place and delve deeper into my sorrow. I'm sure the alcohol had a lot to do with that. I didn't care that alcohol is a depressant. It made me forget. It made me numb. I was depressed and drunk.

Sitting in my chair with the shears, I started playfully, in time with the music, cutting my leg with slashes everywhere. I watched in fascination as the blood slowly trickled down my leg to the floor. I found some weird satisfaction. I never knew why I cut myself at that moment. As much as I have tried to analyze it and figure things out a little bit, I still don't know why I did it. I know I felt hopeless at that moment, but I always felt that lack of hope from having to hide who I was every day.

When the blood started pooling onto the floor, I jumped up to wash it off my legs. I went into the bathroom, taking the scissors with me, and instead of just washing off the blood, I filled a warm bath for myself. At the edge of the tub, I took the scissors, and I cut a gruesome gash in my leg about four inches long and probably a quarter of an inch deep, maybe even more. I stepped into the tub and sank down into the welcoming warmth of the water. First, the water was pink, then it turned red, swirling around me as the hot water continued to fill the tub. This was perhaps my first real attempt on my own life because the others were planned but never initiated.

Megan walked in, and once again, she saved my life. Later on, when I came to my senses and had to patch myself up, I couldn't believe what I had done.

In some ways, maybe my codependency with Megan, both of us loaded with self-hatred, created some of my issues, but in other ways, maybe it saved me because that's what I needed at that time in my life. I don't know. I don't think any of us can know for sure about things like that, but I do know that looking back, I can acknowledge and say thank you. Thank you, Megan, for saving my life twice.

Megan pulled me out of the bathtub, got the wound to stop bleeding, and bandaged me up temporarily. She made sure I made it to the bed. While I slept, she cleaned up the bathroom and kept an eye on me. We woke up the next day, and, in the sober light of day, we had a serious talk. She wanted to know, "Why did you do that? What happened? When I went to bed, you were fine."

I looked down and away and admitted that I was trying to kill myself. I thought Megan would yell, but instead, she cried, "Why, why, why, why, would you do that? Why would you do that to yourself? Why would you do that to me? I'm your best friend. I need you. I need you!" Megan's cries reminded me that someone loved me. I was feeling so much shame.

I didn't even have enough bandages in the house. We had to buy gauze and cleaning materials and realized that the wound really should have been stitched up. It was an extremely large gash in my leg that, later, when I learned more about anatomy, I realized was only about two inches from a major artery. If I had made my random cut just two inches lower, I might have bled out in the tub before Megan found me. Instead, I have to live with the guilt and shame of this thing every time I look at the scar. The scars of my cutting remind me that I'm a survivor. Somehow God and this universe have bigger plans for me.

GOD'S ADULT BOOKSTORE MESSAGE

After we got all the bandaging materials and went home to fix up my leg per our basic first aid knowledge, we went back out. We went downtown to Nashville and wandered into an adult bookstore. The store was in the shadiest part of Nashville. I felt scared and nervous, but I was so happy to realize there must be other people like me. My logic said that if there was a whole gay porn section of the store and an entire bisexual section, then I wasn't alone.

I think it was God leading me to the adult bookstore, not for the porn but to remind me that I was not alone. God can find you sitting on a beach in paradise, but God can also find you in a porn store in Nashville, Tennessee. God was in that moment, lifting me up and reminding me that I'm okay just the way I am. That I'm loved just the way I am.

EMANCIPATION

For Christmas, the second year I was living in Tennessee (my senior year), I was staying at my grandparents' house because my dad and my stepmom were out of town. My friend Robert came to town from college for the holidays. I picked him up to introduce him to my weed dealer, J.D. I felt like those were my dudes, and I wanted them to meet. So, we went over to White House. That turned out to be the night I got arrested.

The cops saw us all at Kroger Market. I'm sure they targeted us because they knew who Robert was. Everyone knew who he was. Robert is a fun guy, one of my favorite people ever, but he was definitely notorious for getting into not-quite-legal shenanigans. We'd already smoked, and I probably wasn't driving my best, so when the cops pulled us over, they arrested me for being underage and high. Robert and J.D. were over eighteen, so I claimed, "All the shit's mine." So, they arrested me. At seventeen, I was still a minor, so we knew that my records would be sealed if anything was prosecuted.

My grandma and grandpa picked me up at the police station and were truly upset. They cried. I never really fought with them, but I had a fiery discussion with them about the situation. The next day, of course, I apologized. I did not want to disappoint them. They were the only family that seemed to care about me.

I went to school or work or whatever I was supposed to do because I was always staying busy. I had one extra rolled blunt in the car that the police didn't find. It was in the side pocket. I found the blunt on my way home, and I smoked it, used eye drops, and went home to deal with whatever my dad would dish out.

Obviously, I was grounded again and in a lot of trouble. My father and I got into a physical altercation, and he pushed me down. I grabbed his arm off of me and snarled, "Don't you ever fucking touch me, ever! Do you think that you have a right to touch me? Don't think that you can step in and try to be my dad now after all these years. Especially after living here a whole year-and-a-half and you not even spending time with me or taking any type of fatherly role in my life! Don't even think that you can step in now. It's too late." Those words, spewed out with nary a breath, were like a knife to him, I'm sure. Nothing between us has ever been the same since then. It wasn't great before that incident, but we had to redefine our relationship. I still knew he loved me, but he didn't like me, and any father/son bond I thought we could cultivate slipped away from me like sand through my fingers right at that moment.

That physical altercation happened because I was coming down from drugs and alcohol. I know people say you can't be addicted to weed. Well, you can surely be addicted to weed. It's definitely mood-altering, and when you have it for a long time over and over again, and you go a couple of days without it, it affects your moods, especially since I was self-medicating my bipolar, ADHD, anxiety, depression, and other mental health issues.

That was the end of the road for my dad. I'd pushed his last nerve. My dad told me he wanted me out of his house. "You have to go, but we have to do it the right way. I'm going to emancipate you," he said.

I had wanted to be emancipated from my mom when I was younger, so I had already looked into it. It was a very lengthy and difficult process. You have to prove all these things, and it's expensive. My father said, "I want to emancipate you. I don't want to have to deal with you. I don't want you to be my problem." It was obvious to me that my mother wouldn't want me to be her problem either.

It was odd to go through all the legal paperwork and expense since I was turning eighteen in two more months and wouldn't need it. I said, "Well, technically, you can just kick me out when I'm eighteen." He looked at me with disgust, his pupils so dark and enlarged that I couldn't see more than a sliver of white, and he said, "I don't even want you here until then. I don't want you here in between Christmas and February. I'm emancipating you."

I said, "Okay. I'm going to pack my stuff up and go." I was so deflated. Before I could get into a long think about having no parents who wanted me, I went to stay at my grandma's house for a day or two, where I felt appreciated.

My plan was (again) to go stay with my friend Megan at the University of Kentucky because she had an apartment there. I stayed with her for a few weeks and then went back home to visit my family in Cincinnati, where I went to my mom's for Christmas for the first time in a long time. The prior year I hadn't been invited to my mother's for the holiday.

I entered the house with great hesitation. I had just gotten arrested and knew I was in trouble. My mother told me, "Hey, your dad wants me to sign these emancipation papers. I don't really have a choice because, you can't live with me either, so you're going to be emancipated."

After hearing this, I was so emotional that I just went back to Megan's for the rest of Christmas break. She held me as I cried for hours. We talked about all my options. She told me she would be there for me. I told my mother that I had found a short-term solution. "I guess I'm gonna live with Megan at her college, but I don't know where I'm going to go to school."

Coincidentally the semester I arrived, Megan was having a hard time at college and was really sick with migraines. She had other things going on around her, multiple mental health issues as well. She told me she was moving back home to Cincinnati to take the spring semester off to deal with everything. She was moving back in with her parents. She asked her parents if I could move in as well and they, being good Christians, graciously agreed. I moved in with them and started working with Megan at the airport.

I went back to my original high school, but because I was working full time, I attended night classes. Then I had to take summer classes to finish all the coursework that had never been required in Tennessee but was indeed required in Northern Kentucky to earn a diploma.

15

THE AIRPORT

Megan introduced me to some people she knew at the airport terminal, and I got a job working as a customer service representative in a little store called Toto.

I was hiding my gay porn at Megan's house and scared about what would happen if her very devout Catholic family found it and kicked me out.

I was trying to turn a new leaf since I was living in Megan's family home. These are the same people I knew wouldn't accept me because of Jesus and God. I didn't smoke for the first couple of weeks, and then some new friends at work had access to weed, and I started all over again.

I was a month into sobriety, and after just a few weeks working at the airport, I had started smoking every single day again. Ultimately, it turned into an even worse addiction because I was smoking alone (sometimes with Megan). With my family rejecting me and hiding my true self, my mental health was in a bad state. I just couldn't stay in the real world for too long. It would have been like someone coming off an anti-depressant. If you read the cautions on those prescriptions, they warn that suddenly stopping can make people suicidal and have physical withdrawal complications.

SERIOUS GIRLFRIEND—LIZ

I had dated several girls throughout my school years. I had lost my virginity to Robin, an older girl. I was eighteen, newly emancipated, finishing up high school, and about to begin college. I lived with Megan and her family when I met Liz. She worked in the same airport terminal as a teller at Fifth Third Bank.

Liz was a couple of years older than me, a sophomore in college. I came in daily to drop the store deposits. We started flirting with each other across the counter at the bank teller window. She started including little notes in the bags when she returned them empty to me. I'd put in notes for her with the deposit. Nothing earth-shatteringly unique, more like, "I hope you have a great day."

My adorable, kind, but firm and efficient store manager, Marshall, knew I had a crush on the bank teller, so Marshall became my cupid, sending me to get change and other small bank-related duties more often than necessary.

I looked forward to going to work because every day, I went to the bank and had another opportunity to flirt with Liz. I brought her chocolate bars and flowers and little gifts that I would pass through the cut-away in the bulletproof glass.

I finally asked her on a date. I wanted so badly to reach out and hug her. I wanted to feel her standing next to me. I was so excited.

For our first date, I asked her to go hiking, and she said yes. We hiked at a local park and then played frisbee golf. We fell for each other immediately, and neither of us could stop smiling. I don't necessarily know if I fell in love, but we became instant best friends, and within three months, we were inseparable.

At this point, I felt like I needed to share my whole truth with Liz. I loved her as a best friend and didn't want to hide anything. I wanted to make our relationship work. For a whole night, we talked until about 4:00 in the morning. I told her that I liked and was attracted to men, but I had never actually been with a man. I had many girlfriends, mostly petting and affection, but I was not a virgin. I identified to her as bisexual.

Liz shared, too, and I found out just how difficult my reveal was for her. It turned out that her previous boyfriend had come out as gay when they broke up. My confession was a triggering thing for her as she spiraled into the thought that *all* the men that she loved are gay. If Liz chose to be with me, my bisexuality wasn't going to drop like a bombshell later. I came out at the beginning of our relationship, so she knew early on and could make her decisions fully informed. Ultimately, my lifestyle choice around drugs and alcohol was going to be more of an issue in our relationship than my bisexuality.

Our relationship evolved; we had a lot of great times and came to love one another. Liz didn't really drink or do drugs, so that was a bit of a disconnect because of my history, and I was still involved in a bit of that. My mother liked Liz because not only was she a sober person, but I was also spending less time with Megan, and that was good in my mother's eyes.

JAGGED EDGE

I was nineteen years old, sitting in my first apartment. I had a job at the airport, was in college, had a car, a steady girlfriend, and a little bit of residual student loan money to help mitigate some of my extra bills. From an outsider's point of view, I was actually doing okay.

Liz and I had been dating for almost six months when we got into a huge fight over something so trivial that I can't even remember what it was about now. It was probably about me being a pothead. I just remember the fight escalated quite quickly, and I just snapped. I had such ferocious anger that I broke the cable remote in half. You have to understand that the cable remote was a pretty thick, heavy-duty gadget meant to withstand just about any abuse, so it's amazing (and scary) I had that anger-fueled strength to do that.

Out of nowhere, watching myself from afar in slow motion, I took the jagged edge of that broken remote, and used it to cut diagonally up my arm in front of Liz. There was a lot of blood, my skin was rough and mangled looking, and I just watched as my girlfriend burst out in tears. Then I started crying, looking down at my bleeding arm as if it belonged to someone else and immediately apologized. "Sorry, I don't know why I would do this. I didn't mean to do this. I don't know what happened! It's almost like something came over me and made me do it." I remember that moment, that day, as one of the worst times in my life.

Thinking about that now, how traumatic was that for Liz to have to watch? At that moment, I guess I knew it was bad because I kept saying, "Sorry. I'm sorry for the fight. I am sorry for the cutting. I am sorry for the violence toward myself. I didn't mean to do it. I didn't want to do it. I just did it."

The worst part was the healing process afterward. There's guilt and shame that come along when you dive into those moments when you're covering up and hiding when you're lying. For about six weeks, I had to wear long-sleeved shirts/sweatshirts or risk revealing my jagged truth to everyone. The scars were a constant reminder of what I had done.

Even when a doctor saw my scars and asked me, "What are these marks?" I said, "I fell on the concrete and swiped my arm in a weird way." I was good at storytelling, and I got very good at lying. The incident was never mentioned again.

What's odd is that for someone who wanted help in the bad times, I had an opportunity to get help, but I didn't take it. I was still too scared to be myself. What if they found out who I was? Then I would have to admit to myself who I truly was, and I didn't want to have to do that; I wasn't ready. Every time I had come out up to this point, it broke my spirit just a little bit more. I wanted to just "be," but it seemed like I needed to explain myself in order to be me.

Liz stayed. She didn't run. She didn't turn away from me. We cried together. She took care of me. It was like by cutting, I had released some maternal, nurturing, caregiving side of her. I needed her, she believed. Liz needed to be needed. We fit together perfectly.

BIG NEWS

I moved to Bowling Green, Kentucky to go to college. Liz stayed in Cincinnati to finish her bachelor's degree in special ed. We had been together for about three years.

In the beginning of May of our third year together, I talked to Liz's father and got his permission to marry his daughter. I bought a ring and was planning on proposing to Liz on her college graduation day. Her dad told me he couldn't have picked a better person to marry his daughter. (This was a little amusing because the rest of the family didn't much care for me.) Her father passed away right before graduation, and out of respect for her mourning process, mixed with graduation, I postponed my original proposal plans.

At this point, Liz already knew I had the ring; she just didn't know when I would propose. As corny as it sounds, I proposed at the end of our friend's wedding that summer, on the baseball field of the Catholic Church during the time between the ceremony and reception (I got permission from our friends to do this). My little brother Cody was my partner in this production.

I had Cody place eleven dozen roses in big vases around the baseball diamond. (Liz and I shared an interest in numbers and favored ones and twos.) I got on one knee on the pitcher's mound and proposed to Liz. She nodded, "yes," and I slipped an engagement diamond on her hand in the middle of the baseball diamond. Cody recorded a video of the whole proposal.

Our friend's wedding reception thus turned out to be a special celebration of our engagement (how convenient). We had eleven dozen roses and candles surrounding us at home as we celebrated our engagement with a romantic lovemaking session.

Liz joined me in Bowling Green, Kentucky, after our engagement. Within a few months, Liz, who was prone to spotting instead of having full periods, told me that she was missing her period. She said she felt "off," so I took her to the doctor.

The doctor asked if we were planning on having children and what kind of protection we were using. Liz had been on the pill for a while, and then we switched to condoms. The doctor reprimanded us, saying, "If you're having sex and you're not using birth control, then you were planning to have kids, and good thing you were planning, because you are pregnant!" Our response? "Oh my God! Really?" And we sat there in shock. We calmly set up the next doctor's appointment, got in the car, and we both let out screams!

Liz had literally just graduated college, and I still had a couple of years left in school. I was still smoking weed and doing hard drugs every now and again when I could find them. We were not living the lifestyle conducive to having and raising a kid. We were still playing! Honestly, our sex life was not very wild, as we didn't see each other that often with our commute before she moved to Kentucky, so it was safe to say, both of us were stunned.

We calculated that our child was conceived during our engagement weekend, which we thought was kind of beautiful. We took a day to process this new information, and then we shared our news with our families. We told Liz's mom first via phone call because we were a couple of hours away from most of our family. The initial response was a shock, but they were not super upset because, after all, we were engaged. Her conservative family expressed their wish that we were already married before this announcement, but what are you going to do?

My Aunt Carol, at first (maybe because she intuited, I was LGBTQ+), didn't want us to have a baby. Then she insisted that we should get married immediately before the baby was born. It could have been because we were so young or just that I was still in college or maybe because the church expects the wedding and *then* the baby, or who knows why or what she was thinking.

Everyone simmered down and ultimately embraced the idea of the new baby that was to join our families. We had a baby shower, of course. It was held at a local church in the Cincinnati area. Unlike most dads-to-be, I wanted to go to the baby shower. I wanted to sit on stage with my baby mama and open presents and welcome everyone and say thank you and be a part of all that. It was really fun and a good experience overall. I think that's one of the ways that gender norms have been hard for me because I've always wanted to go to baby showers and do stuff like that where people would look at me and say, "Uhm…no boys allowed." *Sorry honey, that doesn't apply to me!*

Liz took a job at a bank in Bowling Green, Kentucky, until she could find a teaching position, and, for the first time in many years, I was unemployed and entirely focused on going to school. I always had, since the beginning of high school, had a job. However, I enjoyed a respite from the grind of working and was focused on and embracing my studies.

My break was short-lived, though. Within a month of our startling news, I was able to find a new job. I came home one day and showed Liz my little apron and a menu and announced that I was back to working as a server. We were so excited together. We definitely had a lot going on as we were building our future together.

When Liz was about three months pregnant, I decided to stop smoking marijuana, and I gave away all my weed. I kept one blunt for myself, just for that time…that time when I might need something more than just alcohol. I was proud of myself. I did really well. I didn't smoke, and our relationship was getting healthier. It seemed that the pregnancy was bringing us together. Arguments were calm, and there were more discussions than fights and definitely no physical altercations in any way, shape, or form.

MOMMY, I'M GAY OR BISEXUAL OR WHATEVER

We were in the Cincinnati area visiting family when Liz was about five months pregnant, and we started to argue about something trivial. Somehow it came up that I wanted to come out to Liz's sister because I felt her sister might be affirming and open-minded. I thought Liz might need someone to talk to openly and having her sister know all the details would be helpful. Keep it in the family, as they say.

I had an intuition that Melissa wouldn't judge me, and I knew she would allow me to be me. I asked Liz, "Can I come out to Melissa as bisexual or whatever?" and she said no. I realize now that Liz was likely worried about what people would think since she was pregnant with my baby. How could a gay man be the father of a baby? What would happen to being a family?

However, her rejection at the time only intensified our fight, which progressed to even nastier levels. "But I'll go ahead and tell your mom if you want to tell somebody! Let's just tell her!" she threatened. This was old history; she would repeatedly threaten to out me to my family in conversations and fights.

To be fair, my relationship with Liz was abusive on both sides. I had been taught a lot of abusive, dramatic, and codependent behaviors, which led to my self-abuse years. Liz and I were just doing the best we could with what we'd been taught (or not taught, actually) about being in a relationship. We both wanted control over the relationship and over the other person. Liz's control tactics included threats: "I'll call the police on you for doing drugs," or "I'll tell your family (or everyone) you're gay."

I had walked away from her and was sitting in the bathroom and crying when she came in to talk to me. I pleaded with her, "Why won't you just let me be me? I want to tell your sister. I want you to have someone to talk to about this, and I think she'll understand me."

Liz shut me down, saying, "That is embarrassing. You're not telling any-body in my family. I *will* tell your mom if you want to tell somebody!" Once again, throwing a threat in my face.

I said, "Give me my phone," and I stormed off, got my phone, and called my mom. Mom answered and asked, "What's wrong, honey?" She could tell I was crying.

"I'm gay or bisexual or whatever."

"Okay."

"Okay?"

Liz was sitting there for a while, but when I started telling my mother why I was sharing, Liz got up and left. "Liz and I got in a fight because I wanted to tell Liz's sister that I was bisexual, and she didn't want me to, and she told me that she was going to tell you. So, I'm telling you. Okay?"

"All right. Well, I mean, this isn't like 'breaking news' to us, Ryan. We thought this your whole life. I mean, you used to go around dressing up in high heels and dresses, and you've always been a little feminine, arts and crafts kind of kid. Me and your stepdad had this conversation years and years ago. What if, you know. We've always said that we would love you boys, if you were gay or straight."

"Well, okay." I deflated at that point and sank to the floor. This big balloon in the room that had been pushing on me, crowding me into a corner, was suddenly empty, and I could breathe. I didn't know what to think. I'd waited all this time to share this important news, and they suspected all along? It was a bit shocking that they weren't shocked!

Mom continued, "Ron was worried that you might have a more chal-lenging life, and he didn't want that for you, but we talked, and we said that it is what it is, and we'll just support you and love you like we do already. And we do, Ryan. We love you so much."

I know that I'd been told many times while growing up that it doesn't matter. Ron and my mother always told my brothers and me, "We love you for who you are; we love you just the way you are." But it was harder for me when I realized my truth, and it came time to actually talk about it. I just couldn't. I may have known that I was going to be accepted, but it was just something I couldn't say out loud. I had a really hard time.

I had only come out to three or four people, total. It wasn't something that I wanted to do except in this moment I wanted to come out to Melissa, and I wasn't able to. I came out to someone else I trusted (my mother), and it ended up being really wonderful! Our conversation was very uplifting, and we cried together.

I said, "I don't know why I have to be this way. Mom said, "What do you mean?" I started sobbing again. "I just want to be normal. Like Brent or Cody or my friends growing up! Why do I have to be different? Why did God make me this way?"

"You know it doesn't matter. We love you just as you are, and God must have made you that way because that's who you are. It's okay to be different. You have to celebrate being different."

With that, my mother had started planting seeds in me a long time before I was able to understand that myself. It was okay to be me, okay to be different, okay to not fall into the categories that my brothers or friends fell into. It was okay to be someone completely different than anyone in my family.

When I woke the next morning, I felt so much lighter! But despite my normal heaviness lifting, I still carried so much shame and guilt around my identity that I made my mother promise that she wouldn't tell a single soul. I went over the whole list just to be totally clear. "I don't care who it is. I don't want you even telling your own therapist about it!"

I started to stress about whom she might tell. What if she told her husband or my ex-stepdad (Ron), who was still a big part of my life? What if she tells my dad? What if she tells my brothers? Or her friends? And from that moment forward, we never spoke about my coming out. I think my mother called me to see how I was doing. I said, "I'm doing okay," and we didn't talk about it ever again.

I often think about other people and their coming-out stories. They're much different from mine. I had a father, grandparents, extended family, and other people who had said and done things that made me feel unsafe, so I understand what that feels like, and yet I always had a loving nuclear family that supported me. And I *still* didn't feel like I could be myself and come out.

You could have the most loving, accepting, wonderful family in the world and still not be ready to tell them because it has nothing to do with your family but has more to do with you. Maybe the timing has more to do with where you're at in life and about accepting it yourself. If you can't accept it yourself, you can't expect anyone else to accept it, and I wasn't at a place in my life at that time where I could really fully accept it.

I wanted to hide. I felt like it didn't really matter because I never acted on my interest in males. I'd never so much as done any more than touching a guy's hand, and that was an odd experience. I was on my senior trip to the Canary Islands when I was eighteen. My best friend Megan was with me, and since she knew my truth, she wanted to support me and took me to a gay bar. We drank a lot, and I wound up touching this guy's hand in the bathroom. It was such a weird feeling, and I felt once again ashamed and dirty while simultaneously feeling free. I had a thought that what happened had felt "right." And yet, despite being halfway around the world, I was still scared that someone would find out that I'd even gone to a gay bar, so obviously, something still felt wrong and illicit and needing to be kept secret. In the end, I pep-talked myself into believing I was in the clear. "I think I'm okay. I think no one saw me." I hope that eventually, no human will ever have to feel shame or embarrassment about who they are.

16

A NEW LIFE

Life was calm for a while after I came out. No more threats. After our trip to visit family in Ohio, Liz confided in me how much she wanted to move back to Ohio. She wanted to go home and be able to raise our child around our families. We would need their support if we were both going to be working, she rationalized.

One day I came home from school and told my bride-to-be, "Guess what?" as I handed her a typed-up page. "Here is my school schedule for next semester for Northern Kentucky University. I'm transferring back home, and everything's in the works. WKU and NKU are both aware. We're moving back home!" She was elated. I just had to finish off the semester. We were about to move!

I had stayed sober for a large piece of Liz's pregnancy. It was like I was having a sympathetic pregnancy. Liz and I worked through this transition period over the next few months and moved back to Cincinnati. During this time, I started to feel overwhelmed at the idea of being a husband and father in just a few months. I was disconnected from everyone and dreaded moving back, close to extended family that had always been challenging. I coped with these pending big lifestyle changes by starting to use drugs again.

Brent still says that a huge negative shift happened to me when I found out Liz was pregnant. He didn't know about my return to drugs when I moved back home, but he could see a gloom had descended on me.

BIRTH

In April 2011, Liz's water broke. She was dilated, so we went to the hospital. She stayed five centimeters forever and would not dilate any further. Eventually, the doctors decided to do a C-section.

I was beyond ecstatic when my daughter was born! I was in the operating room and able to hold little Harper for the first time. People tell you that things change when you hold your baby for the first time, and you don't know what that means, but I definitely felt a shift within me. One look into my child's eyes, and in that instant, I knew my life was not just my life, ever again. As a parent, you're not living your life for yourself. You're living your life for your child. It took me about a year to really get that under my belt and to fully embrace the lifestyle changes I needed to make to be a good dad and partner.

When we returned from the hospital with our new baby, I was tempted beyond my control because the doctors had given Liz some pain pills for the emergency C-section healing. I had abstained from taking pain pills for maybe six months, but I admit that I snuck a bunch of Liz's pills. I didn't take them right away because I didn't want her not to have them if she needed them, of course. So, I waited a couple of weeks, and around the first part of May, since she hadn't even used her extra-strength Tylenol, I pocketed all of her pills.

I didn't want to do them around her and the baby, so I took them when I went to work. I went to work for four or five days straight, just totally messed up. I'm surprised no one noticed, but maybe I had been so high previously that this seemed on par with my regular demeanor. Or maybe they correctly deduced that I'd started getting high again. I don't know, but

I was loaded, and over time I finished the whole bottle of her pain pills. At one point, Liz said, "Hey, where did those pain pills go? Did you take them?" I answered, "No. I threw them away just so I wouldn't be tempted to take them." She believed me, or maybe she didn't. Either way, she knew I wasn't smoking weed, and things were going okay between us.

Living back in Cincinnati again, with a baby at home, trying to balance school, work, partnership, and fatherhood, something would often trigger angry disagreements, and our fights escalated to the point of disturbing the neighbors. When you don't feel in control, or you don't feel you have control over a situation or power over the other person, the way to gain that control is through abusive actions. I learned this from my mother, and it just seemed natural to me. Add in Liz's hormonal shifts from pregnancy, breastfeeding, and post-natal depression, things were not good.

One time we were sitting at the kitchen table, and Liz started making fun of my weight. Then she wished aloud that I would get in a car accident and die on my way to work so that it would be much easier to raise this child by herself. I had heard enough, and something in me shifted. I thought *I have to get out of this situation.* I didn't know how. Having a child makes everything much more complicated. I didn't know what to do. Eventually, I started smoking weed again as I tried to come up with a solution.

Weed was definitely my coping mechanism for the abusive cycles. In general, being honest with myself, it was good to go back to feeling I could be free for a few moments.

Liz would occasionally stay at her family's house, which worked out well for me to smoke weed. That was my number one priority. I had another priority with a child, but my child was number two because number one shifted back to drugs once again. Drugs were always in the back of my mind. *When can I start smoking weed again? I miss it. I miss it. I miss it. Something's missing from my life.* And suddenly, I had fallen back into my addictive cycles and behaviors.

I was smart enough to recognize that the situation with Liz was what drove me to do drugs and alcohol again. I said an addict will always find a reason to use, but I was definitely aware enough to see the source. This situation wasn't healthy for my child or me. Liz wasn't happy. I wasn't happy, and I needed to go.

BREAKING THE CYCLE

When Liz and I met, our relationship was so sweet. I was so young. I broke up with her to move away to attend college, but Liz wouldn't let me end the relationship, and we started commuting. Once we got engaged, she came down to where I was and moved in with me. After that, every time I tried to leave or she would try to leave, usually after a big fight, we would pull each other back in. Perhaps the dynamic of addiction and/or our childhood traumas played into the need to keep up with this mutual abuse. Now that we had a baby, this needed to stop. Otherwise, this would be what the rest of my life would look like! Nothing good could come of living like this. Worse, what would our toxicity do to a young, impressionable child? What would it teach our daughter?

I'll say again that I don't believe we should villainize anybody in these stories because we're all people, and we're all learning and growing. For every bad thing that someone did to me, I did to someone else. In this case, anything Liz directed at me, I did just as bad to her (if not way worse) at some point in our time together.

Karma has a way to even things out. Sometimes instantly, and sometimes it takes a while to catch up with you. Karma doesn't know good or bad; it just knows. Your behaviors are going to be paid back to you. You're going to be treated how you've treated other people.

For anyone out there struggling, I think that if I wasn't so stubborn and determined to keep things private, Liz and I may have found some help in couples counseling. Both of us probably should have been going to individual therapy/counseling to learn how to cope with all the challenges of addiction, dependency, parenthood, financial responsibilities, and everything else.

I'M COMING OUT AGAIN

I woke up one day, deeply depressed, alone in my bed. Liz was out of town with our daughter. I was finally fully recognizing that I was not my best self. I was in an unhealthy, unfulfilling relationship with a woman who kept threatening to out me to everyone. I was a father but could not fully be present as I was concealing my authentic self behind a drug-induced alternate personality. I had a confrontational relationship with my family members. What was I doing? I was a grown-ass man and needed to act it. I needed a career, family, stability, love, and to feel peace. *How could I get there?* I wondered as I stared up at the ceiling.

It seemed that everything I did *not* want for myself was coming from hiding the real me. If I let myself shine, I could lose everything I had, but really, what was that? What would I be losing? The only thing I did not want to lose for sure was my child. But staying on the path I was on was a sure way to lose her, and that was not acceptable. I decided that I was finally going to come out to everyone. It was time to remove the huge rock on my shoulders that was holding me down.

As I stared in the bathroom mirror, brushing my teeth, in my mind, I became sure that the only way I could break this abusive cycle was to do something dramatic. I needed to come out from behind the false me and reveal the real me. I needed to stop "acting" and start "living." I looked for the real me behind the eyes staring back at me. Heavy stuff for first thing in the morning!

As I moved into my day, I thought more and more about how this would work. First, I needed to remove myself from the toxic, self-destructive things in my life. My relationship with Liz was top of that list. Come out to everyone and stay out was next.

Then, I would need to embark on a new path for a career instead of just jobs to pay the bills. I wanted to do something that inspired me. I always, even as a child, felt like I wanted to help people. I needed to find a way to do that.

And lastly, I would need to change the way I treated my body and mind. Stop destroying my body with chemistry-altering drugs, alcohol, food, etc. I needed to move more, eat less garbage food, gain more energy, and feel stronger. My mind was perpetually curious, and all I did was numb it with toxins instead of stimulating it.

All of these steps would bring me closer to my true self. But the biggest thing missing, I realized, was a connection to something bigger than just my earthly form. I needed sustenance on a spiritual level. A reason for getting up each day. A purpose. I would look into that.

NEED TO KNOW FOR SURE

I had never been with a man and needed to know for sure that this was my true nature before I outed myself to the world. With Liz out of town with Harper, I got on Craigslist because I didn't know any other way to meet a man. I didn't know about gay dating apps. I had never heard of Grindr and Adam for Adam and all those other options I found out about later on in life. So, I made a personal ad and posted it.

I was not really sure what to expect from the ad, but I got a lot of replies. That seemed reassuring. Men desired me. The whole situation was a little unreal, to be honest. It felt like I was going through something from out of this world. I didn't know if I was going to fall in love with the first man I met or be repulsed by sex with a man.

Marcus piqued my interest, so I invited him over the Friday night after I placed the ad. I was nervous. We had sex, but there was nothing in the least bit romantic about our encounter. I didn't know anything about gay sex at all. I was left afterward with feelings that gay sex felt like I was having sex with a girl (since I was on top).

We had to use lube, which was a new experience for me too. I didn't even own any, but Marcus found cucumber melon-scented lotion under the bathroom cabinet that he said would suffice. And he had brought condoms. I was able to process the experience enough that Marcus came over the next night, and we did it again. More escapism, no doubt.

I was texting him later that second night and suggested, "I would love to hang out or go on a date or something." He texted me back to say, "No. I really just want to fuck, and that's about it."

I was totally confused and had thought (hoped) maybe we would begin a relationship or be more than just a booty call. He didn't even want to be friends. He didn't want to talk. That was not the kind of life I wanted. Was it?

I quickly realized I wasn't walking away from the situation with Liz. I was avoiding it. I had invited a man to the home I shared with my baby mama and child. What was I thinking? I lost my gay virginity with a stranger in my family home. I wouldn't recommend this to anyone.

All of this occurred while knowing I had a fiancé and my baby on the way back home to me! The codependent tendencies that kept me tied to Liz (and other toxic relationships before her) had me reaching out to create a new relationship before I got out of the existing one. Not becoming connected and yet being so intimate with a stranger, a man, was deeply uncomfortable. Marcus rejecting me as a person, just wanting sex, wasn't right. I wanted someone to hang out with me, someone who would be my friend. How to go about finding that was, to me, really scary.

The residual from that experience is that anything with a cucumber melon fragrance makes me a little nauseated!

DOUG

Liz and I had an unhealthy relationship, but she knew I was bisexual. How would she deal with the knowledge of my experience with Marcus? I figured I needed to have another go. Marcus didn't inspire me to want to live a gay life. After feeling rejected by Marcus, I immediately latched on to another person who responded to my personal ad. Doug was a bit older than me. He had a sort of grunge meets surfer dude look with wild hair and thick-rimmed glasses and wore an untucked T-shirt over faded jeans with a zip-up hoodie and baseball cap.

I didn't know anything about the gay world, as Marcus made clear. I knew about other gay kids growing up, but I was never friends with them. I didn't even communicate with any of them on social media. I literally had no idea how to connect with other gay people.

Doug and I sent messages and then spoke on the phone, all in a matter of several hours. He seemed nice, and I drove an hour to pick him up. Doug and I spent the next two days together in my apartment. The guilty feelings were accumulating! At the end of our two days, we had already decided that we were going to move in together. We loved each other. It seemed, in retrospect, I «loved» everybody, but it was a codependent thing, not real love.

By the end of those two days, I knew for sure that I was gay, not really bisexual and that I was determined to leave my daughter's mother when they returned to town. Logic and decency said that if I craved a relationship and more sex with a man, I shouldn't be in a relationship with a woman. The manly thing to do, the right thing to do, was to set Liz free. She shouldn't be tied to me. Liz was still young and deserved to have a fulfilling life with someone who could truly and passionately love her. I wondered what Liz was thinking about our relationship and if maybe she secretly wanted out as well. If she wasn't thinking that, then this was going to be very uncomfortable, I predicted. I gathered my strength and resolved to do what needed to be done; to act like the man I knew I could be.

Liz was coming back that Tuesday afternoon after an extended weekend away. When Harper and her mom walked into the apartment, I had prepared for battle. I knew Liz would fight me because it was her nature to do things her own way. We had been unable to separate many times before, and I did not think this time would be any easier. I told her she had to move out. "I am leaving you," I declared. I coldly explained, "My name is on this lease, and I need a place to live. I'm going to school here and have a local job. I'll be able to support myself, but I need to have you leave. I can't live with you anymore!" I finished with, "Do whatever you want with the engagement ring, but I prefer to have it back." Nothing like going straight into practical details before even processing the emotional part of the confrontation! Way to go me!

Not surprisingly, her reaction was not gracious. "You're never getting it back," she snarled.

"Well, that's fine," I said, "I just need you to go. I can't do this anymore. Our relationship is abusive; it's just not healthy. I can't do it. I'm not doing it; we will work out custody with Harper…"

She interrupted, suspicious, "Why? Where is this coming from?" And she got really angry. As if to prove to me I was doing the right thing, to show me how toxic our relationship was, she punched me in the face. Then she broke all the picture frames I had made for her containing custom collages. There was one from every year of our relationship and others for special occasions like our anniversary or Christmas. She went to the wall, knocked them on the floor, and broke all of them. In truth, I don't blame her. I kept my cool. This is what I had to do. It was not a choice anymore. I clenched my fists and let the fingernails press into my palms to keep me based in my humanity instead of letting anger or other emotions carry me away.

Liz persisted in her questioning, "Why? What's going on?" She was confused. She looked around the apartment and found my phone. She opened the screen and saw that I had new contacts in my phone. "Who's Doug? And Marcus?"

I had deleted all my recent messages, but Doug texted me in the middle of all this, "Hey, how are you? How's everything going?" Liz started to connect the dots.

Liz started spouting out hateful, nasty thoughts while our child was sleeping not too far away, still in her portable car seat. She wouldn't allow joint custody.

I had to end our engagement and relationship, and I knew that if I told her my new relationship was the result of only two dates, she wouldn't accept that as a valid reason for her to leave and never come back. I had to make her want to leave me forever because I just couldn't break the abusive cycle any other way. It was better for Liz to have a full life. Get everything she deserved.

I had to make it seem like I was in a relationship, having an affair. Make her want to leave me. Help her understand that it was better for her to go. I told her that I had been with Doug since we moved back home to the Ohio area, which was a lie. I told Liz that Doug and I had been seeing each other for months. Lies only make you look and feel worse.

Liz is someone I respect and someone I feel is a good person. We were best friends before we became a couple. I did not want to lie but felt I had no other option in order to have joint custody. I may have wanted to partner with a man, but that didn't mean I didn't want to be a father to my incredible daughter. I was hoping we would work out the joint custody arrangement sooner rather than later.

She moved out and got tested for all kinds of things. I can imagine it was probably traumatic for her. We met up a few days later because Liz wanted something she had forgotten to take when she moved her stuff out. She begged me to come back to her, and I asked her why she would even want me back after everything? I said that it made no sense. I told her, "I'm out now."

Liz, in her anger, outed me to my whole family right after our fight. She called my mother immediately. I had already told my mother. She called my grandma. She called my dad. She had all my deeply Christian aunts, my other grandma, and everyone's number she could get a hold of, and she called them. She called her family and told everyone about the situation. "Ryan's been cheating on me with a man." I was getting calls and emails all day and night.

Not satisfied yet that she had hurt me as much as I hurt her, Liz outed me to all my close friends. So, at that point, I just came out publicly to everyone.

I think I made a Facebook post. I had been thinking about how to go about opening that cliched closet door anyway, but Liz basically took away any finesse I may have chosen to use and pushed me into the center of the room under a spotlight instead. The alternative would have been to post something and tell everyone myself before telling Liz. I thought that would be worse for her. I couldn't see an easy or harmless way to do this at the point we were in our relationship. Let's face it, as I've said before, hurt people hurt people.

I even came out to my journalism class at school. One of my class assignments was a group message. I used this assignment to share my truth. I got reprimanded at school because I used a lot of vulgarity (fucks and shits and stuff) in my group message. (I was still angry about Liz's harmful outing when I started writing.) The professor made an announcement to the whole class that we can't use that language, but she also made the comment, "I'm super proud of you for using this as an outlet, but probably just not the appropriate outlet." I had to have some way to announce it in order to make it more real for me. You know how once something is in print, it seems permanent?

John, a classmate, reached out around this time. He was an on-air DJ for one of the local radio stations. He often did "celebrity" appearances at local events and festivals and suggested we get coffee together.

Before I went to meet John in person, another friend looked him up and found out that he was gay. After sharing that he was proud of me, John said to let him know if I needed anything. And suddenly, I was feeling part of an instant community of people rallying around my decision to be me finally. It was intoxicating and a huge relief. I truly was not alone any longer.

The flip side of the coin is that there was also negativity coming from various people and organizations that thought they knew me. From this point onward, whenever I would tell people I'm in the LGBTQ+ community, I wondered, *are they judging me? What are they thinking about me?* It always came back to, *what do people think about me? Why do they like me (or not?)? What makes them like me?* I was out, but I wasn't yet happy. I was still self-medicating all my stress and anxiety, and the anxious feeling shifted to wondering if people knew I was gay in every new encounter.

During this whole reboot of my life, I was again feeling disconnected from God, more than ever. I began identifying as an atheist because I just wondered why God would create me this way? And why would He make me be this way when, according to the Bible, He doesn't even love me this way? That piece was hard and rather internalized. I didn't talk about it much because I felt like no one would understand. I didn't have anyone to talk to about religion or spirituality. So, I cocooned it inside and left it there to fester and evolve.

SEARCH FOR CONNECTION

After my separation from Liz, I was able to connect more often with Doug, even though he lived quite far from me. My relationship with Doug definitely was not love. When anyone told me they loved me, I latched on to that, and I answered with «I love you too.» As we got to spend more time together, I came to know that Doug was not a very nice person at all, but he said he loved me, so it was, «Oh, okay. Well, this is fine.» In my mind, this was better than Marcus, who only wanted sex.

I was jumping from one end of the spectrum to the other. I did not know what gay relationships would look like compared to heterosexual relationships. I had only been with women, never men. My mother had several marriages and relationships. My father had a wife and children who I never really got to know because they pushed me away. I had never truly had an adult relationship until Liz, and that was toxic beyond measure. My expectations were limited to whatever I got in the moment. What should a healthy relationship look like, never mind a gay one?

The sex with Doug was fine. Nothing to write novels about. In bed one night, trying to be romantic like I saw in the movies, I kissed the tip of his ear, and Doug freaked out, yelled at me, almost rolled me off the bed, pushing me away, and said, "Don't ever, don't ever do that!" And then more vociferously, "Don't ever fucking play with my ears!" Shocked at his reaction, I pulled back and said, "Okay, I didn't know! What's going on?"

"I was abused," he admitted.

"Oh my gosh. I'm sorry. You know I didn't know, obviously."

Doug had not opened up to me. I knew sexual abuse happened (it happened to my mother, after all), but I think it was the first time I realized that sexual abuse was also in the LGBTQ+ community. In fact, I've come to know that it's probably more likely than not that if you're a member of the non-hetero community, you might have suffered some form of sexual trauma or abuse or molestation, etc.

Luckily, abuse like that had never been a piece of my story. When I was younger, I tried some stuff with an older friend of mine. We didn't mess around or touch each other, but we were experimenting with ourselves in front of each other. It felt a little bit weird because he was a few years older than me. It had a predator vibe, but I didn't understand what it was I was feeling at the time. At the same time, I was quite aware of what I was doing. Taking ownership of the part I played, I was probably instigating because I was curious. I wasn't being taken advantage of or anything. I think I was the one leading that situation.

Back to Doug, I'll say that relationship opened my eyes. I didn't know much about sexual positions and relationship roles. The first time I'd ever bottomed was with Doug. I was literally prone on the floor, trying to crawl away as he was lying on top of me. He made a joke about me escaping. It didn't feel right to me with him. I bottomed because I felt like that's what I had to do. *That's what gay men do*, I thought. And that was that.

Doug and I, just like Liz and I, had arguments and did some fighting, but I was used to that. I felt that he judged me a lot, and he would comment about the way I did or said things. He talked disparagingly about my weight. Doug said he was once my size and how I should look at him as an example since he had lost a little bit of weight from when he was that bigger guy. It was uncomfortable talking to him about that. I never talked to people about weight nor about relationships.

I came home one day, looked at my email account on the computer, and saw some emails from Craigslist in response to my ad. I had posted my ad on Craigslist for a month under Men Seeking Men. I thought a new response was weird because my ad had been canceled and stopped running. I opened the multiple messages and started really looking at them, I thought, *I don't even know if this is from me!* Then recognition, *this isn't me*. Right then, I looked at the top of the Gmail account and realized, *Oh, not my email. This is Doug's e-mail!* That's when the anger set in. Doug was using my computer to try to hook up with someone else! *What the Hell?*

I was fuming as I hoped to find a rational reason for looking at what I was looking at! *When is this from?* I wondered. *Oh, no! Not good. It was posted earlier that day.* I went back to look at the original posting. It said, "My boy-friend is in class. I need to make sure that this is quick and…" I confronted Doug about it. He said, "I just wanted attention. I just wanted to see if people wanted me. I wasn't going to act on it. I didn't act on it. I didn't cheat on you."

I said, "Pack your shit. I'm taking you home." I took him to his house without either of us saying anything in the car and dropped him off. I did my version of talk-to-the-hand goodbye and drove the hour back home. I had no intention of seeing him again. Betrayal mixed with anger stung my eyes as the occasional oncoming headlights created blurs and streaks in my tears.

About three days later, Doug messaged me, claiming he was sorry. I had cooled off and missed having a boyfriend (or the idea of a boyfriend), so I said, "Let me come pick you up." At that time, I believed everyone deserved a second chance. I picked him up. Things were okay for a week or so. We still argued every now and again. Our sex life was subpar, but I was super inexpe-rienced and didn't know any better.

Sex with women always felt forced. It didn't necessarily feel wrong, but it just felt that I had to work at it. Then again, I was now having sex with men, and that felt forced too. Hmm. That was weird. I waited all that time to have sex with men, and then when it finally happened, it was still subpar, and I didn't understand why. I felt I was missing something essential.

Doug and I went to Gatlinburg that next week for me to experience my first vacation with a gay boyfriend. I paid for everything! I even gave Doug one of my credit cards for when I wasn't there to buy himself cigarettes and food or whatever he wanted. We were on vacation, and I was determined to have fun, so I smoked weed every day of our trip.

I smoked weed all the time at that point. Doug didn't really like that, and it was one of the reasons we argued. He would smoke with me every now and again, but in general, he made it clear he didn't care for it. We would drink together sometimes, but it just wasn't something we did together. He was smoking cigarettes every day. I got the feeling that he condemned me for the weed and alcohol. He felt superior, even though he was addicted to cigarettes.

We were leaving Gatlinburg, arguing in the car, and one of my tires blew out. As I pulled off the road, Doug said, "That's why you don't want to make me mad."

Confused, I asked, "What do you mean?"

"When I get mad, bad things happen."

"Okay. Supernatural bad things? Or just in general, your negativity creates it?"

"At this point in my life, I'm still pretty damn negative. I don't like myself. I don't like anybody around me." And that negative energy, he explained in great detail, was why my car's tire blew out. Imagine the power of that? What else could energy do? What could positive energy do if negative energy could blow out a tire?

I had finally come out of the closet, but I still wasn't feeling any better about myself. I was still confused, maybe more confused than I'd ever been in my whole life, I think. And I don't know if that's why Doug's comments stuck with me. It was weird. Negative energy, how did that play into my life?

We went back to my home for the next week or so, and things were calm. I came home from class one day and found a note on the counter from Doug that said:

> I'm leaving you. You deserve better. You're a better person than me. You have your life together. You're trying to go to college. You have a child. You have much more going for you than me. And you deserve way better. I have to leave. Here's your credit card back. I could have taken it, but I'm being a nice person returning it.

I thought, *well, that's illegal if you take my card, but whatever.* I tried processing his note. I finally put it on my fridge as a reminder that I deserve a better partner.

Since Doug, the more relationships I've had, I've come to understand that wanting to give people a second chance is a good and generous philosophy. Still, we also have to have enough faith in our gut instincts and the wisdom that comes from experience to know that not all people are worthy of a second chance because of what it will do to your peace of mind and self-confidence. Without trust, open communication, and feelings of being safe, you can't patch up a relationship.

17

HERE WE GO AGAIN

I first met Kellie in middle school detention. She was a cheerleader, really pretty, and one of the coolest kids in school. We didn't have any classes together throughout middle school, but we connected and became friends. When middle school ended, we lost contact. When I moved back to Cincinnati after Harper was born, we reconnected and started smoking weed together.

The first time we got together, she asked me, "Do you ever do pain pills?"

I said, "I've done them on my own since I was thirteen or fourteen, and so yeah, of course."

"Okay," she said. We didn't really talk much more about it.

We smoked weed and hung out every other day or every day sometimes. I still thought she was cool because she was this blast from the past and a real straight shooter. I admired her. Then one day, Kellie asked me if I wanted to do pain pills with her.

"I don't really know. I'd rather just get high," I answered.

"Okay, well whatever," and she slipped her arm around me, and then eventually I said, "Sure, I'll take a bump. Normally I swallow them."

I was sick for days after I took my first bump. She introduced me to Opana, an opioid. Some people say this is just a pain pill, but nothing else that I'd ever had in my life (and I'd tried Oxycodone and all kinds of other pain pills, uppers and downers) was so strong that it made me physically sick for days. And yet, as soon as I wasn't ill anymore, I called Kellie to ask for more Opana.

We went out and bought one. Kellie had $20 to throw in, and I had $40, and we bought a thirty milligram Opana, if I can remember correctly. This could last days and days if you were taking it by yourself, but sharing, it would last a day-and-a-half or two. We were taking a bump here, a bump there. I told her, "I took way too much the first time. I'm going to take a little tiny bit because I love the way that it made me feel, but I was sick for days." Kellie agreed to my plan. We smoked a blunt, and we did a line, and, yeah, that's how I started snorting pain pills. Opana and Oxycontin, sometimes Percocet.

The pills had to be pretty strong because I'd been taking them for five months every day by this point. At that time, I got fired from my job. I stopped going to class. I was not doing well. I started hanging out with other people who were doing drugs all the time, not just smoking weed but also using harder drugs. My rental became a "trap house" because it was a place where everyone came together to party. I had parties with fifty, sixty, seventy people in a two-bedroom apartment. I had parties where people were selling drugs. I came home one time, and people were doing a nude photoshoot in my bedroom. People sold their bodies out of my space. It was just a freaking mess. But once I got into that lifestyle, I was trapped.

OUT OF CONTROL

I didn't take any pills with me to visit my grandparents that year for Christmas, but I knew they would have some lying around. What did I do? As soon as they went to bed, I started going through their medicine cabinet, looking for my grandpa's oxycodone. It was five-milligram strength. That's nothing. I took eight of them! I don't know why I thought he wouldn't notice eight of them missing, but I never got caught. I crushed up eight large Tylenol-shaped pills into this huge mountain and snorted line after line after line because I wanted to feel the way that those Opanas made me feel. My little mountain of oxy actually never made me feel the way I hoped, but I did definitely get messed up, which is what I was looking for as well.

At that point, I realized, *wow, you have a problem*! But I rationalized that with *hey, you're not doing meth, and you're not doing heroin, and you're not shooting up, and you're not smoking crack. You're just doing pain pills. Everyone does those. Look—everyone has them in their house or just lying around.*

I was telling myself it was okay, I was okay. I could afford them. I started with $50,000 open credit, and I started putting all my bills on my credit cards and using all my cash for drugs.

I also went to my mom's house that same Christmas and went through her medicine cabinet and started taking her pain pills. I guess she thought when I did that growing up, it would be the last time; that I would have outgrown that phase. Well, it wasn't. There I was repeating the same fourteen-year-old behaviors as a twenty-two-year-old. Back to where I started, but this was a worse spot.

It's crazy to look back and remember all the times I lied and stole and cheated to get drugs, even just to get marijuana, when I was younger. I would steal change out of my grandma's jar, and my grandma confronted me about it. I said I needed gas, and I didn't want to ask her for money. When I lived in rural Nashville, my grandpa was already putting a tank of gas in my car each week because I was traveling twenty-five minutes to go to school in a different city.

I never stole people's jewelry to pawn. I never took TVs or electronics, but I stole little stuff. I stole from my friends, which was always something I felt guilty about doing. I felt wrong about it. This became part of who I was because I did it all the time. I lied, cheated, and stole for my addiction.

My friend Cecilia had very high-milligram ADHD medicine (Adderall: the ones with little orange balls inside), and I would steal those from her when I was at her house. I would open up the pill case, take the little balls out and swallow them so they would go directly into my system. I thought they would do something different for me. I was so tolerant that they just got me high but not as messed up as I wanted to be.

Everyone's addiction story is different. Some people pick one drug and stick with it and become super addicted to it. And I understand that because that's how Opana worked for me—high-potency pain medication. I was also an equal-opportunity high guy. Anything would do when I needed to escape.

PART II

RYAN AWAKENING

18

TO HEROIN OR NOT TO HEROIN

The spiral down to the end of my relationship with Liz coincided with my increasing use of drugs. The months after Liz and I moved to separate residences, I experienced unintended lessons learned from incidental people that resulted in an entire shift in the focus of my life.

I was hoping to gain immediate joint custody of my daughter after I split with Liz, but obviously falling into the world of drugs, that wasn't the case. Around January, early February, I had run out of cash, and I needed cash to make a buy. I only had credit. From previous experience, I knew there were ways to get money from credit cards, but I preferred to get cash through any other resource before I went to credit.

I was yearning for an Opana, and they were going for up to $70 per pill. Dealers were gouging their clients because the market was there. My daily challenge was all about *how do I get fucked up?* I calculated and manipulated funds in my head. *If I do this, I can buy some gas or the groceries for the week and then get me a couple of Opanas.* It was always a hustle.

I found I had clothing and toys my child didn't need anymore. Anything she could still fit in I kept; fancy or formal stuff, I kept. I could sell the old baby stuff we didn't need because she was outgrowing it. It was all in great condition and good quality as they were gifts from family and friends. We would never need it all.

I brought Harper's clothes, toys, and newborn baby items to Once Upon a Child. I stood there anxiously waiting for the store clerk to count the items and calculate how much it was worth. Usually, you drop the bag off and come back the next day, but I was too anxious to get the cash. Instead of dropping it off, I was pacing around the store, waiting the forty-five minutes she promised it would take to do her calculations.

While I was pacing, I got a call from a friend who offered me drugs. "Hey! I can get you Opana for $70, or I can get you this heroin, and, honestly, I've done both interchangeably, and you're not going to notice the difference. It's going to be way cheaper. For $35, you can be messed up for twice as long. For this being your first time using it, I'll try it before I give it to you to make sure it's a good batch." This friend always had a quality product. With this intro processing in my mind, I rationalized that I was already taking heroin. I mean, they're all opiates or opioids, and this was something new to me.

Here I go again, I thought. I was getting that feeling in that pit of my stomach. Gut instinct. Intuition. My head said, *oh yeah! I want to be high for twice as long!* But my gut was asking, *do you really want to start doing heroin?*

The pills I wanted were starting to get really hard to find. The drug companies began to coat them. These were the ones that were cheaper, but you'd have to know how to handle them, how to fix them, but it still wasn't the same high. It didn't feel the same. I'd done it before, but I wanted the real deal even with this intuition in the pit of my stomach, churning and burning and telling me to stay away. My brain was *yes, yes. Try heroin.* I was addicted.

Once I finished that call, knowing my fix was arranged, I was itching so hard for the drugs I couldn't even wait for the clerk to count my huge bag of baby supplies. I told her I would come back later.

I had money because I had open credit, so I could hustle with what I had. Other people hustle with nothing. There are people who literally have nothing but the clothes on their back, and they still make a hustle to get high. It's an art form in itself, and I got a little glimpse into that, what that feels like, but luckily, I didn't stay there very long.

I came back from a Christmas visit to family and found the stuff in my apartment was thinned out. My "friend" Kellie was on the same need-for-cash-to-get-high train with me. She had used the emergency key I gave her to take $400 or $500 in DVDs and Blu-ray Discs I'd collected over the years, and she sold them. She pawned them along with tons of my clothes. I was frequently messed up, but I was still aware of what was going on. I confronted her.

It was uncomfortable more than usual because Kellie didn't drive or anything, so I still had to take her to her mother's house after confronting her. This whole betrayal by Kellie was really hard for me. She was stealing from me. It just made me scurry down the drug rabbit hole even further.

I was so angry that I went to Kellie's mother and told her, "Hey, your child stole from me for drugs. Your child's a thief, and I just want you to be aware. She's staying in your house but be careful of Kellie, and you should be aware of what she's done."

In a weird way, Kellie selling all my clothing worked out okay because six months later, I would weigh eighty pounds less and wouldn't need those clothes anymore.

Kellie messaged me about a year after I had gotten clean and thanked me for being her friend. "Thank you for getting sober because it inspires me to get sober," she told me. "Thank you for all your positivity." She told me how she had noticed a shift in my life just from watching me on social media. She watched me lose weight, be a dad, and return to school. Kellie also said she was proud of me. I told her that I would always be there for her if she ever needed anything.

I ran into Kellie's family years later, and they told me that she was still in and out of rehab. Kellie has a son a bit younger than Harper. It's hard to be a parent and an addict. I think the number one thing is that you have to want to change for yourself. You can be motivated by other reasons, like for your child, because you want to be better for a child, your parents, your siblings, or whatever, but you have to want a better life for yourself.

You can't provide a better life for your child and family until you help yourself. It all goes back to loving yourself first before you can love other people.

I mean, you can superficially love people and theoretically love people, but love's not a thought; love's a feeling, and love's an action. If you can't act on that love, then you truly don't love because you don't truly love yourself.

I might have a lot of addicts up in arms with that comment, but it's true. Love is a verb. Love is not a thought. It's a feeling within your heart that is a form of actual action: doing kind things, doing acts of service, using words of affirmation, the five love languages essentially[3]. Those are ways to express love. Those are all actions.

Since it all stems from your heart when your heart is clouded and mucked up with the darkness, debris, and decay from drugs, that junk is literally blocking certain neuroreceptors and flooding your brain with chemicals. It's hard to get out of that. It's hard to feel normal again for a while.

I didn't cold turkey stop all drugs and alcohol together because I had too much debris in my system, and I needed to ease myself off and clean myself out. I stopped hard drugs and weaned myself off all the other stuff one day at a time until, eventually, I got to a place where I decided that all of that needed to be gone. It took a long time to make that happen.

I don't know how I had the strength or instincts for how to get myself clean, but I'm sure it had something to do with faith in something bigger than myself. For Kellie (like most people), she needs the support of experts to reach her goal. I have a good feeling in my heart that one day Kellie's going to be able to come to me and say, "I'm sober and clean for good."

---

[3] More about the Five Love Languages can be found on page (240).

19

TRIPPIN' AND RIPPIN'

I did acid maybe a handful of times, but there was one incident that was the scariest moment of my life. Liz left, I was without a relationship to ground me, it was holiday time, and I was spiraling out of control.

I suggested to my friends that we should start the new year out right. We got some pretty strong acid. I took three hits of it, and I immediately started tripping: super hardcore, visuals, and auditory. I went to my bathroom and locked the door because I was freaking out.

When tripping, I left the realm of this world and went to some other type of dimension where everything was really psychedelic. I don't remember what I was doing in my bathroom (I guess just sitting there), but my mind came back, and I felt like I was within a tornado or something. I could see myself spiraling back down to Earth and watched my soul or a life force re-entering my body. I decided I needed to be around people because what I was going through was wild and unpredictable.

The party guests were all coming down off the acid high, all over my apartment. I needed people to leave. I needed only my closest circle of trusted friends to stay and look after me. I named off the people who could stay and demanded that everyone else had to go. Marie explained that they couldn't all go because they'd been drinking and doing drugs, and what if they got into a car accident. To me, this was about regaining my sanity, so this internal battle of what is right versus what I needed raged inside me. Maybe Marie thought I'd be safer with people around who could watch out for me, but it was my home, and I was freaking out. I screamed again, "No. I need those people to leave!" I made them leave and hoped for the best and that they got home all right. I also made them promise to text our other friends to let them know they arrived and were safe.

There were about twelve people left when I seemed to be sobering up finally. We were all sitting on the floor in a circle. I saw lines connecting everyone's belly buttons together through our solar plexus (at the third chakra), our energy source. (Maybe not so sobered up after all!)

Through a string of light, a unanimous group of voices came to me and asked, "Are you ready to go home?"

I said, "What do you mean?"

They repeated, "Are you ready to go? Is it your time to leave?"

And I said, "No. I have to stay. I can't leave. I can't leave Harper. It's not my time to go." And suddenly, all the lines immediately disconnected, and everything popped back to normal.

I didn't know what it all meant. It was very vivid. The voice was very prominent. I don't know if it was God's voice. I'm not going to say, because there are other times God is directly talking to me, and I find that really beautiful. I don't want to devalue that.

This was a really impactful moment for me because I started to see that everyone was connected when all our navels were connected. I'd heard my whole life that we're all connected in the circle of life. Are we all connected? What does that mean? It means that my actions affect you and your actions affect me.

That acid trip stuck with me for a long, long time. I never did acid again. I continued doing hard drugs every single day and made bad choices until February 19, 2012. But to this day, I still have questions about what happened or what the message was about. *Do you want to go home? Is it time to go home?* Was I dying, or was it God or the universe asking me if maybe it was time for me to go? Maybe it was time to go to jail? I don't know. I don't know what the message was. I kept up with bad behavior, but the seeds were planted in me, and I was evaluating and thinking something wasn't right. I kept telling myself, *you don't need this. This is wrong. You're going to end up hurt. You're going to hurt someone else.*

Thank God I was able to have that experience because I think it was a part of my spiritual journey as well. It was the first time I'd actually visibly seen an aura or chakra connection. To this day, I can see white or golden colors/auras around people if I really concentrate. I need to really be in the moment with them. If I have a connection with a person, halos are usually brighter. If I already like that person or love that person or care about that person and they're super excited about something, then the lights are even brighter. What I see is similar to the images painted on the walls and in the stained glass of churches.

I know that this experience helped save me and continues to help me connect with spirituality and God. I think it was an important piece of that puzzle. They say that some people need to hit bottom to start climbing their way out. It was terrifying. I wish I could have gotten the message without going through all that I did. But I needed to see the ugly truth: I wasn't doing well, I was on a wrong path, I could end up dead, I could end up hurt, I could go to jail, I could hurt other people.

20

EVANESCENCE

It was late January/early February, and the winter semester had begun. I had flunked the whole fall semester, and I thought, *well, I better at least try to go to class.* I had been going to classes and getting high on my way there.

I stopped one day to get Opana from this girl, Tess. She told me that what she had available was similar to Opana but not the same. I didn't know much about Suboxone at the time. I didn't do my research. I spent three days of my life vomiting in toilets, feeling totally disgusting. I was nodding off. I felt I didn't have the strength to deal with real life, my life. I didn't deal with boys or lack thereof or the fact that I wasn't seeing my daughter more than once every other week because all I was doing was screwing up my life. Worst of all, I knew what I was doing, but I just couldn't stop.

A lot of people want to do drugs with their friends, to party, and I wanted that, but I also did drugs by myself, a lot. I loved to do drugs by myself.

I loved to smoke weed by myself. I loved drinking by myself. I just wanted to be intoxicated. I wanted to escape because instead of just having fun, I was medicating and numbing myself. I was numbing my pain.

The day before my birthday in 2012, I snorted my last line. I think it was my last little quarter of an Opana or something. I remember hearing the Evanescence song *Lost in Paradise* as I was sitting in my car listening to tunes on my phone. It's the only Evanescence song I had. It wasn't always my go-to music because it's sad and depressing, but hey, whatever came on. I started listening to it, and I had this shifting moment in my life where I saw my daughter singing the song to me.

Harper was Evanescence; she was the lead singer. She was singing the song about how she was lost. She couldn't find her way. I saw myself in prison, dead, a drug addict, a low life, someone who couldn't provide for her, care for her, or even see her. I just kept seeing all these things like a slideshow in my mind. I saw my daughter singing me the song and telling me to look at my life. It could have been wonderful, but it was not.

I've thought about this moment a lot since then, and I thought it must have been God's way to communicate with me because, at that time, I wasn't into spirituality very much. I wasn't into God or religion. I was just into drugs. Literally, that was all I thought about and all I did. My life revolved around drugs and self-medicating through sex.

When I visualized Harper singing me the song, I knew I wasn't going to be around if I kept doing what I was doing. It hit me so hard that it was the last time I ever touched hard drugs.

My epiphany was that I could and wanted to stop all drugs. Well, that lasted about twelve hours before I was smoking weed again and thought, *that's gonna be the last time.* The next day I bought more weed, and the day after, I sold some weed, and then I started actually selling weed. I never sold anything other than weed.

I didn't want any drugs other than marijuana or alcohol in my home. I stood by this commitment, and that was the first step toward me getting clean. I never ever turned back because I had to be there for my daughter. I had to be the parent that my parents weren't to me. Sometimes, even with all the love my parents gave me, it still wasn't enough. If my parents gave me all that love and support and I still was a mess, Harper was going to need more than just love and acceptance and support not to be a mess. And I made that my life mission.

I recognize that I still was an addict. I couldn't fully live out this new mission I had in life yet, because marijuana and alcohol still had control over me. But at that point, I got a job and tried to go back to school. I was already so far behind in the program that I just couldn't make it. I failed the whole semester.

STEPPING ONTO THE PATH

I got a job where God was invited back into my life in the form of spirituality because I worked in this hippie store. This was one of the things that helped save my life (thank you, Tala.) The store sold inspirational and spiritual things.

I was going to work high all the time, and one of the managers there noticed. She warned me to put in eyedrops before the owners came in. I was starting to be more myself; the hard drugs were gone. I started on this path toward liking myself.

I started losing weight. I was around 225 pounds when I made the decision to stop hard drugs. I began eating healthier and sometimes exercising, but mostly, it was just diet. I lost eighty pounds by that summer, which also helped me gain confidence, self-worth, and self-value. Not that our self-image should ever come from our body image, but I felt better about myself. Sticking to a commitment gave me confidence that I could take on something new and see it through.

The acne on my face and body cleared up because I was eating healthier, drinking more water, and moving more, which released the toxins in my system. I could look in the mirror and feel good about the person I saw looking back. There wasn't so much darkness around my visage anymore.

I used the money I wasn't spending on drugs to get veneers for my teeth. My smile positively glowed in the dark! With all the physical improvements, I started to reassess my value. I had to take care of myself first before I could take care of my child, but I was going to be an amazing dad to that kid because I believed I was a valuable human being.

Mind you, I was still smoking and drinking every day but only enough to take the edge off. I was working super hard to turn my life around. I was in the midst of turning things around, right? It wasn't even a ninety-degree turn yet, but it was a forty-five-degree turn. I was making an effort. I stopped hiding who I was and started admitting that I had issues and I needed help.

And this time, I rediscovered God through my drug dealer, through my marijuana dealer, Marie. From then, everything started changing and unfolding, and eventually, my life went from that forty-five-degree change to a 180-degree change.

21

REBOOTING

The effects of my drug days, to the exclusion of everything else, led to me receiving an eviction notice from my apartment manager. With the generous help of my ex-stepfather to clear up the situation, I caught up on my rent and luckily didn't get a ding on my credit report or anything. I still had to move out as part of the settlement agreement.

When I got evicted, my friends on drugs (who had been staying with me) also had to find alternate places to live (and party). I suddenly realized how intertwined all of our lives were, in general. The consequences of my self-loathing behaviors rippled out into several families. The gratitude I felt for having family and loved ones to help me was accompanied by recognition of how not everyone has that, and certain people were left displaced and alone when my little haven for them was removed as an option. I think this planted a seed in the recesses of my mind that I wanted to be able to help people find safe spaces and build a support network. Nothing happens by accident. My eviction had a purpose.

Instead of being angry at a God that the church said would condemn me, I moved beyond my hurt brain and recognized that it/everything really was just about love, a universal love that I had never felt but yearned for my whole life. I planned to begin that expression of love by being loving to my mother. And my siblings. And my daughter.

Humbled by my eviction, I talked to my mom about needing a place to stay. She laid down the law and said if I were staying in her home, I would need to carve out a spot for myself in the basement (with the laundry machines and storage items), and more importantly, there were to be no drugs whatsoever. "We know you are on drugs. You are not allowed to bring them in my house. If I ever catch you high or find any kind of drugs, you're out for good." I agreed to her restrictions and terms, all the while knowing I still had in my possession a quarter ounce of weed. I wasn't planning on stopping my self-medication with weed. I truly felt a weed high was the only thing I had to look forward to most days. But I would avoid doing anything in her house to honor her request.

Cody, my younger brother, was away at college but still had his room there. I brought my luggage and smaller boxes from the car into the house and made ready to reside with my mother who was living solo. I was moving back into the same basement from whence I was removed when CPS pulled me out of the house all those years before.

For the most part, I had already reconnected with God, and I was having these beautiful spiritual encounters, which made me a little less dependent on weed and a little bit more able to be flexible in situations.

As part of my universal love spiritual quest, I had learned the basic principles of "like attracts like" and karma. I thought I would be able to follow my mother's rules. With my mom's help to transport the rest of my belongings over the next few days, I moved back into my family home. Mom graciously had made a space for Harper in a room upstairs for when I had her for a weekend or overnight.

As I worked on making myself comfortable in the utilitarian dark basement and rearranging things, I needed to move the dryer across the room. I was scooting the dryer across the floor when I pulled my back out. I felt the most intense pain I'd ever experienced in my life. Triggered, I immediately wanted pain pills. I said *no* to myself.

I told my mother that I was going out with my friend Del. Del didn't really smoke, but he did drink. I had rolled a blunt and smoked it by myself before picking him up. Del didn't like to be around smoke. I smoked so much weed, so many blunts a day, that I was immune to the smoke. It made me more relaxed, calmed me, and made me hungry (always) and tired (eventually), so it helped me sleep at night.

The universe intended for me to be immobile for this moment in time. Del and I stayed in the car driving around because I didn't think I could physically get out of the car with my back in excruciating pain. If I had been mobile, Del and I probably would've done something like go to the movies or visit friends. Instead, we talked in the car.

We were just talking about general guy stuff, hanging out, when I pulled into the Lee's Famous Recipe Chicken parking lot in Florence, Kentucky. Munchies! We ordered some food and ate in the car. Del is a really spiritual person, and we found ourselves discussing God. I don't want to identify for him, but I think he had more of a Wiccan vibe, with a foundation of a divine presence. We were talking about life and what our purpose was. God was in that car with us for three hours.

SHIFT MESSAGE

For my whole life, all I'd ever wanted to do was to help people. Even when I was very little before I really understood how life worked, and before I was hiding who I was all the time, before the drugs and alcohol, people would ask me what I wanted to do, and I would say this or that profession because that's what they expected. But what I really wanted was to help people. I just didn't know how that would manifest.

As I aged and started simply answering that I wanted to help people, I was asked, "What profession do you want to take on in order to help people?" I never knew.

In reality, throughout the previous several months, I'd been on this journey toward self-love. I went from a place of self-hatred to feeling confident about my personal appearance. The darkness I had seen in the mirror was hardly ever there anymore. I saw that I wasn't a bad, awful, evil person. I was able to overcome hard drug addiction and get clean. I moved through the world with a more confident air instead of hiding who I was. I had come out to the community and my family and was free from the need to hide. I wanted to showcase my good qualities. I wanted people to see that change is possible. You can get sober or clean. For probably the first time in my life, I had started sharing some positivity.

I went on social media to search for inspirational quotes. I looked at Buddha, Gandhi, and many other philosophers, theologians, and spiritual gurus. I came across a frequent quote to "Be the change that you wish to see in the world." But God said to me, "How are you supposed to be the change that you wish to see in the world when you are still an addict?"

I was there to help Del along his journey, and he was there to help me connect. I was eating my chicken and describing the messages I was getting, and Del told me that he felt a shift in the energy in the car and that my voice had changed. He said I became really calm and serious. It was a powerful moment for both of us. Not in a Martin Luther King Jr. kind of power, as it didn't have that roar behind it, but I projected a very sincere, confident voice that came to me with my mission outlined, and I shared it with Del. I knew he wouldn't judge me or think I was out of my mind.

The message I received in that moment was that all drugs, all alcohol, all cigarettes, including marijuana, were not meant to be in my life. I needed all toxins released from my life for me to live my mission. My mission was important, I was told. This message was just delivered into my awareness, into my head. One minute I'm munching on chicken, and the next, I have this sudden revelation. The message I received that day with Del in the car about giving up toxins was so I could be clear of mind and body and become a catalyst for people loving themselves.

At one point, God gave me a really clear message about one of my missions; how I could be of service. *You have to help with water sources for the developing world. You are meant to help with all these things.* I was blown away. I wondered if one person could really make a difference? Can I really help? How do we change the world? And how do I become the change that I wish to see in the world? The answer was, *The change starts with you.* I understood that to mean that you have to change along the way so you can impact other people. You can help people through sobriety challenges. You can help people along the way by teaching the principles you've learned about how to embrace yourself and love yourself.

Through the smoke haze in that car, God gave me clarity. *This is your purpose on Earth, God told me that day. Never forget that.* It was something that had never happened to me to receive that kind of clear directive. I admit it took some time to process. Honestly, it felt like God put the words into my mind and directed me to say them out loud, talking normally, just rambling on and on as usual as if they were just my thoughts. There was no pre-recorded message or notes on a sheet in front of me. I mean, this was just flowing. I had a flash recall of all that had transpired in my life and the experiences I'd had.

I've told this story before, and the response has sometimes been that maybe I was just really high! I thought about that, but the reality was that I used to smoke so much weed that one blunt was not really that much. I would argue that I wasn't really high at all. Maybe some residual buzzing, and maybe my mind was less resistant to messages entering me, but at that point, I really don't even think I was buzzing anymore. It was just this super powerful moment that I will never forget because the words and thoughts weren't mine. It was God's voice; it was the universe. It was my divine, and it was love. And it was all at once, in a sudden knowing; not the way humans talk, sentence by sentence.

I was super serious about stopping and following my new mandate. Before I let Del out of the car that night, I gave him my cigarettes. Del didn't want anything to do with the weed. I had a little bit of weed left, and I think I gave it to some other friends. By letting go of anchors from my past, I began my transformation into the person I knew I could be, the person I wanted to be.

Whatever it was, the impact of that car ride was formative and changed the direction and aimlessness of my life from that point forward. When I got home that night, my mother applied some special alternative healing techniques on my back for me. While she was working on me, I was telling her that something had changed inside of me and that I had shifted; I moved to a different place. I went to bed that night and woke up with my back ninety percent better.

My physical recovery solidified my belief in spirituality and the power of God's healing hands. I was on fire to get started on my mission. For about two months, I didn't touch drugs, not weed, cigarettes, or alcohol. The whole world seemed brighter. Literally, I could look out the window, and it seemed like it was in HD. Whereas my life before was shielded behind fog and smoke, that darkness finally lifted. There were a hundred little shifts along the way, and a whole new world was in front of me.

Sobriety was good for me. My horrible asthma went away, and I didn't have to use my inhaler at all. I used to go through a 200 puff inhaler every two weeks or so. I was using it way more than doctors would recommend. My asthma was out of control, but when I was drug-free and motivated for my mission, my life's purpose, my physical body started to heal.

I noticed everything was rejuvenated. I started to take better care of myself, brushing my teeth more often and washing my face, which maybe is why my skin looked better. I was drinking water. I was eating healthier. My hair had a shine to it and was no longer greasy or stringy. I started self-care routines I'd forgotten for a long time. When drugs come first, that's all you think about. Drugs, partying, and then eating; this combo did not make for healthy skin, hair, and body.

Days after my shift moment, I found some self-help-type videos my mother had on her bookshelves. One was by Wayne Dyer. I had heard of one of his quotes when I was searching for meaningful quotes, but I didn't know who he was. I watched this movie (since without doing drugs all the time and exiting that culture, I suddenly had time), and I promise you, it was my experience that was being lived out on this TV screen! He had a dead-on description of what a shift is and why I shifted and that I must have been ready for it, and how critical it was that I listen to the message that I had received.

I watched Louise Hay talk about how you can heal your life. About how you could use positive affirmations to make things you want to happen, happen. I also watched *The Secret* (based on the amazing book) about the abundance you want and deserve coming to you through your belief that it will manifest. I watched some John Edwards stuff. He's a psychic who is connected with people who have passed. My brain was being stimulated by ideas, philosophies, and inspiration instead of being diffused by drugs. It was almost like a different kind of high.

I attended an event about God and different world religions and had my first interaction with meditation. At first, I couldn't really get into it too much. I left it there. Later, it was a John Edwards guided meditation that ultimately made sense.

I started to realize that these principles were principles I'd been picking up over the previous several months. I'd say the shift was in my positivity and how I treated myself kindly within affirmations that I spoke to myself and that I began incorporating into my everyday life.

I was waking up every day (I still do this daily) saying *I love and accept myself just the way I am. I am beautiful, just the way I am.* I ask for protection. I say a little mantra or prayer every morning, calling on my archangels. Then I encircle myself with a white light of love and protection. *I'll let nothing but positive thoughts and energies affect me. I will not be influenced by the negativity of those around me.* I say these things every single day. I function in the world for the higher good. And I treat myself for my higher good. I have a purpose that is much bigger than just surviving any particular day.

I've created a positive bubble around myself, but not in the sense that I can't see reality. I still see suffering. I still feel suffering. I still acknowledge it. I'm not in a happy bubble by myself, only seeing the good. But I want to be surrounded with good, positivity, and love so that I can be the best version of me that I can be and bring that love and light into the world to reduce suffering and negativity for others. I operate best in a place of positivity and a place of acceptance, love, kindness, grace, bliss, peace, joy, and those have been the most powerful affirmations for me.

Resource:
I want to share one of my favorite channeled-guided meditations with you.

MOTHER MARY HEALING MEDITATION

With this meditation, we will be focusing on Mother Mary's love. Usually, you would be listening to me say these words, but if you cannot find the voice recording on YouTube or my website, take this content and record yourself saying these bulleted words. When you are ready to meditate, you can just play your own voice and follow the instructions to embrace Mother Mary's healing energy coming to you.

Take a comfortable position. Sit with your feet flat on the floor or in a crisscross position with your back straight and aligned. If neither of these positions is comfortable, take a lying position with palms facing upward with legs shoulder-width apart.

Today we're going to let Mother Mary surround us with her love, her healing, and her light. Oftentimes, people see Mary in a blue light or with a white or golden light around her. You can see this depicted in many Mother Mary stained glass or pictures that people have created. This energy is pure love and nurturing.

Meditation

- Take a few moments to take several deep breaths.
- Breathe in for the count of six, hold for three seconds, and then breathe out for six.
- Breathe in: one, two, three, four, five, six.
- Hold: one, two, three.
- Out: one, two, three, four, five, six.
- In: one, two, three, four, five, six.
- Hold: one, two, three.
- Out: one, two, three, four, five, six.
- Again in: one, two, three, four, five, six.
- Hold: one, two, three.
- Out: one, two, three, four, five, six.
- One more time in: one, two, three, four, five, six.
- Hold: one, two, three.
- Out: one, two, three, four, five, six.
- Return your breathing to whatever feels natural and most comfortable.
- Imagine yourself sitting in front of Mother Mary.
- You look into each other's eyes, and you feel the love that she had felt for Jesus. The love she feels for us all. She is our mother. She is our protector. She nurtures us when we need nurturing. Loves us when we need love. And ultimately is always there to bring light into our lives.
- Take one deep breath as you look into Mother Mary's eyes.
- What do you see in her eyes? What do you feel?

- She is a figure of love and light. Do you feel the love and light that you desperately need and want?
- Allow her to hug you.
- As you embrace each other in a warm, beautiful hug, feel instantly protected and safe and secure. You instantly feel love for yourself and for others and for the world. Take a moment just to embrace that hug and embrace that love that you feel.
- Thank Mother Mary for this moment as she steps back. She looks back into your eyes and asks if she can hold you throughout your life at different points when you may need her the most, when you don't feel safe, secure, or loved.
- She divinely guides you to recall times in your life when you needed love the most, maybe as an infant, child, or teenager, or young adult.
- Wherever you may be on your journey that you need love the most, she wants you to know that you are beautiful. You are safe. You are secure. You are healthy. You are happy. You are whole, and you are divinely loved by God and Jesus and her. If, for any time in your life, you didn't feel this way, take a step back into that moment for just a brief minute to sit with Mother Mary in her healing love and her healing light and, ultimately, her beautiful love.
- Step into that moment.
- Let this love pour onto any moment in the past that feels like you had Less Than Love.
- Allow Mother Mary to protect you and guide you and ultimately love you.
- Thank you, Mother Mary, for that love in your embrace. For that time.
- Thank you, Mother Mary. I know that we can call on you at any moment when we need love, guidance, support, safety, security, and wholeness. As we could always call on Jesus and God, we can also call our Mother Mary as she is the protector, as she is an ultimate beam of love and light.

- As you allow her to step into your life and into your energy, you can feel a shift; a calmness.
- A piece of you feels safe and secure, wanted, loved, and pure.
- A pure love that is not tainted by anything of this world.
- A pure love that is from the universe, from God, from Jesus, and from our beautiful Mother Mary.
- Take a moment to embrace Mother Mary once again.

As we say our gentle goodbye because we know that we can call on her at any moment throughout our day, week, month, or year, Mother Mary shall be there with open arms, with her beautiful blue gazing eyes. And, most importantly, that embrace that helps us to feel loved and whole, safe and secure. She provides this love for free at any time, and at any moment, you can return back to her embrace.

If you're ever in need, return to Mother Mary's light, return to her love that she feels for Jesus, and she feels for every single one of us on this Earth, for she sees us all as children of God. Just as she saw Jesus, she loves and embraces us all as a Beautiful Love.

Sometimes it's hard to even understand. But allow that embrace and allow that love to trickle in and to fall into the crevices of every aspect of your life: past, present, and future. And though it's okay to focus on the past and the future, it's also important to focus on the present moment.

- Allow Mother Mary's love for this moment.
- Allow her love and her light to sink into you; to be a part of you; to be merged together.
- Allow Mother Mary's love to be your love and allow that love to spread out into this world to every person, plant, and animal; to every being on this planet.
- Allow Mother Mary's love to live through you. You are a beacon of her love, just as you are a beacon of God's love.
- When in doubt, call upon God.
- Ask to return Mother Mary to you that you may feel her love and her light.

- You could also call directly on Mother Mary as now you have formed an intense bond with her.
- She will always be there by your side, but you can call on her when you need extra love and support or guidance.
- She will hold you and let you know that you are beautiful and loved and wanted and good enough just the way you are in this moment, in the past, the present, and the future. She always loves you, and she will always be there for you.
- Now, let's take a moment to thank Mother Mary for this opportunity to connect with her, for her love, for her life, for her graciousness.
- As we do this, we can also thank Jesus and God for their eternal love.
- For all the Miracles they bring into our lives.
- For all the lessons and learning opportunities that they plant seeds that turn into the most beautiful flowers in the most beautiful garden. That Garden is your heart. That Garden is your mind. That Garden is your soul. Allow them to plant those seeds of love and light and of beauty.
- Thank God. Thank Jesus and thank Mother Mary for this experience.
- Thank them for all that they are and all the love they bring into this world.
- Be a beacon for this love; be a beacon for their light.
- You are, in essence, pure light.
- You are, in essence, pure love.
- You are loved.
- Love, love, love.
- As you take a deep breath, you can open your eyes.
- Wiggle your fingers and wiggle your toes, maybe even wiggle your nose.
- Maybe stretch your arms.
- See the beauty that surrounds you.
- You are filled up with the beauty of Mother Mary and her heart.
- Allow that love and light to stay within your heart as you go into the waking world.

The waking world is simply the world that we live in; nothing peculiar or unusual. It's just our day-to-day life. You are allowed to take that love you felt for Mother Mary into your life to help others feel love and light and for you to feel safe and secure.

Remember to call on Mother Mary whenever you're in need, for she will always be there for you.

Just make sure to thank her at the end of the process, though. She won't be offended, either way. She knows you love her just as Jesus and God know that you love them very much. Mother Mary is important for healing and for growth and safety, and security.

Just as we call on Jesus, remember, you can always call on Mother Mary. Don't feel insecure. She loves to help, and she loves to make you feel safe and loved just as you are in this moment.

Go throughout your day and spread this love that you feel. Smile.

When in doubt, you can simply ask Mother Mary to return to your presence. Even if it's just for a brief moment when you feel sadness or when you are triggered to feel any way that's less than love call upon her.

She shall surround you and her love and her beautiful blue light often. This light can also be seen as white or yellow, or even rainbow rays. Either way, it's beautiful, and it's perfect just as you see it and just as it is for you.

Thank you for this moment. Thank you for this time together. And thank you, God, for the love that you bring to every aspect of our lives and our hearts.

With much love, we say goodbye for now.

Know that YOU are pure love.

Love, love, love.

22

MESSAGES IN THE DARK

I stayed sober for a couple of months after my big shift. Marie (my drug dealer and faith guide) no longer lived with me. I felt safe with her and missed our time together outside of work, so I suggested, "Hey, let's get high. I'll do it. I've been sober for a couple of months." She knew my journey and was proud of me. "You're going to be fine. Just getting high once, you're good." So, she said she'd pick me up from home. Some people are so sensitive to intoxicants that they can't just get high once and then stop. I had reached a point where Marie and I both felt confident that I could handle this.

When Marie pulled up in her car, there were already several other people I didn't know in the back seat. We were heading to another friend's home. After spending a little time with everyone, I got a really bad vibe; my heart started to burn physically. I was high, but that wasn't the cause.

I snapped out of my high and checked in with myself, and felt I was not safe. I had learned this concept of checking in with myself from the spiritual world, which just means seeing how you're feeling. What's going on? Why are you feeling this way? The message that entered me upon feeling that burning was my intuition coming from my gut. My heart was connected to that burning sensation, and the message was, *you need to go home. You're not safe.*

We had planned to go to a bar after smoking some weed, drinking some gin, and everything. I just told everyone sitting in Marie's friend's home, "I have to go home. Something's not right. I don't really know what it is. I just have to go home."

I called another friend and asked him to pick me up. He was on his way. I was freaking out a bit because my friend was hesitant, saying, "I'll leave in ten minutes. I have to get ready." I asked him to call me if he changed his mind. He assured me he "probably wouldn't." There's nothing more unnerving than someone making you a promise using the word "probably!"

Sitting underneath a darkened streetlamp on the curb, waiting for my friend to arrive, the streetlight suddenly came on. I took that as a good sign. I thought the light meant I was where I was supposed to be. I started to second-guess the burning feeling I had and thought maybe I should just go back inside. The light was probably on a timer to save electricity, right?

I was worried about inconveniencing my friend, whom I had asked to come to get me, and then also started to feel crappy about abandoning Marie and all these new friends I just made. I stood up and was going to walk back inside, but as I turned toward the door, pulled out my phone, and was about to call my friend to tell him not to come, the light went off again. That was weird. As soon as I moved away from the door back toward the curb and stood underneath the streetlamp, the light came on again. My mind processed the instincts I had and came up with the idea that *I'm not supposed to go in that home again; something's not right. I'm supposed to be near the light. I need to get out of here.*

A collection of messages downloaded into my brain, and I could feel them land in my gut. I just knew—not logically or practically—what the message was.

Something bad has happened, is gonna happen, and you need to leave. You need to get out of this situation.

Going into the house is not a smart idea.
You're not supposed to do drugs.
You were given your mission; you were told what to do.
You need to abide by what you agreed to!

Boy, did this all sound ominous to me and kind of like an elder reprimanding me. But was it God reprimanding me? Or was it my instincts?

My rational head, the one that was not so spiritual, was saying *you're just being paranoid*. But it was different from the paranoia I had in the past during the time with my dad. With him, I felt I was going to get arrested every time I passed a car when I was smoking a blunt, or people were looking out their windows and were going to call the police and report me. I smoked weed hundreds of times in my car, and I never once got pulled over. Never did a cop say, "I saw you smoking weed." Nor did a cop pull me over saying, "Someone reported you for smoking weed." Mostly it was baseless, intoxication-induced, paranoia all in my head. Maybe it was keeping me safe at the time. I don't know.

But the messages at that party house and then at the curb felt different. These were strong messages and even included lighting effects! The summation of all the messages was *you need to leave*. So, when my friend showed up, I got in the car, we left, and he dropped me off at home. I was safe.

MAKING GOOD CHOICES

When I got home, I was about to put a frozen pizza into the toaster oven, but instead, I had a few chips and salsa and found some lunch meat in the fridge, doused it with some hot sauce. I had lost a lot of weight around that time, and I was trying to keep the weight off and maybe even lose a little bit more, tone up, get lean.

Once I was safely home, the messages shifted, and I was feeling/hearing:

Good job, Ryan. We're proud of you. The universe is proud of you for making healthier choices, even when you were high, and for not sliding back to your old behavior of just grabbing onto unhealthy food.

Food had become a huge part of the addiction process for me because I usually wanted to smoke weed and then eat, or smoke weed, drink, then eat or drink again. Food was always at the end of my other addictive behaviors. Get high, eat. Drink, eat. Smoke, eat. Random sex, eat. Not a great pattern. Here I was demonstrating to myself (and God) that I could break my pattern. I was treating myself with respect. That was a new experience.

After that incident with messages, I didn't smoke weed for a while. We get messages all the time, but most people are oblivious to them. We're not paying attention. There are too many distractions in our lives. Once you start to take notice and use your mind/body/gut check-in, you realize that you are not alone and that you just have to be open to interpreting what is happening around you. Anyone can do it.

MAKING BAD CHOICES

I went out with Marie again about a month after that streetlight night. I got really drunk and high with her even though I had remained sober/clean since the last time I had seen her. I was allowing myself one bad-boy night a month.

On my cheat days, the behaviors I allowed were not in my own best interest. I'd buy a bottle of wine and drink it in one sitting. Why do homework? Sometimes I would go out with my friends and get drunk. One time, I got drunk with Harper's mom, which ended up being a not-so-great situation because I realized that when I drank, I wasn't myself, and I could get mean and nasty. Sometimes, I got overly promiscuous. Mostly I just wasn't in control of myself, and it led to things that weren't advantageous to my well-being. Why I did this to myself is related to the feelings of needing to be accepted (getting high was what I did with friends) and feeling some kind of masochistic need to feel terrible about myself.

I wasn't at the point yet where I could totally give up everything and stay clear of people who triggered or enabled my bad choices. In any Twelve Step program, they teach you to stay away from the people who were part of your addiction life. I wasn't in a Twelve Step program. I hadn't learned that lesson yet. And Marie was my drug dealer, a co-worker, but she was also the person who brought me back to God, and I felt we had a spiritual connection that was not so easy to dismiss.

That particular night, everyone met at my home, and I drove. Fortunately, someone else drove my car back to my house because they had to retrieve their own vehicle. I was black-out drunk, which I had told myself I would never do again. I threw up all over the floor of my basement-style apartment. The next day, cleaning it up, I was feeling that shame. *Why did you do this to yourself? You're better than this. You're stronger than ever before.* I resolved again that I was not going to drink or do drugs anymore. *I'm not smoking or drinking for at least a year.*

For the rest of the year, I was supposed to be getting clean.

I was getting high on a second date to which I'd brought weed. This new guy and I had talked about smoking, and he wanted to smoke with me. As we were about to get high, I got another message that came as a thought. Once again, *you need to go home. You're not safe.* I left the guy's home and instead went to smoke weed with an ex at his house. When I was there, I got the same message again! *You're not safe! You need to go home.* It was always about going home and that I wasn't safe. The meaning I absorbed was, *this is not what you're supposed to be doing. This is wrong.*

A non-spiritual person might say that these messages were my subconscious talking to me. Some would say that it was my logical brain adding up the harmful pieces (drugs, strangers, and people facilitating unhealthy habits; potential consequences of doing illegal things; health dangers; etc.) But I felt it was directed to my mind by forces outside of myself.

Usually, drugs and alcohol blocked out all thoughts, all emotions, except for the most pleasant, disconnected feelings. Suddenly, repeatedly, the messages were jolting me out of my inertia and bringing me front and center to deal with my reality.

After each drug/alcohol experience, I felt shame around it afterward. *I can't believe I smoked weed again.* When I woke up, I had the same feeling I got when I was little and had done something wrong, knowing I would get in trouble. Well, now I wasn't getting in trouble. No one said anything. My mom never caught me smoking weed or even drinking. I don't think I really told her in-depth about my sobriety. I think I just said I wasn't doing any drugs and trying not to drink.

I would go for a couple of months without drinking or smoking. I wouldn't smoke cigarettes in my day-to-day life, but I would smoke when

I was doing drugs or drinking. Have you ever noticed that bad habits seem to bunch together?

I was at my friend Alex's house along with my good friend Del. I felt safe at that moment because I trusted Del and Alex. I was in a trusted home. Since my shift experience with Del, I was getting a daily Bible verse on my phone through spiritual and biblical apps. The daily Bible verse that popped up while I was smoking weed that night was about how a man shall not lie with another man. It was one of the clobber verses! I didn't really get the universe message to go home and be safe as much as I did at other times. But I started being flooded with all these instant negative thoughts. I went into panic mode. I started questioning everything: my path, my mission, even God. *What are you doing?* I thought. A series of doubts invaded my consciousness like I was on a speedway with cars coming at me from the opposite direction and speeding by so fast I barely had time to process. I was obviously headed in the wrong direction.

- *What if this guidance you have been getting, to go from darkness into light, is not light at all?*
- *What if my God isn't my God? Not the Christian God?*
- *What if I'm still on the wrong path?* repeated several times in my mind.
- *What if I'm steering myself, and I'm following a false prophet?* My grandpa always said the worst thing in life is a false prophet, and that stuck with me.

I was in a full-blown panic attack. It took me a long time to process that. I didn't get an immediate answer. I kept praying and working in that area, and I knew I would get the message if I just kept doing what I'm supposed to do.

Stay sober.

Stay away from drugs.

Do the things you need to do.

GETTING BACK ON THE RIGHT PATH

One of the things I needed to do was make sure I got back into college. I didn't know how after failing two whole semesters (a full year), I didn't get kicked out. I knew some people who failed just a couple of classes and got kicked out of school. I was afraid. Would they let me back in? And yet, I got in. My student loans came through so I could pay for college. Wow! It was a miracle. I don't know how it happened, but I knew I was making the right choices again. I credited all my "luck" to the hand of God.

I was so grateful for school that when I went back, I made sure I got mostly A's. I was making the dean's list every semester. I put a lot of my heart into my schoolwork.

I got a job at Red Lobster, and I worked there for four years. I was grateful for Red Lobster because, although it might sound weird, Red Lobster helped keep me sober. I made some really close friends who lifted me up.

One of my best friends, Stacy, was this beaming ball of joy and innocence, and as much as I tried to corrupt her a little bit, she helped revert me back to my innocence in some ways. I was grateful for genuine friendships that weren't built around drugs and alcohol or sex and gay bars.

FREEDOM DATE

The last time I ever smoked weed, drank, did drugs, or smoked cigarettes was July 11, 2013. The date will forever be etched in my mind. I had been on my journey to get and stay sober/clean. My whole lifestyle to stay healthy and keep my weight off is a top priority. My diet is low carb, low fat, low sugar, and not eating much red meat. I have found meditation, the School of Metaphysics (see page 149), and Oneness (see page 155) as spiritual outlets. I am sure that all of these healthy resources played into my motivation and ability to level out.

Right before my sobriety date, I was on and off with an ex, and we got drunk together even though he knew that I didn't really like to smoke or drink that much any longer. Once again, I fell into that I-can-control-my-addiction falsehood, a belief that because I hadn't had anything to drink or smoke for a couple of months, it was okay "just once more." There we were in the middle of the night eating big, juicy hamburgers from a fast-food joint. I was back to my triggering habits.

Eating two big burgers along with the drinking left me with a hangover. I don't think I blacked out, but I know I wasn't one hundred percent in control of what I was doing. The next day I didn't throw up, but I felt sick to my stomach. I kept running my tongue across the roof of my mouth because I had a very unpleasant residual taste of meat and alcohol. I spent the day greasy burping. I said, "I'm done." I could feel that I was ruining all the good work I had accomplished toward being healthy.

This decision wasn't like my big shift, but this one night was enough to see that these negative behaviors didn't align with my new lifestyle and what I wanted to accomplish. My body was rejecting my "fun" indulgences, which affirmed to me that I was much healthier overall. That's when I knew it was time to stop everything.

Why did I slip off the wagon? I asked myself. Perhaps I was scared that I couldn't have fun without drugs and alcohol. Certainly, being with my ex brought out the need to party. The thought occurred to me that if I needed all that extra stimulus to have a good time with him, shouldn't that provide a clue as to why the relationship hadn't been working?

The intoxicants were always my way of helping me deal with all sorts of uncomfortable feelings. So, when I got sober (or at least was on my path to sobriety) that first year, maybe I just felt I wouldn't be the me that people liked anymore; that I couldn't relax enough around people without tuning out all the noise in my head. I don't know what it was. But I had relapses on my path to sobriety, and I eventually was able to get to a spot where I just didn't want weed or alcohol anymore. I've not had a drag on a cigarette, a drink of alcohol, or a puff of weed since 2013.

I know everyone's path toward sobriety is different. I used my spirituality to get me through. I am thrilled to be living a healthy life overall, surrounding myself with vibrant people. I find myself now drawn to relationships with people who are loving and kind, and supportive. As I get healthier, I've been in *no* abusive or hostile relationships. Love took over my life.

The biggest love of my life is my daughter. I wanted to be sober/clean and healthy for my child, so we could have a positive relationship, and I could be a role model. I had to love myself first before I could truly love my child, and that's something hard to say aloud and admit even to this day. But when I was actively in addiction and using, I didn't love anyone or anything except my drugs.

When you make a change about loving yourself, then you're able to rebuild your life. You are able to have your kids in your life in a healthy way. If you are focused on change for the sake of another, what happens to you when that person does something to disappoint you or doesn't appreciate all you're going through? You'll slip up and go back to where you were comfortable.

Because drugs, alcohol, and the party lifestyle were numbing me, I couldn't fully live my life. I couldn't share myself because I hated myself deeply. When I reconnected with God and started reconnecting with spirituality, the universe, and my heart, then I realized that I didn't hate myself at all; quite the opposite, I loved myself. And that, to me, is powerful.

Self-love isn't arrogant; self-love isn't selfish; self-love isn't needy. Self-love is mandatory for a healthy life, for sobriety, for true success. Self-love isn't egotistical. It's not being self-centered. Self-love is the key to unlocking your best life.

Success is getting everything you want and need and still being happy. How many times have we heard stories of people winning a lottery or getting the big job they worked so hard for, and they're still unhappy, depressed, anxious? And sadly, how many times do we hear of people who appear to have-it-all, are the envy of those around them, and yet those people show up in the news, tragic stories of overdoses, suicide, or homicidal behaviors? People who feel self-love don't battle with insecurity demons to the point of wanting to destroy themselves. They move toward resolution, work with counselors/therapists or talk to friends and family, express themselves (perhaps through art), and eventually make changes to get to where they have the strength and coping mechanisms to thrive.

23

SCHOOL OF METAPHYSICS

As I was having my big shift, I came across an organization called the School of Metaphysics, based out of Missouri. They had over a dozen campuses, mostly across the Midwest. The school taught world religions, philosophies, belief systems, and how to meditate, visualize, and manifest things. The basic coursework for level one was on training your mind to concentrate.

The program has four stages. I made it through the first full year of the program to the end of the first stage. There's a community service component that I was unable to complete because of work and my college course load, so I never officially graduated from the first stage.

The program consisted of classes, weekly quizzes, exercises, homework (up to two hours a night), and activities. Despite the woo-woo-sounding name, this was a serious education program!

One of the most helpful tools I learned was a common daily zen exercise we did for the year that involved staring into a candle flame for ten minutes.

The school had us mark down every time we had a thought and then refocus back on the candle. When I first started doing this, I put down seventy-five marks in ten minutes! That meant I had a thought every couple of seconds. By the end of the practice, I was able to go ten minutes with only about fifteen to twenty marks. I was getting better all the time. Now I have the skills to still my monkey mind and get back to clear-headedness!

The program also included dream interpretation. We interpreted our dreams and other people's as well. One time, I worked at a farmers' market (part of my college internship while I was simultaneously attending the school of metaphysics), and I spoke to a woman about her repetitive bad dream. It was a very quick conversation. I told her what her dream seemed to mean to me. When I finished, I asked, "Does that make sense?" She said it did. Since her dream was recurring, I told her to think about what I'd said to see what happened with future dreams. When I saw her again the next week, she said she hadn't had that frightening recurring dream one day since she had spoken to me. I felt so great that I was able to help her!

The school taught me a baseline understanding and one way of doing dream interpretation: one way to help people, one way to help myself. I recorded my dreams every night, and I found I wasn't as good at interpreting my dreams as I was at helping others. I probably remember about ten percent of what I learned at the school at this point, so when I help people with dreams, I'm pretty sure I'm also adding my own intuition into the interpretation.

The school has a few rules. You can only miss every other class, and you can't miss two consecutive classes. Attendees could not use any drugs or alcohol. Since I was newly sober, it was kind of like joining AA[4]! The regimen of classes, activities, and homework helped keep me sober and brought me closer to God.

I'm one of those people who usually does something if you tell me not to do it. I don't like traditional rules. I went swimming with sharks, and they said not to touch the sharks, but boy did I want to. Those sharks have sharp teeth, so I didn't touch, consequences greater than reward! But at school, the fact that they said no drugs or alcohol almost made me subconsciously need

---

[4] Alcoholics Anonymous.

to do something just to defy the rules. Fitting into societal norms does not instinctively work for me (nor my mother, by the way). But we need to fit in to have and keep paying jobs, graduate from school, have interactions with our community, etc. I remained completely sober after I stopped going to the school because I had learned how to meditate and other skills that enabled me to maintain sobriety long term.

Learning about all the different world religions was amazing. It enabled me to think about what spoke to my heart. I found a correlation between all the world's religions. They all stand for love, kindness, peace, joy, and meditation. When Christians question my meditations, I point out that it talks about meditation throughout the Bible. In some translations, it may have been noted as praying. Deep prayer is a form of meditation. Semantics. The results are the same. The school taught me more about God, my God, not the God that anyone else wanted me to choose. My God would hear what I felt in my heart.

No matter what horrible things happen in the news, there are thousands, millions, of positive love things happening all over the world at the same time. There's no one right way to do anything. There's no one right answer to anything. Anything done with love, however, can be the answer to everything. Love and light will ultimately win.

It doesn't matter if you go to church or find a meetup group based around God or religion, or you do community service outreach; you're going to learn and grow. That service can be for yourself (which makes the world a better place to live), or it can be of service to other people (in giving you also receive). I think when you work diligently at something and focus on something bigger than yourself in the moment, it leads to self-growth. I had to work on myself so that I could help other people be their best selves.

Around week seven of the twenty-nine-week program, they required participants to attend a weekend retreat. We could choose between camping outside in a tent under the stars or sleeping on the floor indoors. We meditated alone and in groups. Community service involved helping with animals and planting/gardening on the farm. We connected our work with the Earth to the food we prepared and ate communally.

I felt proud that I came prepared because when the rain poured down while I was camping outside, my plastic bags saved the day! At the end, I feel like we didn't just learn life's practical skills, but we were given the gift of connecting to our basic core needs of sustenance, shelter, spirituality, caring for the Earth, and friendship with other humans. I'd like to teach these things to young people early in their education cycle.

All of us meditating and praying together sent out a higher tuned energy. Add in all the Earth-bound connections we made through the farm so that when you leave the property I was told it's quite normal to have a physical withdrawal response. I got physically sick to my stomach after I left because of the higher energy grid around that school and farm property. I learned that we don't consciously see or feel everything around us. Scientifically, we know that we only see the lowest part of the spectrum of light and sound. So why not energy?

The school shared with us the Universal Law of Tenfold Return. They challenged us to put a certain amount of money away (you determine the amount) every day in a jar (or some receptacle). It's a lesson in prosperity and abundance. They offer an abundance affirmation, something along the lines of, "I ask and receive a tenfold return on this X for the goodness of all concerned." I was a server, so I always had cash and could spare $1 per day ($28-$31 a month).

You don't give expecting a return. You give freely, knowing you karmically get returned at ten times what you give. There's enough on this Earth for everyone to have what they need. We're isolated by this scarcity theory that we have to hold everything in and keep all our money and not help other people.

This program taught me about abundance thinking, and though I put cash away, I didn't expect to get cash back. I was comfortable sitting in the knowledge that the universe would repay me in a value worth tenfold to my life and existence. The return on investment (ROI) could be free services, a board member who can help my non-profit, a scholarship or grant opportunity, volunteers offering time, a mechanic telling me, "Honestly, you don't actually need new brakes," or anything that helps me be the best person I can be in offering service wherever I'm needed. It comes back in a non-quantifiable way mostly.

Every quarter or so (and I did this for years), I would go out into the world and distribute the money I saved. I gave it to homeless people on the street or people in need, or an organization asking for donations.

When we give, we make room for new to come in. Marie Kondo in *The Life Changing Value of Tidying Up* talks about clearing your home and office of clutter and junk and unloved objects to open the energy in your space. It is the same abundance theory with money, with giving of time and service and supporting family. The powerful lesson is that when we give, we receive from the universe.

We cannot be fearful about helping people. Whatever is meant to be, whatever the universe sends our way, having a generous heart should remain a priority. We can't take money with us when we pass, so why be stingy? Of course, take care of your needs. But recognize that helping others helps you too, karmically and energetically. Generosity affirms your value in the world. The School of Metaphysics taught me that I *need* to give. I've taught that to my daughter and friends, and family.

I knew I would not go without because I was giving. As an example, in the first year of my sobriety, I was down to my last $100, and I spent it on buying my daughter Christmas gifts and a stocking and things to make the holiday memorable, even though she was only two years old. I had to do it. I realized it would leave me with no food for the week, but my daughter was more important. I sponged off my roommate's food and left an IOU. I went to my grandmother's for Christmas, and she gave me tons of delicious leftovers. Then, I got Christmas gifts in the form of gift cards from my family. (No cash since I was just into sobriety!) I had what I needed and did okay. The universe provided.

There's a classic *Seinfeld* episode called "Even Steven" where Jerry loses a comedy gig and gets another one later that day; he misses the train but catches a bus immediately. Elaine, hearing these stories, tosses Jerry's $20 bill out the window of his apartment to demonstrate that it will come back to him, somewhere, somehow. And it does. He finds $20 in the pocket of a jacket he hadn't worn in ages. I bet if you think about your life, you will realize that this kind of thing happens to you.

I know what it's like to go without. When I was seventeen and emancipated, I lived at Megan's house for a while. I left Megan's house in the middle of the night, after a really big fight. (Sometimes, walking away from an abusive situation is the best and only thing you can do.) As a result, I had to live in my car for about a week. I went to the community pool and jumped the fence to bathe in the pool water. I slept in my car or on a blanket on the grass. Sometimes, just a dollar or two can be so impactful to someone. I understand the scarcity view because I've been there, and it's no way to live. Learning about abundance and prosperity in an energetic way was enlightening. Because I struggled, now I know the value of having a safe space. Because I lost my family at times, I value the relationships I have with my family now. I have been given the opportunity and desire to now help others find their safe haven.

My favorite Saint Francis of Assisi quote: *It is in giving that we receive.*

This Metaphysics program helped me on my spiritual journey. I recommend this program or something similar to everyone ready to explore spirituality. It will offer perspective outside of the familiar and your preconceived ideas. Visit www.som.org for more information.

Commit to the following daily exercise for thirty (30) days. At the end of the thirty days, you can assess your ability to clear and focus your mind for extended amounts of time. If you find yourself interested in more about metaphysics, visit the school's website at www.som.org.

A) **Stare into a candle flame** for ten (10) minutes and markdown with a stroke or a check every time you had a thought, and then refocus back on the candle. You can mark this on any paper or, a more long-term option, keep a journal so you can see how your progress improves over time as you continue practicing this exercise. An alternate way to do this is to use a jar of rice or pennies or pebbles to move them from one pile to another each time you have a thought.

B) **Take the Tenfold Return Challenge**[5]: Commit to putting a specific item/amount in a jar every day for a month. Repeat the following as you make your daily contribution: "I ask and receive a tenfold return on this [*fill in what you are putting in the jar*] for the goodness of all concerned."

Now mark down how you feel each day when you make your contribution. Mark down anything that happens that you might feel is related to your contributions.

---

[5] Sample challenge form in the workbook.

ONENESS, MEDITATION, CONNECTION

Ryan Luken, a Facebook friend who had connected to me through the spirituality community, reached out in a direct message to me. He messaged, "I see that you posted recently about meditating. I have this very cool meditation event that I think you'd be really into. I hope I will see you there." He attached a link with the details. I'd never been part of a hands-on meditation program. According to the website, the facilitators (including Ryan) were trained in the Oneness Movement out of India.

I didn't recall ever meeting Ryan in person, but I looked at the link, thought the event seemed somewhat interesting, so I messaged back and said, "Okay. I really want to go. Thank you for reaching out. I'm excited." I put the info into my calendar and basically stopped thinking about it. And while my intention truly was to go, something came up, and I had to work that Sunday night. I wasn't able to participate. No problem. I would go at a different time. The website said they had regular events.

A few days after, on Tuesday, my mom texted me to call her. When we talked, she told me, "I went to this really, really amazing meditation on Sunday night. One of my friends told me about it, and it was awesome. They did hands-on blessings, and I really think you would love it." I'm thinking, *oh my God, that's weird.* I asked her, "Is the person in charge of that named Ryan Luken?"

My mom, surprised, responded, "Yes!"

In amazement at this coincidence, I said, "Shut the freak up! I was supposed to go to that event that night! We would have shown up at the same place, the same time, not even knowing that we were both going there!"

I found it remarkable that we were both drawn to this same thing called Oneness, right at the exact same time in our lives but from different sources! We were guided there by different people. It was the universe at work! For me, it was one of those God moments where I realized, "Okay, I'm supposed to be there."

That coincidence (which was more like destiny calling) pushed me to want to attend. I was still busy with school and work and Harper visits for the next week or two and wasn't able to fit it into my schedule. I finally arrived at the center three weeks after that first call. I was a little hesitant to enter.

I didn't really know about hands-on work or how I would react. Would the space feel like an ashram? A massage studio? A cult? Would the hands-on work feel uplifting or draining, or just weird?

Meanwhile, my mom had been going every time they had an event, which was every Wednesday and Sunday or something like that. When I finally got there, I was identified at check-in as, "Oh, you're Cathy's son! We've heard about you and are glad you got to be here." Was it peculiar that they seemed to be waiting for me? I'm not sure that I could absorb their intention of welcoming me and making me feel at home. I was a bit cautious.

I walked into Oneness, sat down, and more coincidences kept on coming. I picked up on a familiar energy from the person next to me. I knew that I knew her. I kept looking at her and snapped my fingers in my head as I realized I hadn't seen this person since I was in high school! Of the twenty or so people that were there that night, who was it that happened to be sitting right next to me? I said aloud, "Oh my God, it's Emily! It really is Emily!" A friend from my original high school, the one Mom pulled me out of before sending me to Catholic high school, was at Oneness on the same night! She was such a cutie then, and she still was cute as a full-grown adult.

She told me that it wasn't her first time at Oneness. She'd been a couple of other times. God brought us together originally, and then we reconnected and hung out a couple of times twelve years later! This is how the universe works. If I had come any of the weeks prior, if I hadn't been too busy, I wouldn't have arrived the night I reconnected with Emily.

I think some skeptics would just say it was a coincidence. But, just like the time when my mother and I were both invited to Oneness on the same night, I am convinced that this too was God intentionally pulling people together. When you are ready to connect these types of coincidences together to realize that there's an intentionality about them, you will suddenly see all the connections clearly.

There's no question in my mind that I'm being directed to be exactly where I'm supposed to be all the time, at the time I'm supposed to be there. God is present in my life, and I see/feel Him all around me, all the time. After having a mini-reunion at Oneness, Emily and I reconnected and "friended" on social media. I didn't even know she had moved back up to Cincinnati after she had gone away to college. This is how Oneness has a way of working in people's lives. This is how God has worked into many people's lives. Random connections lead to meaningful relationships.

Emily and I got along at the event and afterward. I'm still not sure of the greater purpose of our reconnection, but I'm happy that it happened. Maybe it was simply to have a friend there to help me transition through my first hands-on experience. Maybe there is something coming up in my life that will make Emily's role in my life clear. It doesn't really matter. It was intended, it happened, and I feel great about it. Maybe it was more about what meeting me did for Emily (that she hasn't yet shared with me).

Ultimately, I later attended a Oneness meditation event in Sedona, Arizona. I went to a Fort Myers/Tampa-area Oneness program. Bigger cities all have Oneness. Ryan Luken has a Master's in Education and instills meditation practices into the public school system. Keith Boyd, Oneness co-leader, is a nurse practitioner. They are both hyper-intelligent and walking beams of love and light. When I first met them, I just saw mythical creatures of love. *You are not real. You are just love! Pure love! Just beings on fire!*

This really awesome Oneness experience occurred in 2013, and it impacted how I think about myself and my relationship to God. Oneness means we are one; we are whole. We are one humanity.

A new friend, Nick, from one of the events, explained that while we may be different people with different personalities, we are one humanity, and we have to stand together. We have to stand up for love. I totally embraced that energy and focus.

Oneness made me aware of so many new ways of thinking and revealed many spiritual doors and avenues for me to explore. I'm forever blessed for that in my life.

24

JOEY

In the midst of my self-improvement and thirst for education, I was actively looking for a man to love. To be up-front, I dated a lot looking for the right partner. I admit that not all my relationships were healthy, and in this, I'm sure I'm not alone. I kept finding myself in serially monogamous relationships hoping that *this* one could be made into *the* one. These relationships were pleasant and loving enough for the time they lasted. I dated men who fell in love with me, but I never fell in love with them. I may have loved them, but I wasn't *in* love. This often led to break-up drama. I really did not enjoy that part of the romance cycle!

While romantic relationships were (and are still) important in my life, my priorities are clearly stated from the beginning of any relationship. Harper is my first priority, then my mom, after God always, and then my partner. Without God, nothing matters in my life to me. I was perpetually learning how to care for myself within my family, my spirituality, and my romantic relationships.

I met Joey through a mutual Facebook friend. Mindy seemed adamant that we should meet, and though I wasn't enthusiastic about the idea of a blind date, I trusted her opinion. It was a peculiar first date and ultimately a fun story to tell in that I wound up sneaking into his middle-of-nowhere Ohio grandmother's home because she didn't know he was gay!

After we had gone on a few dates, I realized I thought of him as my best friend. We had a strong spiritual connection. When I had a great day, I wanted to share it with him, and we celebrated together. When I had a bad day, I would turn to Joey. He knew that I needed prayer to get centered. He would encourage me to pray and prayed with me. Joey is a truly good person and was a trusted and loving partner. Additionally, he didn't need me to provide for him financially. We were equals. Ultimately, Joey and I dated for two and a half years. For two of those years, we lived together.

This was the first time in sobriety that I got to take real vacations and do everyday relationship things. Joey and I rented a cute little condo together. We had regular game nights with our friends and date nights and did sweet things for each other. He was very kind to me, and we took care of each other. We loved each other very, very much. Newly sober, I was still learning how to have healthy relationships.

Joey and I parented Harper for a couple of days each week. Harper was still very little. She knew Joey and I lived together and that we were friends who loved each other. "Boyfriends" was not a concept she could yet grasp. Liz and Joey actually developed a bond, which was so helpful. We occasionally went to dinner all together and would go to Kings Island and other amusement parks. We worked around the logistical challenges of any couple with shared custody of a child.

There were times when Joey and I argued, but it never turned physical, violent, or abusive like some of my previous drug/alcohol-stimulated relationship disagreements. We had boring, common, standard couple disagreements, which helped us discover and then define our boundaries.

Overall, I felt it was the healthiest relationship I had ever been in. All was going well, but I still didn't feel right; something was missing. There was this one thing, which turned out to be a pretty major issue; I just wasn't falling in love with him. He told me he was in love with me many times and every time I would try to answer in the kindest way you can say this to somebody: I love you as my best friend, but I'm not *in* love with you. That was difficult. I mean, it was hard for me to say it, so I can only imagine how it was for him to hear.

About a year into our relationship, we formed **Love Must Win**, a non-profit, with one of our best friends, Mindy, who had introduced us. I started as Vice President and eventually became the Executive Director. The three of us had a passion for helping people and giving back. We shared a mission and vision. That usually provides incredible strength to a relationship.

Despite all the good there was, we had a falling out due to my disturbing discovery of a series of lies Joey had perpetuated through our entire relationship. On the most basic level, Joey had told me that he had his college degree, and I discovered that he actually didn't. I didn't care that he didn't have a degree. I was hurt more by the fact that he lied than the content of the lie itself.

I questioned him, "How could you lie to me for so long? It's been two years, and you've lied to me every single day. This lie isn't just about you not going to school. What about when you answered my question about 'how was your senior year of college,' by saying it was great and then sharing all these stories of things that happened at school, telling me stories that were all false. None of them happened because you didn't go!"

We could sit here and analyze why he would lie about his college degree. There are a million reasons why people do what they do, but I will say that in the LGBTQ+ community, a lot of times, trauma causes people to say or act in ways not normal to ourselves. Joey attended the very conservative Ohio Christian University. I'm sure it was super challenging to be gay at OCU since he told me you weren't allowed to be openly gay there. When I went to Catholic high school, I had the same restrictions, so I totally understood what he must have gone through.

In the end, it really was more about feeling that I couldn't trust him. If I couldn't trust him, I could never fall in love, and that was the missing piece. Knowing he had been lying the whole time we were together broke my heart and left me feeling betrayed.

Hurt as I was, I still gave the relationship a few more months, even after I knew the truth. I actually told him, "I'll give you three to six months for us to try to work this out. Maybe go to therapy?" Neither one of us made an effort to go to therapy. I guess in the back of my mind, it was his responsibility because he was the one who broke our trust bond.

I was feeling guilty because I started reverting to behaviors that I had promised sober me I would never repeat. I came to the realization that I just couldn't become that person again. I had worked so hard to become a better person, to be who I wanted to be, how I wanted to present to the world. After Christmas that year, I asked Joey to move out. This was hard on both of us but probably more difficult for him, to be honest. We were family, living together, sharing our lives, spending time with my mother, and parenting my daughter.

After he left, I moved on rather quickly since I had already taken about six months to figure out what I wanted to do. When he moved out, it was closure for me while he still had processing to do. I wish I would have been kinder to him, looking back. He's not a bad guy. I still see Joey as a very sweet, good person despite how things ended between us.

In the end, what I took away from that relationship helped me learn and grow, which was invaluable for my relationships to come.

25

Healing Affirmation:
I am kind to myself and others, and when I feel like I might do
something out of alignment with my core self, I pause and reconsider.
I allow for mistakes and will take those mistakes and mold them
into learning opportunities!

EDUCATION

By the grace of God, with some help from family, I ultimately finished my undergrad years and earned my bachelor's degree. I originally studied at Northern Kentucky University in Ohio. I then moved to Bowling Green, Kentucky, and went to Western Kentucky University to study meteorology. When Liz and I had Harper, I moved back to Kentucky/Ohio so we could be closer to our families. I switched my major to broadcast journalism and cultural geography because that's the only thing at all similar to meteorology coursework I had been studying at WKU. I just wanted to finish my bachelor's degree! Then, being an overachiever, I earned a second bachelors in electronic media broadcasting.

Like many students who graduate, I struggled to find meaningful work that was in any way related to the degrees I had earned. To supplement my bank account while I searched for the right fit, I was also a server. It was phys-ically difficult and exhausting work, but I was making pretty good money. I could work thirty hours a week and earn enough money to survive while I was trying to figure out how to balance fatherhood, dating, work, non-profit duties, family, fitness, and everything else going on.

The biggest joy and challenge at the time was that I finally was able to share custody of Harper more than I had in the past. When I had been doing drugs and then going through the first year of sobriety, things were a little rocky. Ever since I left Tennessee my senior year of high school, my birth dad had not really been much in my life, so I understood how having no access to a father would feel. I asked Liz not to make Harper go through that. Liz knew what life was like without a dad as her father passed away when she was younger. We actually agreed that we didn't want Harper to experience that loss of balance from not having a father figure in her life.

I told Liz that Harper needed both parents, she agreed, and we negotiated an agreement without lawyers. Our agreement was verbally finalized after lots of discussions, lawyer threats, and crying nights. Harper would spend two days a week with me and would stay the night in between. In this way, Harper could get to experience what having a dad was like. She also got to see me in a relationship because I was with Joey around this time. This gave Liz a chance to be a single woman for one night a week and enjoy time on her own to see friends or date if she wanted.

CULTIVATING MY OWN STYLE

Even with a double bachelor's degree, I couldn't find a nine-to-five-type job that would match the cash I was earning as a server. To get a starting position for a forty-hour-a-week job and make enough to pay my bills was almost impossible. I felt stuck serving, but I didn't hate it. I mostly worried about slipping back on my sobriety. The restaurant atmosphere can be toxic because there are some nasty customers, and people smoke and drink all the time, but thankfully hard drugs weren't present where I worked.

Work can be stressful as a server, but you're done for the day when you leave. I made good money and could go home after work and not be stressed once I left the premises. At this point, I started thinking about going back to school. My hours and schedule as a server were flexible. I considered going back for a degree in clinical counseling (follow in mom's footsteps) or maybe education. I thought I would love to be a teacher. It's something I felt I was supposed to do since I was little.

My intention was to teach at the college-age level, but I thought perhaps I would love to work with young kids after having Harper. I envisioned being an influential figure in emerging lives to help youth or young adults grow and not just learn the curriculum but learn about how to treat people, be kind and fair, and instill some spiritual practices in there. I watched how the parents interacted with their children at my serving tables and thought about how kindness, love, and acceptance should be taught at the school level, but it's not typical (unless you are lucky enough to have self-motivated, amazing teachers).

Then, as I carried trays back and forth between the kitchen and the patrons, I toyed with the idea that maybe I should get a Master's in Business Administration (MBA) so I could learn more about the business world, entrepreneurship, and leadership. I was primarily interested in leadership, perhaps combined within the world of clinical counseling, helping people and kids with their problems. There were lots of different thoughts going through my mind while I was serving with a smile and earning tips and a paycheck.

I prayed and meditated about all this for a good six months. I kept getting signs to go for the MBA. It was crazy. I could look up at a billboard when I was thinking about what I should be doing, and I'd see an ad for an MBA program. I'd turn on the radio in the car, and the first ad would be an invitation to join an MBA class online. I would look at my phone and see an ad on Facebook for MBA programs. (On a side note, it is a bit freaking crazy weird that Facebook ads pop up when you're talking about things. Right?)

I finally said, "Okay! I get it, God! I have to do my MBA." I was a little resistant at first because I really didn't want to study for the GMAT. I hate tests. I'm not the best test taker. But I started studying for the GMAT. I registered to take the GMAT with a plan to apply essential oils to my skin and hold a crystal in my pocket! (I know—*hippie!*) When I arrived on the day of the test, they made us leave everything from our pockets in a locker. So I applied my essential oil all over my head. I was deep breathing in the aromatherapy, and before I closed the locker, I held my crystal and prayed, "Give me strength!"

I prayed and meditated a lot before I went into the testing room. I didn't do as well as I wanted to, but it worked out that my score was perfectly fine to accomplish what I needed to accomplish. God, the oils, the crystals (oh, and studying too) helped me get accepted to the MBA program back at Northern Kentucky University.

I picked NKU because I had attended the school as an undergrad. I thought they had a really cool cohort program. You stayed with the same students all six semesters. It was year-round for two years, pretty intense. We went fall (September to Christmas), spring (January through May), and summer (June to August) semesters without a break. Some MBA programs stretch out over three or four years, but I chose this intense two-year program. I definitely didn't want to take on more than two classes per semester. Two classes in a master's degree is full-time. I still had to work close to full-time to cover the bills.

My first day of class, I was a ball of nerves. Observing the other program participants around the room, I began thinking, *oh my God, all these people have professional jobs. I'm pretty much the only one in this class in the service industry.* I went through that self-doubting phase of feeling like I didn't really know why I was there. Based on how people treat servers like we don't have importance or value, I thought maybe these professional cohorts in my class wouldn't think I had a *real* job. I started the self-doubt train that I wasn't as qualified as all the other students. This is that judgment voice (perhaps ingrained by interactions with parents, other relatives, teachers, religious leaders, media, peers, employers, and so on) so many of us use to diminish our accomplishments and value.

When God sent me all the messages to go for my MBA, it felt like more than a suggestion. This message was not to be ignored. Do you know how some people joke that if they don't do what is demanded, they will get struck down by lightning? I felt this message had that kind of force. "God," I questioned, "Why did you make me do this?" I found out why once I started the program.

While going through my MBA program, many amazing things happened. I met one of my best, most kind friends in the world, Erin. Erin is an adorable, blonde sunbeam who radiates ethereal light wherever she is.

She owns a successful all-natural, organic airbrush spray tanning business. She even spray-tanned Miss America at one time.

I learned a lot about myself and about who I am as a leader and was able to ultimately define what was important to me. Let's be a mid-level manager. Nope! I need to be a leader. There's a difference between a leader and a manager, and I'm not a manager. I don't want to manage people. The people I met, the experiences I had, and the education I received in that specific MBA program led me to recognize that I want to lead.

Our non-profit (the one I started with Joey and Mindy), *Love Must Win*, received our 501(c)3 status while I was in the MBA program. We became an official IRS non-profit and started doing big events in the city and small events around the community. It was a glorious gift that I witnessed the direct impact we were having in people's lives. As someone who thought about leadership, teaching, and influencing, I found I was in my perfect zone for happiness in my work! *Love Must Win* provided me the opportunities to develop as a strong leader.

I want to share something about me and finances; I admit that numbers are not my strongest skill. The master's program taught me how to follow my heart and not to follow the numbers all the time. The program did focus on the bottom line and finances in the beginning—the basics. Later we learned, to my great joy, that improving the bottom line for a business included revenue, of course, but it is also related to environmental and human impact— the triple effect.

A business impacts your clients/customers/patients/guests, the people purchasing your product or service, your employees, your management or executive team, your board members, your stakeholders, and your shareholders. It's not exclusively about money. Businesses impact the communities in which the business sits and operates. The concept of a triple bottom line stuck with me because it provided an image of what any business needed to look like from a more holistic view. I shifted my leadership approach to a more organic style, and I am still developing that, which led me to continue my education even further.

I wanted to share my education journey because I felt that this decision was God-driven, and there was not really an option for me to say *No*. It was pushed in my face, it was not easy to accomplish, but it ended up being perfect. I didn't know why I was there in the moment, but I knew I was guided to do it. And because I did what I was guided to do, the outcome was something really beautiful. Even if I just did my MBA so I could help start **Love Must Win**, it was worth it because of the thousands and thousands of people we've impacted since we began.

In addition to learning about myself as a leader and meeting Erin, I also stepped out of hiding and decided to be authentic; however, I had no idea how it would be received. When classmates asked me to go to happy hour, I always declined. How were they to know that I can't be in bars? So, during the third semester, I shared with my MBA cohorts that I was on a sobriety journey. I told them I'd been sober for about three years and a lot of them seemed shocked. My sharing helped them understand why I said no to happy hour outings. People may have thought I was antisocial or didn't like them, or that I thought I was better than them, or maybe that I had too many obligations with my child and being a server. There were probably a lot of reasons they may have attributed to my rejections of joining them for happy hour. Once I shared, they didn't need to assume or wonder any longer.

After I shared my truth, when my classmates invited me to happy hour, they'd always say, "Well, they have food too, Ryan. You know you don't have to get a drink." It was nice to know that people cared. It also was a great reminder that people don't know unless you share and that sharing your story can be really impactful. Sharing your story is also part of how you can communicate better with people. Once people get to know more about you, they feel less confused or conflicted.

Alcohol is everywhere, and drugs are everywhere. Caffeine is everywhere. Technically, I can go to a bar. I keep open alcohol in my home. I have wine and beer, and I even have some liquor bottles. I'm not tempted to drink it. I'm okay with it being in my house. But I wouldn't necessarily keep it out in front where I see it all the time, reminding me of what I'm not having, what I used to be like, taunting me on bad days, etc.

I thoroughly enjoyed my MBA cohorts and maintained my sobriety through all the studying, tests, and social experiences. Three or four years prior, I was snorting lines on the way to class and really struggling. However,

I'd finally gotten to a place where I had the opportunity to further my education, and I was killing it!

As I had shifts in my life, the work I do with ***Love Must Win*** has helped people have little shifts in their lives. The opportunity to do this is something that you can never put a financial value on. The importance of being there to help guide fellow humans in crisis moments cannot be underestimated. The two years of blood, sweat, tears, and money that I put into that MBA program were worth more than I can even put into words.

I heard that just nine percent of US citizens over the age of eighteen had achieved a master's degree or higher. So really, not many people get that opportunity, nor have the drive or resources or even want to accomplish that goal. I was guided to do it, and I did it! I feel really blessed for that. I hope that you will find what lifts you up, gives you purpose, and helps you live in this world authentically.

The accumulation of experiences from childhood to adulthood, combined with the ongoing education through schooling and work/volunteer efforts, added to what all the people who came through my life taught me and brought me to a place where I felt crystal clear about what works and doesn't work in my life. We all have that. It's human evolution.

Once I was free of chemicals that muted my mind, I was getting messages and knowings that the things I was learning were meant for me to share with others; not just keep the lessons for myself. I was filled with the understanding that people struggle to get through challenges. However, they may not be aware of why those challenges appeared and what to do with what they learn from them. I was meant to teach, support, motivate, and lead. It has become my mission.

In the following chapters, I will share with you some of what I have experienced and have been directed to impart to the community, in general.

PART III

THE ADDICTION
TUG OF WAR

26

RECOVERY FROM ADDICTION

I had a caffeine addiction, there was my food addiction, and my drug and alcohol addictions. I don't know if my dating life could have been considered a sex addiction or more of an addiction to attention. But addictions ruled my being for a long time.

"The first step is recognizing and admitting you have a problem." I did that. I had several addictions, I realized. In my work, to clear myself of all my addictions, I came to believe that tackling one addiction at a time is more manageable than trying to stop everything simultaneously. An assessment (self-assessment or done by a professional) is important to know where you are, what you're currently doing, and what you want your life to look like overall.

Maybe you've never felt the need to explore sobriety, but perhaps you're addicted to caffeine? Well, let's check that out. Self-assessment:

Why do you think that you're addicted to caffeine?

How does caffeine make you feel?

How does caffeine make you feel when you don't have it?

Can you cut back your caffeine?

Can you look at more natural sources for that energy you crave?

- What about food addiction? Go through those same questions too.
- Cigarettes?
- Drugs—answer them all
- Alcohol—same thing
- Exercise
- Sex

(There are some people addicted to exercise and/or sex because they substituted the high of drugs and/or alcohol for the endorphin and serotonin rush.)

An assessment gives you a starting point and a picture of the challenge ahead. It will let you know where to focus your energy.

There's no reason to feel bad about your intention to rid yourself of an addiction. If you feel wrong about something you're doing or the side effects are impacting your quality of life, that's a sign that you need to change some behavior. We're just here doing the best we can do, and I think that's my challenge for you. It's about just being the best version of yourself that you can be. That's all I ask of myself, and that's all I ask of my child. We're not going to be perfect, and we're going to make mistakes; we're imperfectly perfect when we make those mistakes. I find that thought reassuring in my journey because recovery from an addiction is hardly ever a straight line to the finish!

RECOVERY FROM DRUGS AND ALCOHOL

I will share with you my thoughts on my recovery from drugs and alcohol. For me, it is what it is. I've heard people say they don't like that saying. I prefer saying *it is what it is in the moment.* It is what it is today, but that doesn't mean that's what it has to be forever. Tomorrow might be different; maybe a week from now, or maybe a month from now, a year from now, ten years from now, who knows? But it is what it is today in this moment. In five minutes, you or the situation might change, but there's no reason to beat yourself up over it.

First, let's be clear that each person's chemistry is different. What is easy for me might be quite impossible for you. There are people who find that drugs/alcohol makes them feel better, gives them the confidence to come out of their shell, and makes them forget what they don't want to dwell on, but if, like me, they are told they can't have the drugs for a month (like what happened when I got grounded), they can handle it. It's not fun, but they handle it. A support group, counseling, or advisors can all help someone get over the bumps on the road to sobriety.

On the other hand, some people are chemically addicted, and they cannot just stop. Their system goes into shutdown. They go through physical withdrawal that can be excruciating and miserable. The body starts screaming to be satisfied by the chemical that changed the way the addict functions. For those people, the best solution is a medically supervised program. People with a chemical addiction cannot just have "one." Their body will go into full craving mode and won't let up until it gets more and more. Like the blood-thirsty plant in *Little Shop of Horrors*, the addiction screams "FEED ME!" more and more once it has a little taste, and it doesn't stop until it's consumed the master.

MARIJUANA

I think there's some good science behind marijuana. It's probably not healthy for your lungs when you smoke or vape it, and it can potentially create holes in your frontal cortex. Luckily, in your frontal cortex, those holes can be healed when you stop smoking, but long-term smoking marijuana is not good. I think that's why most people and a lot of doctors are turning toward edibles, oils, and CBD tablets/capsules and pills. I don't know much about that. All I know is to stay away from all of it when you're trying to stop your addiction.

What if? If I ever had some type of illness where I needed some pain relief, I believe I would choose marijuana instead of opioid pain medicine. Marijuana is way more effective and healthier for the human body than some of the drugs doctors are prescribing. To be completely honest, I would try my best to do without anything. However, if it's medicinal marijuana and prescribed by a doctor who's monitoring me after understanding where I fall on the addiction spectrum, I would see how it went.

As a recovering addict, I am aware that one joint or pill, or drink can start the cycle all over again. If you are an addict or in recovery, inform your doctors and clinicians about your addiction so they can make sure that whatever they're prescribing is not harmful or going to rekindle your desire to abuse drugs again.

I will never touch drugs again. I usually fight health challenges on my own (even strep throat) with a blend of vitamins, herbs, tea, healthy food, and meditation. That's healed me many, many times from upper respiratory/ lung illness. I live in an area where allergies are a big thing, and often allergies morph into other things. I'm not anti-medicine. I'd say I'm just anti-quick fix if there are healthier ways that could possibly resolve an ailment.

Pharmaceuticals are a mess. I stay away from all prescription-based medications for anything unless I have an infection. In 2018, I had horrible chills and a weird fever. I have found natural remedies that work really well for most things, but this was not a time where any natural remedy was working. I needed a doctor. I went to my physician and, lo and behold, had scarlet fever. There you are. I promise you people still get scarlet fever; it's a form of strep.

Full disclosure here: When I lived in Bowling Green, Kentucky, I wasn't actively attempting suicide, but I was thinking a lot about it. I felt I was doing better, and then a sudden realization would hit, *oh no, I'm not doing better*. So, I reached out to my mom, and she helped me reach a psychiatrist in the Cincinnati area. I had to get on medicine for depression and anxiety because my go-to self-medicating with marijuana was not working. I remain a big advocate for mental health medications through a psychologist, psychiatrist, nurse practitioner, or doctor. They are aware of what they are prescribing medications for, based on what's going on with their patient. I feel that helps us a lot.

I tried the medication alone first, but they take forever to kick in (as much as four to eight weeks). I had to take those pills along with smoking marijuana. I think it helped get me over the hump.

I met with my therapist once a month at first, then every other month once I was stable for medication management. I stayed on that medicine for eight months until things got better. I don't know what happened, really, but one day I told him I'm going to wean myself off the drug. We came up with a plan, and we were officially done. It was over. Again, I'm not advocating for purely holistic methods for resolving mental health issues. I think mental health remedies sometimes need to come in along with prescribed medication and therapy.

ALCOHOL, CIGARETTES, AND DRUGS

Most of my journey with alcohol and drugs is throughout this book, so I won't go into it again here. My on-again and off-again nicotine addiction, however, was something that started when I was around sixteen and lasted until I got sober. I went through phases where I would smoke for six months to nine months or even a year, and then I would quit for a year, then start back again. It was a constant push and pull. What I will say is that you have to find what works for you. Not everyone is the same. Not everyone needs a support group, but most people find it very effective to get through the roughest parts and keep you motivated and accountable. Most people cannot go cold turkey. Some people find weaning off is easier. Some people reduce by one addiction at a time. Some people smoke more cigarettes until they can stop drugs. People who drink often smoke when they drink, and they need to quit both simultaneously because they are each triggers for one another. And so on. I'm only saying that no one solution works for all. But find what works to keep you on the road to being your best self, to finding freedom from the shackles of addiction. Don't be afraid to ask for support, advice, or direction to finding resources.

CAFFEINE WON'T CONTROL ME ANYMORE

"Can I please get a decaf sugar-free nonfat pumpkin spice latte?" That would be my most preferred order, but they don't make a sugar-free pumpkin spice, which is a travesty! They can make it with skim milk; they can make a caffeine-free version, but they can't make it sugar-free for you. So now I don't even drink that anymore. As I write these thoughts in October, with the crisp air hitting my face when I walk to the car, the leaves swirling around my feet, I am sad because (and I'm not gonna lie) I love pumpkin spice lattes! I wish I were heading to the coffee shop to pick one up for my morning walk.

I haven't had caffeine in over five years as of this writing. I don't know the exact day, but I decided to cut caffeine out of my life when I realized it was a stimulant. Caffeine is a form of drug. I'm not here to caffeine-shame anyone, Lord knows. My brother used to spend a hundred hours a week hiding from my out-of-control behaviors, and he became addicted to caffeine drinks and supplements. He then carried that addiction into the rest of his life. So, I'm here to tell my story but not with the intention of placing judgment. These are just my opinions and views based on my life and the knowings that I've picked up from other people.

Caffeine had a powerful pull on me. Girl, I used to score some pain pills, but caffeine was harder to give up. To some degree, probably, because it's so readily available. Caffeine sources are everywhere. When I had it all the time, it changed my mood and altered my state of being. That's why I decided to get rid of it. I was extra moody all the time. I'd wake up in the morning and have a cup of coffee, which would help me get my system going, and then I would have a cup in the afternoon around 2:30. I didn't do energy drinks and stuff like that, but drinking coffee was a thing to do. You get rid of holding cigarettes and smoking and replace them with a cup of coffee.

Caffeine use is prevalent. It's one of the hardest addictions to break because it is everywhere, and it's embraced as part of our culture and embedded in our daily routine. It's like an activity, a distraction, a bonding thing, and a chemical rush all wrapped up into one mug. It's a piece of the corporate culture. "Grabbing a cup of coffee" at a coffee house has taken the place of the martini lunch for business meetings. People sit in coffee houses to work, create, and people watch. It's affordable luxury.

Everywhere you go, there's coffee or tea or caffeinated drinks. But there are also caffeine pills, mints, soft drinks, and gum now. There are "shots" of caffeine in little single-serve containers at the cash registers of gas stations, convenience, and stationery stores. Caffeine is a legal high that is more readily available than any other stimulant you could ever think of.

Kids get caffeine in their snacks, including chocolate, ice cream, flavored cereals, hot chocolate, iced tea, and more. They offer caffeine at schools in soft drinks, Monster, and Red Bull-type beverages.

A study published in the Journal of Pediatrics[6] found that low doses of caffeine could affect a child's heart rate and blood pressure. This is even more enhanced in teen boys. Side effects include difficulty sleeping or concentrating, headaches, nervousness, and even an upset stomach.

Using caffeine to make it through exams, prepping for a presentation, staying awake for a meeting, or getting through a long drive, is accepted behavior. Getting pumped up and energized is addictive, the same way taking pills would be. But coffee is accepted. I would argue that a lot of Americans right now are battling a caffeine addiction, and they just don't know it or wouldn't see it as a problem. Maybe I would say a lot of the world, too: the caffeine cult.

When we share our sobriety story with other people, it helps them open up about whatever they may be struggling with or what they've struggled with in the past.

AN ADDICTION YOU CAN'T LIVE WITHOUT

My mom took a job at St. Elizabeth Medical Center in their weight loss division. She did intake and psyche evaluations for people who are considering weight loss surgery. One of the doctors running the program had told her that he was addicted to food, and she laughed and said, "my son always says that."

"No, really. I'm addicted to food," he said rather seriously. Then he explained to her it's a hard addiction to have because you have to eat to survive.

I told my mother, "Oh my God, I've been saying this for years, and no one believes me, and here we go with doctors saying the same thing."

Here's an example of how food addiction shows up:

> My mother and I were at a formal dinner. We were at our assigned seats. The staff put two rolls laden with sunflower seeds on the bread plate at my seat. *Interesting.* I ate both of the tops of the rolls because they were delicious. The

---

[6] "Pediatrics: 133 (3)," American Academy of Pediatrics (American Academy of Pediatrics, March 1, 2014), https://pediatrics.aappublications.org/content/133/3.

waitstaff wouldn't take away the uneaten parts or the full breadbasket with an assortment of freshly baked, fragrant rolls and breadsticks and flatbreads; they just sat there the whole time, taunting me.

My mother was busy talking to the person on her other side, which left me staring at the bread. I was too distracted to talk to anyone else at the table. Self-control, when something you love is right in front of you, and you can't just walk away, is the most daunting thing! I kept picking up the basket and picking rolls out of it. I know that most people say, "Okay, it's just food. You're allowed to eat." Well, yes, it is food and food sustains, but the problem is that once that bread was set on the table, that's pretty much all I could think about, all of dinner. Well, not only rolls but also dessert, because we made our selection with the waitstaff when we first sat down. Getting through the full dinner was absolute torture.

If you're not addicted to sugar or food, none of this is a problem. You think my description is exaggerated. For those of us who have addictive tendencies and/or have food restrictions or weight concerns, this simple scenario is an actual nightmare, and carb addicts have no doubt experienced this very same or similar situation themselves. Addiction is addiction, but food, oxygen, and water are needed for survival. Food addiction cannot end by avoidance of consumption.

There are people who eat to live, and there are people who live to eat. Which are you?

FOOD SOBRIETY

Since my drug and alcohol sobriety, I lost eighty pounds. I was proud of my accomplishment, but then the yo-yo effect started. I gained thirty, and then I lost thirty-five; I gained twenty-five, and then I lost twenty; I gained fifteen, and then I lost thirty; I gained ten. I rocketed between crash dieting and binging. I was not anorexic or bulimic. I never threw up what I ate. But I would make deals with myself and then feel guilty. It was not a healthy mental attitude to begin with, and the impact of yo-yo weight on my body and health was not ideal.

My initial significant weight loss happened while I was still smoking and drinking. One night I drank at my friend's house, and the next day I was super depressed. Obviously, alcohol is a depressant, which makes sense. I also smoked a whole pack of cigarettes that day, and then I went to school, but I skipped one of my classes because I just couldn't get out of my car because I was crying. That's the last time I ever remember feeling just hopeless. You don't realize that everything you put into your system processes differently when you lose that much weight. While I eventually stopped the drugs, alcohol, and smoking, I couldn't stop eating.

To try to stop the yo-yo, I decided that I was going to allow myself cheat meals once a week. This works for some people, but I found that I became obsessed with my cheat meals. I thought about food *all* the time! For a cheat meal, I would order a large pizza, hot wings, and a carton of ice cream. I would eat the entire pizza, the hot wings, and about a third to a half of the carton of ice cream at one meal. That's a lot of food. What I ate could literally feed a family of four!

The binging turned into an addiction; I couldn't stop. It got so out of control that I joined the web Overeaters Anonymous program. Though I had planned to go to live meetings, I never went to any. I did learn about limiting carbohydrates and what sugar does to the body.

I really knew there was a problem when I realized that my partner (Joey) and I would plan out my cheat meals all week. It was on our minds all the time. Planning food was an activity we did together! Where are we going to go and what will I order when I get there? Maybe we're going to Chili's, and I'm going to get a salad with extra ranch dressing, and then I'm going to get the hot wings or the chicken tenders with extra sauce, and then I'm going to get loaded mashed potatoes. We have to ask for that free appetizer that comes with that. Choose the loaded cheese fries with extra ranch! Yeah! And then for dessert, let's make sure we have ice cream at home. What!?

If I stop now and count up the calories for this "meal" I fantasized about at Chili's, I bet it would be more than I burned off for three days of everyday living. It's not like I was training to run a marathon where I would burn off the calories. But, besides that, these food selections were not healthy. I don't usually have problems with acid reflux or indigestion, but when I over-eat or eat food that my body is not used to eating, stomach issues are always a sign that I've gone in the wrong direction.

I stopped the binging the same way I stopped the cigarettes and the drugs; I eased myself off. Now, I allow myself to eat certain things, but I'm just very aware of what I eat.

I limit starchy bread and carbs. I limit fats and oils. I have learned that certain foods make me unwell physiologically but also impact me mentally, so I don't eat those foods in general. When I indulge (like with the rolls and dessert at the fancy dinner), I'm not going to beat myself up over that. I've maintained a consistent weight since 2017. To be honest, I may gain ten pounds around the holidays because sweets are everywhere then! But I stay within a pretty good range.

It's rare that I binge now. When I do, I catch myself binging on healthy food. It's really about making a lifestyle change. I eat a lot of fruits and vegetables and lean meats. However, I do allow myself to have desserts and to snack on something when I want it. If I want a bite of something, I'm going to have a bite. I have said (joking-ish) that I can live without food, but not ice cream. I wouldn't dare. Ice cream is important to me.

For me, at this point, it's not about weight. It's more about being healthy. It's also about body image because I struggle with that a lot.

PART IV

ADULT—RYAN

STEPPING INTO LOVE AND LEADERSHIP

27

> **Healing Affirmation:**
> *I am doing the best I can, and that is the **best***
> *anyone can ask of me (including myself).*
> *I bring out the best in others and in my experiences!*

PERFECTLY IMPERFECT

People who don't truly know me, those who are just friends or follow me on social media, or have known me for a few years or less, think that my life is just some type of beautiful, no-problem life. They might imagine that I grew up without trauma, that I don't now, nor have I ever had any issues. To them, I'm just what they see on Facebook postings. If you've read this book until this point, you know that it is far from reality.

When people define me as perfect, it makes me feel really uncomfortable because I'm not perfect in the way they pedestal me. I still have my own learning, growth, and challenges in many areas of my life that I'm working on diligently. No one always shows up in the world (as society defines) as perfect all the time. I want to argue that everyone's perfect in any single moment. We're all *Perfectly Imperfect* all the time.

Social media has made it seem like others are always better than you are. This puts unattainable visions in our heads and can lead to depression and anxiety. You are perfect just the way you are in this moment, but you should strive to be the best version of yourself at all times.

I've been working on my body image issues. At one point in my life, I had body dysmorphia, which makes you see your body as something completely different from what it is. When I was bigger, I saw myself as an elephant. I didn't see myself as I was. I thought I was obese, lumbering around, waddling from side to side, sending vibrations through the floor with every step. At 225 pounds, for my height and build, I wasn't obese, but I was definitely over an ideal weight. I still, to this day, don't see my body as it really looks.

Now, I never feel fat. I've worked through that aspect of my life, but I have moments where I realize, *oh my gosh, I'm bloated,* or *I ate too much today, and everyone can tell!* My clothes fit me better at certain times and in different seasons because I flow with five pounds of weight. I might notice a difference in the way my clothes fit me, and there's a part of myself that reacts to that. I've done a lot of work around accepting that there are moments in life when I'm going to gain five pounds, and there are moments in life when I'm going to be at my goal weight.

I'm still working on not looking at a scale. I don't jump on the scale every day by any means, but I will jump on the scale once a week or so just to make sure that I haven't gained weight. I've been hitting the gym to tone my muscles and improve my cardiovascular endurance.

Harper and I joined a rock-climbing gym where we go climbing together. Just between you and me, I will tell you that climbing is the best upper body workout I've ever had, and at some point, it's almost aerobic as well (in case you're looking for some not-boring exercise program)! My goal when I go is always to do every rock wall that I've done before. Then I try to do one more. I'm constantly challenging myself to improve, even at the rock-climbing gym. I don't have a meticulous plan of what I do when I go there, but I have fun. I enjoy challenging myself to be the best version of myself that I can be.

That's not perfectionism. Perfectionism, in my mind, is walking into that rock climbing gym and falling off that wall and then beating myself up over it later or not being able to finish what I set out to accomplish and then beating myself up over it later. With a quest for perfectionism, you have a repercussion for not being perfect. Whereas doing the best that you can do in the moment or being the best version of yourself is not perfectionism. It's about improving and doing better, and at some point, maybe there is no further to go. Maybe you've done that piece. Perfect. Move on to a more challenging piece. That's how we learn and grow and how we come to live this life to the fullest.

Next time you're stuck in that perfectionist mindset, remember me, and that there was a time when I did act that way, and now I've shifted. I'm happy just to be me and okay to recognize this day might be different from the next day.

One day I might be the best parent in the world, while the next day, I might be seemingly a crappy parent, but overall, I'm a good parent. I think that's what we have to focus upon each day. Do better next time. **Bestism is the idea of being the best version of yourself in that moment.** That's my aim, every day, in every moment.

28

Healing Affirmation:
*I am a beacon of light for others and allow others to help light
the way when I'm down or my path needs illumination.
I am a lighthouse of **love**!*

SAFE HAVEN 2015

*L*ove **Must Win** was formed in the springtime of 2015. As we were getting things together, forming our 501(c)3, and working on official paperwork, we wanted to design what our programming would look like overall. We were still getting our bearings.

Erin was in my MBA program with me. Paula, one of Erin's organic spray tanning clients, joined our meeting at Erin's home. We started talking with Paula about the organization, and she got super fired up about the concept.

"We want to create a safe space, offering events where people can just come in and be themselves," we described to Paula.

Paula said, "Sounds like a safe haven."

Erin and I had this lightbulb moment, one of those divine moments where you knew that you were being guided by God. Paula had encapsulated in words exactly what we were trying to accomplish! We adopted her language and called our physical space Safe Haven.

After participating in the Northern Kentucky Pride festival as an organization, we were ready to get everything in the works to open Safe Haven by mid-summer. All we needed was the actual space.

With a modern, curved, mostly glass edifice, Boone County Library features a huge glass dome in the center of the building, which imbues a very open and airy feeling. The café sits below. The clean lines, grounded earthy wood trim, helpful staff, and various meeting rooms and spaces were perfect for us.

"Ask and You Shall Receive" was our prayer and energy. We asked the leadership at the library (which was conveniently located right up the road) if we could use their community space. While we were in ask mode, we boldly added a request to use it for free since we were a local non-profit organization. They said, "Yes!" Once we secured the space, we needed to collect food donations from the community. We had people volunteer to make finger foods to have food for people attending our first event. Then we thought we should have some raffle prizes to get people in the door; this would help us collect monetary donations and gather contact information. People went to retailers, and we found ourselves with a bevy of raffle prizes!

We deliberated on a topic that would be helpful and appealing for our targeted community and decided that the first event should be a collective show rather than only one keynote. The focus of the evening was on mental health in the transgender community. A lot of people don't understand the transgender experience, and we wanted to make sure that the LGBTQ+ faction knew we stand strongly with that community. In the past, we had watched as other gay organizations left the trans community out of programming and support efforts.

We found an author who had written sport-related books, including a book about a wrestler who had completed suicide. The author was actually one of my professors, a wonderful writer and storyteller, Ryan Clark. A transgender woman, Sarah Kabakov, came to share her story publicly for the first time. Our final speaker was a transgender veteran. They all graciously donated their time and expertise. The program was complete!

We distributed Safe Haven materials at Pride events, displayed them at the library, and posted them wherever we could for two or three months. I guess in my mind, the room sat around 100–250+ people, and I thought *I don't expect 250 people, but I expect fifty to seventy-five people to show up to this: it's free, including food! We have respectable, professional speakers with great stories to share.* We wanted to spread some love, and I was just excited to create those ripples to help love flourish.

On the night of our mental health event, about fifteen people showed up. Honestly, this is how many people still show up for Safe Haven events to this day. We've had audiences as large as sixty people and as small as ten. I remember getting in the car at the end of that night and crying. I emceed the event, and it went okay, but I was a nervous wreck overall.

My life partner at the time, Joey, was the president of the organization. I was the Vice President of Operations. He hugged me and kissed me, and asked what was wrong? He assured me that everyone enjoyed their time and we really did a great thing. He said it was a great first event. Through my tears, I whined about having put so much time and effort into the event and that one of our board members drove there from way out of town, all for only fifteen people. In addition to all the board members and volunteers working on the event, I'd spent a lot of time working on the event because, between school and work, I had the most flexibility in my schedule. I had spent innumerable hours doing the bulk of the logistical work and felt like a failure that let down the team. If I didn't create an event that brought more people, that had a larger impact, what good was I? I felt it was my fault because I was the one who was doing the marketing, had gotten a lot of the raffle prizes, and had planned out the evening. I was speaking. I was the emcee. So, I thought I'm a failure. Okay, yes, I was running myself a big ole pity party!

"No, Ryan," Joey calmly said as he put his hand over mine, "If one person in that room heard what they needed to hear tonight and being at our event helped, then we helped bring love and light into their life. Just one person— then everything we did was for a beautiful reason, and we should feel wonderful about the work we were able to do. Ryan, this is God's work. We don't get to choose how many people we help. You have to know we were sent here for this mission. You did wonderfully, and we did wonderfully." I stopped crying, and I've held that uplifting idea with me ever since then. He changed my whole perspective.

In everything we've done since that first event, I now focus on doing what we can to help even one person. If one person's life is better because we came along and were in that life for a moment, maybe we stay in their life forever. Maybe they only came to one event and never come back to another. Maybe they received a hug at one of our **Hearts & Hugs** events. Maybe they didn't even come over and get a hug, but they saw it happening, and that impacted them regardless. Whatever the maybe, we're doing great work, and we're doing God's work.

I've taken that piece of knowledge into everything in life, including my paycheck job, school, and family. If I can impact one person every day at any point in my life, then I'm impacting seven people every week. If the organization can impact someone at every event, then we'll impact hundreds of people from the hundreds of events we put on over the years. If any of our event participants became inspired to help someone else, we've put that great energy out there in the world.

I would say that everyone in that room was affected to some degree that first night, and at some point, they were helped. I'm here to serve, and as long as I'm being of service and serving others, then I'm doing exactly what I'm supposed to do.

29

LGBTQ+ BIBLE STUDY

I love the spiritual energy I find in churches, even when they aren't accepting or affirming of who I am. Four years completely into my sobriety, I was seeking an accepting house of worship, and I started to really look at several churches in my area.

I was having some problems with my partner that stemmed from his family. He was really struggling with them not accepting him because he was gay. I visited one of the mega-churches, and it wasn't bad. I attended the church service by myself and went up at the end of the service to ask, "Would you pray for my boyfriend?" One of the deacons handing out prayer folders that evening had an immediate energy shift that I could feel in my core. I recognized that, while this congregation might be loving and accepting (and they would surely love and accept the money I put in that offering plate), they were not affirming. This was not to be the right place for me.

I came to find out that there are a lot of houses of worship that feel that way. I'm not here to church bash. You go to worship wherever you feel connected to God. I just know that most churches didn't feel like home for me. I love music, especially any type of church music or gospel music. I can sit in the pews, listen to the music, and I'm instantly connected to God. My heart's on fire.

I go to a beautiful Church in Cincinnati called Saint Xavier when no one's in there, and I pray and meditate and bask in the wonderful energy. There's something to be said about places of worship where people have kneeled, bowed, prayed, and worshipped together.

Someone watching me may wonder why I have a smile on my face, but mostly it's because, on my headset, I'm listening to meditations out of India while I'm in the Catholic Church, which I find humorous. If no one else is in there, I turn it on without the headset, and I just pump up the volume. The doors are loud and creaky, so you can hear if someone comes in.

The energy in most empty churches is phenomenal–empowering. It's when you fill the church with people that the space loses that sparkle for me. I will say there are churches out there where there's still a magical feeling to everyday service. I was lucky enough to find one eventually.

The people of Florence Christian Disciples of Christ are a group of amazing, affirming, loving, kind people. They just marched in Cincinnati's Pride Parade. They've supported Lawrenceburg, Indiana's Pride Parade and Festival. They're about love and support for all. No matter who you are, they believe that God made you just the way you are.

Several parishioners started an LGBTQ+ Bible study group. I was invited by some of my friends and was honored to be a part of that. The first hour we did communion together, followed by breaking bread and learning about each other's stories and sharing, and then we spent the next hour diving into some quote or portion from books in the Bible or planned topics for discussion. These discussions were beneficial to me. I still held on to that piece of the Bible that said I was going to Hell, which made it hard for me to connect to the text, but I love the Bible despite it.

I attended for about a year on and off. I got to meet so many different people from different walks of life who identified in different sectors of the LGBTQ+ community.

NICK'S REMARKABLE MESSAGES

Nick and I went on a few dates over several months because he lived quite a distance away, but I didn't feel romantic feelings for him. He would have preferred a relationship with me, but instead, we became friends.

On one of our dates, he and I took a walk and sat on my favorite bench to look at the sky on the shore of my neighborhood lake. Nick shared a Bible verse with me: Genesis 1:1, "God created the heavens and the Earth," he read and then, right above us, exactly when he said that sentence, we watched the longest-lasting shooting star I've ever seen in my life span the whole length of the horizon!

That was a remarkable moment! I could have been singing "I like big butts, and I cannot lie" when it happened, but whenever I've seen a shooting star, it's never been at a time when I was just having some basic conversation. It's always been when I've had a thought about something that's critical either to my life or the world or experiencing a true meant-to-be connection. I received a gift with a message, and I knew Nick was in my life for a reason I had yet to learn.

Initially, Nick was able to remind me of the beauty and love in the Bible. He helped me reconnect beyond my fear of the clobber verses to appreciate and love the Bible again.

A few months later, I took Nick to my LGBTQ+ Bible study group, where he connected with everybody. And then he left my life for a long time.

About a year later, Nick came into town and asked if he could see me because there was something really important, he needed to share. I hoped it wasn't going to be that he was angry that we weren't a couple. I did not know what to expect.

When I saw him, he gave me the biggest hug and gave me a kiss on the cheek in a friendly way. Then, Nick gave me the most beautiful compliment one could ever receive! He explained, "When I first met you, I was in a really dark place. On any given day, I could have just decided to kill myself. I planned it multiple times. I thought about it in-depth, wrote my suicide letters, everything. I was ready to do it, and the connection I made with you literally saved my life, and for that, I'm forever grateful and forever will love you."

I answered, "I love you too, and God loves you."

That would have been enough, but Nick continued, "I got this message from God for you." He told me, "I want you to know what God wants you to know. He said you were supposed to help many more people like me. You helped save my life, and you're here," as Nick demonstrated by putting his hand lower near the ground, "but where you're supposed to be is up here," and he raised his hand as high as he could. "You keep following God and God's guidance, and you will end up where you're supposed to be, up here, helping to impact many more people than you could ever imagine." We both started crying. I had massive tears running down my face.

I didn't really know what to say, so I just said, "Well, thanks for telling me. God does love you!" I was speechless. I'm forever grateful to Nick for being strong and courageous enough to share that message and his story with me.

You never know why someone comes into your life; what reason the universe has for you to meet at that particular time. There may be people now who you wonder about, but, as I learned, at some point, you will have those "whoa," "aha," "now-I-get-it" moments of clarity.

Though you may not know it, as I didn't realize with Nick, sometimes you are the person who will impact someone else's life in a significant way. Giving a seat to the elderly or a pregnant woman, helping someone up when they fall, smiling at someone who looks sad, providing advice in the grocery store check-out line, sharing your cancer story with a stranger, all things matter more than you know. So, just be kind and patient all around and think of all the ripple effects of goodness you will have in the world!

SHEPHERD OF SHEPHERDS

I was about twenty-seven and in the healthiest relationship I'd ever had. Karl and I connected spiritually as well as intellectually. We wanted the same things. We enjoyed going for hikes and long walks. We enjoyed healthy eating and were both sober. And, in addition to our romantic chemistry, we could talk for hours about God and meditation, the universe. I felt comfortable sharing with Karl.

One day, after I shared several of my life philosophies and what I was learning in school, and how I wanted to use that to help people, Karl turned his blue eyes toward me and said thoughtfully, "I don't know. It's like to me you're a shepherd of shepherds." I immediately had a flashback to when I was only four or five years old, sitting in my Aunt Jewel's apartment, maybe a five-minute drive from my home. My Aunt was a devout, devout, Christian and I'd go to her home to visit. She read her Bible every day, sometimes prayed for hours at a time, and watched a lot of evangelical TV. Everything about her home and personhood was Christian-based. Everything was about loving and serving God. I always admired her. She was a very divine and pure soul.

Aunt Jewel told me a story (details are vague since I really was only four or five at the time) with a memorable kicker at the end. She told me, "Some shepherds lead sheep, and that's important, but some shepherds lead shepherds, and that's you. You are a shepherd of shepherds." I felt something move inside me when she shared that message, and here Karl was saying the exact same thing!

Asking my Aunt Jewel about God and everything related to Christianity was my regular habit when visiting. About a year after she told me that shepherd story, she baptized me in her house and asked me if I would take the Lord as my savior. I said yes. All the conversations we had until then suddenly seemed to mesh together and make sense. I was still so young, but I felt important. I had a purpose.

Maya Angelou said something along the lines of how you don't remember what people say to you or what they do, but you always remember how they made you feel. It's true. I was young, but my Aunt, with my baptism ceremony, ignited a special fire in my heart, a beautiful flame of love.

I went to church with Aunt Jewel often. I enjoyed it. I wanted to go. I felt connected to the rituals, her, and God. I didn't always connect to the messages I heard from the pulpit, and to be honest, sometimes I still don't understand the message when I sit in church services! I would (and still do) get a feeling from the service.

I loved that people sang songs to God. It was beautiful to join in all together. All those voices in harmony. Hands clapping together. Toes tapping. It was a spectacle to me! Maybe some people go to a Broadway show or listen to music or watch a movie to get lifted up like that. I didn't feel this level of love with anything else but being in the presence of God.

People put on their best clothes to worship God. I found it uplifting to want to dress and look your best for God but in reality, what happens at churches is that people are often dressing up for the people around them, for their pastor or the Deacon, or their friends and family. They may be dressing to impress, not dressing up for God. I think when I was little, I didn't know that. All I knew was what I felt. I felt such a powerful presence of God and of people loving God that I associated with dressing nicely. I felt God was okay with me, but all these dressed-up people praying were not going to let me join in with them.

What mattered most was that God had (has) this unconditional, everlasting, undying, infinite love for me and for everyone. I felt that then, but I was confused. I felt on fire for God, but then I'd hear the message that I didn't . belong because the way I was would lead me to Hell. So, church ultimately didn't make me feel at home or welcomed until I got older when I found an accepting congregation.

30

Healing Affirmation:
I am constantly attracting healthy relationship dynamics within my friend group and also my family. I have a plethora of healthy relationships in my life!

FALLING FOR A MARRIED MAN

The second time I truly fell in love, I had been using the dating apps Tinder and Bumble (for young professionals). Essentially, it's the same people on both. At this point, my Tinder account (which I used on and off) had about 1,600 matches. One would think that my husband-to-be should be included somewhere in that 1,600.

When you're in the LGBTQ+ community, it's more difficult to find people to date. There are a variety of challenges. I was online because I had exhausted all the friends of friends, and I wasn't into hanging out in bars. As a gay man, when you meet people out and about, I wouldn't want to just walk up to a man and presume that he's straight or gay or bi or pan or whatever. And, specifically in certain more conservative communities (like Cincinnati, where there's a large German Catholic base, or in Tennessee or the South where there are so many evangelicals), it typically means there are a lot of people in the closet. There are young professionals who are out, but they're not out at work per se, so they're half out.

Geographically in my surrounds, there's the Southern Baptist and Southern Evangelical Church to the south and then the Conservative Christian Catholic base to the north. We're right on the Mason-Dixon Line where there's this dichotomy of Southern Baptists and Catholics, and they're different but both conservative. They create a lot of shame within the community.

We don't have a strong LGBTQ+ center in Cincinnati. To start, we don't have a physical location, but more than that, we don't have a cohesive community that would gather if we did have a center. Our communities are disjointed, and thus, it's difficult to meet people or find support groups.

Tinder seems to be the go-to app for people in the LGBTQ+ community. I don't judge anybody for using an app. My mom even was on Tinder for a short time (she's going to get me back for including that here! LOL).

I met Will on Tinder. His picture was cute, he seemed sweet, and we virtually connected on a deep intellectual level. We had lots in common. He was a restaurant manager, and I had been a server since I was able to start earning money. We both worked nights. He understood the stress of the job. By the end of that first night, after chatting with him from basically 11:00 p.m. to 7:00 a.m., I promise you, I'd fallen in love with Will. Before meeting him. Before even talking to him on the phone. I never thought I could fall in love with somebody just by texting with him. Don't get me wrong, I'd been super excited to talk to other guys before this, but it's not like I fell in love with them before I ever touched them, heard their voice, or looked at them in person.

Will and I exchanged phone numbers and started texting, which led to talking on the phone. We seemed to be of one mind. As if to prove it, we both sent each other the same screenshot of deactivating our Tinder accounts at the exact same time! I had sent it to him, and he sent it to me, without either of us knowing the other person had sent it. It was one of those moments where you think *this can't be real*. Well, it *was* real, and it seemed that the universe was facilitating our connection. I knew something was different.

On the night I was finally going to meet Will, our date fell through because I had an unscheduled visit from my daughter. So, Will and I rescheduled for the next night. It was the hardest thing to wait to meet him in person!

Instead of meeting in a public place, Will showed up at my condo because the most convenient time for both of us happened to be later at night. My schedule was back-to-back. I hadn't started my doctorate yet, but I worked a paycheck job (which often leaks into the late evening). Then I had my non-profit volunteer work, which took up a large chunk of my days and weekend time because of programs/events. Any free time I had, I treasured with Harper. I literally only had maybe one day off a week or, mostly, a few hours in a block of time.

When Will showed up at my building (that sounds like a booty call, but it wasn't), we stood in the driveway lit only by the half-crescent sparkling moon, and mostly we hugged. The air was brisk but not yet cold. I felt like I was looking at almost a mirror of myself. Will was as tall as I was. He also had blonde hair and a goatee. He was lean and fit with muscular arms and legs. Will said later that when he looked into my blue eyes before we said a word to each other, he felt like he had known me his entire life, my entire life. I felt the same way.

We talked, leaning against his car in the driveway for an hour. By the time we kissed, I'd confirmed my original instinct; I was in love. Our teeth clinked together like two glasses of champagne toasting, and a tingling explosion, bubbles, went straight to my heart. I felt flush with warmth and had an irrepressible I-can't-stop-smiling kind of glow (which didn't leave me for days after).

I had fallen in love just once before and was grateful to have that feeling again. I was scared that after my last ex (and the guys I dated in between) that I hadn't fallen in love, so maybe I wouldn't be able to fall in love anymore. I thought, maybe you can only fall in love once? Nope. I fell in love twice. I felt very lucky.

I invited Will inside, and we hugged and shared simple kisses that set off fireworks in my body for two and a half more hours! We were bonding and connecting, but it was like we couldn't let go of each other. It was the longest hug I've ever had in my life. Hugs release all those feel-good chemicals like oxytocin. I experienced my first drug and alcohol-free high. We talked about this bizarre euphoria we were experiencing and that was before we ever went to the bedroom.

When Will and I eventually came together, another night, physically, I finally understood the difference between making love and having sex.

All the movies, songs, books, and poetry with the descriptions of what sex was supposed to be, how it was supposed to make you feel, made sense. I could no longer imagine my life without Will. I wanted to be talking to him, holding him, all the time.

Admittedly, after the initial novelty, our relationship was a little rocky from time to time, possibly because he was married. But hang on, don't judge. He was going through a divorce and was separated. I made you think he was having an affair! I guess, technically, before he was divorced, our relationship would qualify as an affair. He was in the divorce process but hadn't even filed yet. The other issue was that my back-to-back schedule made me a moving target, difficult to pin down.

We hit a spot where we started having communication issues. We didn't even talk. He was dealing with a lot of life stuff and working through a divorce and needed some space. He said his life was chaotic, and he needed to get everything in order. I definitely wanted to spend every free second I had with him, but my time availability was more limited and less flexible than was his.

When we did see each other, we went on hikes, drives, worked out, and spent time talking and eating meals. He met my family, but not my daughter. He came to a few of my *Love Must Win* events.

In my mind, it made sense to me that Will would want to spend time with me every second that I was free because he would still have other free time outside of that. Well, it just didn't work out that way. Juggling schedules was very complicated, and this issue seemed to become a bigger and bigger obstacle and ended up pushing him away. I think the idea of "us" scared him. I had a child. I had a home. I had responsibilities. He was so much younger than me. He pulled away from me instead of telling me that he didn't want to use our relationship as an escape from his marriage.

I had tried to help him with his marriage issues, the separation, and how to get back on his feet, but Will didn't want to hear my advice. He had to heal. He needed to figure out how to get back up after being knocked down and out. Will pushed me away and wouldn't let me show him that he wasn't the awful person his soon-to-be ex-husband was making him out to be.

We discussed all of this in-depth both during and after our relationship ended. He had a lot of fear about getting divorced, coming out, and being in another relationship when he wasn't even finished with his marriage, which led to us breaking up after a very intense month. Will said he had only been looking for something casual on Tinder and didn't expect to fall in love. He claimed he didn't even know who he was; Will had gotten married when he was twenty to someone he had met while he was still in high school. He was still only twenty-three when I met him. Will was six years my junior, and that timing, the place we were in our lives, was not syncing.

Lord knows I could not stay away from him for more than a couple of days without feeling physical withdrawal pains. We reconnected and decided to just talk and date, but not be a committed couple. To me, it was all semantics because we were still making love all the time and hanging out together. It was the only way I could be close to him because he was not letting me really get to know all of him.

Part of the reason that it was so hard to let go was that the sex was the best sex of my entire life. E-V-E-R! We would have sex multiple times in one night, and (booty call or not) I was okay with it because I was definitely still in love, and I never thought I would have an intimate connection like this in my whole life.

I have a lot of complexities around sexuality (the whole top and bottom thing) and how I like to be treated, and Will and I just meshed perfectly together. I had really good orgasms—as good as any chemical high I'd ever experienced. Intoxicating.

You know you're in love when you can't imagine your life without that person but also when things that normally irritate you and that you find unacceptable with other people don't bother you with your current lover. I knew I was in love because I don't like when anyone gets sweat on me. With other men, I would say, "Don't get your sweat on me. It's gross!" but with Will, I didn't mind. If I could have bottled his sweat and kept it in my bedside table to smell when he wasn't there, I would have. Is that strange? Is that what love does to you?

I learned and grew. I came to realize that we are all sexual beings (unless you're asexual) and that sex is important in a relationship. Whether you have a low or high sex drive (I'm in the middle), I think we all have a desire to bond with someone physically.

One of my favorite moments with Will was waking up together after a thirty-minute nap to find our lips were still together mid-kiss when we drifted off. It was a pure, innocent, unforgettable, magical moment.

And yet, even with our great chemistry and all the love in the room when we were together, we didn't work out. It was bad timing.

Will went on a cruise with a female buddy after telling me that he wasn't ready for a relationship. When he came back, we met up at a little ice cream shop to talk, and I shared that I had spent some time with an old boyfriend while he was away. I could see him become visibly angry. He stood up to leave and said that I had disrespected our relationship. It was our first actual fight. He walked out. I sat there dumbfounded.

Later he told me that he was afraid he would say something so hurtful that he didn't mean and wouldn't be able to un-say. We agreed that we hadn't defined clear relationship boundaries. I truly didn't intend to do anything to upset him. He was the one who didn't want a relationship, or so I thought. Sometimes what we say and what we think or feel is not the same. Lesson learned; clear communication is essential.

Will moved away shortly after that fight. He moved back to his home-town, about three hours away from Cincinnati. About nine months after he moved away, Will came back into town, and I got to see him. I'd wanted to see him ever since we broke up. I didn't know how I would react to seeing him. Once again, he came to my house, we hugged for an hour in my drive-way, and we kissed. I didn't fall back in euphoric love. That was a sad realization for me. I most likely stopped myself because it hurt so much when he left, and I didn't want to go through that pain again.

Standing in my driveway, feeling the chemistry heating up, I wanted to pull him inside, throw him on the bed and share amazing sex again, but I also didn't want to get attached to him, and I didn't want him to get attached to me. I didn't want us to form a union when I no longer felt that head-over-heels feeling. Maybe it's because I was scared. Maybe it's because I knew true love would have still been there. I felt the novelty and infatuation was over. Perhaps, I rationalized, if the situation was different and timing was better, we could fall back in love, get married, and raise children as many people want to do in life.

I do know that if I fell in love twice, I can fall in love again. If I fell in love once with a particular person, I can re-fall in love with the same person. I can also fall in love with someone else, and I'm okay with that. I allowed myself to dream and fantasize.

Everything happens for a reason. If Will and I were supposed to share our life together, then it would organically come to pass. I needed to sit in the knowledge that it wasn't supposed to happen at that time. One or both of us needed to do some learning or have some experiences before we would be able to blend together. Separation time would be advantageous to making our relationship work in the long run if it were meant to be. I believe and trust God. I trust my feelings. I trust my heart. I trust love. I will leave you with that.

God is love. I am loved. You are loved. We are loved.

31

INTENTION OF BELIEFS

Some of who we are and how we present in the world is based on nature (including our genetic make-up), and the rest can be attributed to nurture (who is around us, how they treat us, and where we live). The words we hear and read and the actions we see go to our nurturing experiences, which leads to how we evaluate and react to every situation. We grow up believing that what we see and hear in our home, schools, and from religious leaders must be the truth, that everyone else must also believe. Therefore, unless we come in conflict because of our genetics or education, or experiences, we function in society from that basic core value system.

When you come to know someone who is not following the same core beliefs you hold dear, then conflict, judgment, and even hostility can rise to the surface. This is what happened in my life. My family, the church, the school system, went against my nature, so I reacted by changing my environment through chemical means. When I was able to step out of my box and meet and experience people with different viewpoints, I was set free to truly follow my nature and become true to my own being. I was then able to change how I nurture others (my daughter, my family, my partners) and become more authentic; I was finally feeling whole and actualized.

I want to share a few brief stories about remarkable people in my life who evolved beyond their indoctrinated thoughts and opened themselves toward becoming more authentic.

COUSIN BILLY

I had a distant cousin named Billy. He was one of my Tennessee grandma's (aka Nanny) favorites, and she would help him from time to time with his bills or drop by to visit him. I only saw Billy in person a couple of times in my lifetime. However, I noticed the way my family would talk about him when he wasn't around.

"Oh, Billy!" they'd wail.

"Pray for Billy!" they'd implore as if something horrible happened to him.

I would ask, "Why are we praying for Billy?"

My bold Aunt Debbie, who also took me to church all the time and seemed to love everyone, blurted out what they were all feeling. She said, "Well, he's probably gay, and it says blatantly in the Bible that if you're gay, you're going to Hell. We better pray for him." And someone would say, "I just hope he is not. I just hope he is not!" When I was really little, this stuck with me. My family was praying that Billy was not gay.

To put this in context, it's not like my extended family was protesting at Pride festivals with posters filled with anti-LGBTQ+ slurs or chanting Bible verses but knowing that they would not accept Cousin Billy if he were gay (and by pure logic, that meant me too), was weird.

On the one hand, they laughed and enjoyed me putting on high heels and a dress from my grandma's dress-up clothes and walking around the kitchen, using balloons to create fake boobs and everything, but then, on the other hand, they would still say those nasty things. So many mixed messages! My brothers and cousins joined me in dressing up in the "costumes" we found in our elder family's closets. It didn't seem like anyone minded that.

God says it's not okay to be gay, but I'm okay to play dress-up with the girls? My family seemed to accept me for who I am. My logic went, *Well, I can't be gay if they accept me for who I am, and they accept dressing up and my femininity and me taking time to fix my hair and whatever. If they don't accept gays, then I can't be gay. Right?* I thought I must just be some other kind of different.

Some people marry someone of the opposite sex to prove that they are not gay. If your religion and the government certify you as heterosexual by nature of your marriage, and you're doing the right things according to the books, then you aren't gay, and you can deny, deny, deny. But we know that the pain of denial and living an inauthentic life comes back to haunt you one way or another.

Later in life, my Aunt Debbie supported me and shared stories about her affection for Billy. While she may have towed the party line when younger, her heart still felt love for her family, and she wanted to make life easier for anyone facing challenges. She is very loving and supportive of me.

THANKS NANNY

My father's mother was diagnosed with Alzheimer's before she died. Right before they diagnosed her dementia, I came out to my family. I traveled from where I lived in Cincinnati down to Tennessee to visit her to make sure she knew about me from my mouth, in my own words, so she could ask me anything she needed to.

She looked me dead in the eyes and said, "Ryan. I love you."

"I love you too, Nanny."

She said, "I love you so much. I know that God created you Just-the-Way-You-Are. And you're perfect just the way you are."

I looked at her and started to cry. She was a sweet but feisty little lady, so she said, "Let one person in this family say one word to you about that, and they'll be hearing from me!" This is the same grandma who, when I was growing up, would say prayers for Billy because homosexuality is a sin.

By the end of my grandma's life, she was able to be supportive and loving, as I would never have thought possible. I don't think I would have received that same level of love and acceptance when I was growing up if I had shared my truth then. Then again, Nanny did visit Billy and help him financially—all the while, she worried about his soul. She followed her heart, but her words echoed the teachings of the church leaders. People evolve. Some people don't change, but God has a beautiful way of working into people's hearts and lives. I have a thought that the closer you get to the end of your life, the clearer certain elemental truths become. Priorities become more crystalized.

Sometimes just knowing someone who's different from you and your neighbor; someone who's gay or black or transgender; disabled, Asian, Jewish, Hispanic, or Islamic; someone who's rich or poor or homeless; or someone with an illness that often makes people uncomfortable (like Down's Syndrome, Tourette's, Autism, Multiple Sclerosis, Parkinson's or Alzheimer's disease) or whatever it may be, changes how you think about them and changes your viewpoint on the whole category of people. It's why we fight so hard to make sure media depicts all kinds of people. We're all humans—the same on the inside—we all bleed red blood and have the capacity for love.

There's a Facebook posting I enjoyed that showed a group of dogs. There's a black one, two shades of brown ones, a beige one, and an almost white one, and they are all Labradors. All the same, but also different. Another meme shows a box of eggs in shades of browns, blues, white, cream, and even pink/purples. They're all eggs when you crack them open, and if fertilized and left to hatch, they would all create chickadees. Humans may all be different on the outside, but we're all humans. Why does that seem so hard to accept? God loves all living creatures.

I've told the story about my Nanny time and time again, and I will continue to tell it because I want to remind people that our family, friends, and selves have the capacity to change. It doesn't mean we should sit around and expect other people to change. It's each individual's journey. It's their heart. It's their lives. But what we can do is hold hope that they change for the better when it's good for them, when it's good for the world and divine timing.

GRANDPA BILL'S LOVE—MY PAPAW

My grandpa passed away in 2015. I wasn't awfully close to him, but he was one of the first people who actually took me on any type of hike or walk at the local creek. I was three or four when he took my brother Brent and me down to the creek, which was only a tenth of a mile down the road from his home. We would go through this tunnel and find fossils, collect rocks, and connect with nature. We would talk about what he knew about trees and plants, what they were called. I still hike that creek, though not in the same place.

As I was going on a hike one day, about three years after he passed, I knew I had to be ready for the Cincinnati gnats and would be walking into an extensive network of spider webs. I hate running into tons of webs, and they, along with gnats, thanks to recent rains, had been pretty abundant. I probably had to swat off anywhere from fifty to seventy-five, or maybe even a hundred, webs just on my regular hike. But on this day, I chose to take my grandfather's walking stick with me. I wouldn't have to swat the webs and bugs away by hand. I started my journey and thought, *the creek today is beautiful because the water's up a little bit, which creates a mystical view through the filtered sunlight.*

Walking stick in hand, I hiked the creek grandpa introduced me to all those years ago and started thinking about my grandfather's past, how he grew up, his rocky journey, and my connection to him. At the end of his life, my grandfather was a deacon in his church. He was married to a woman (his second wife) named Marty, with whom he was crazy in love and treated her really well. They had what seemed to be a healthy relationship.

Grandpa Bill had a bit of a temper, but from what I observed, it was mostly controlled. Listening to my mother's stories about her father from her childhood, all the familial trauma my mother experienced at her father's hands, I understood quite a different story. He was significantly mentally ill. I know people don't say that anymore; they say he had mental health issues. But he needed a lot of mental health care. It wasn't just where he needed to go to the doctor and see a psychologist. It was to where he needed to be hospitalized. It was bad.

The gun story my mom shared in the prelude is a piece of my mother's journey. That's probably her most traumatic memory of being a child, but it has nothing to do with her immediate safety and security being threatened as an adult. Were her parents totally throwing a wrench in the whole trust and love thing? My mom's PTSD can flare up when she gets into situations that trigger something about that memory—a feeling, a smell, something sensory or energetic.

My Papaw tried to kill himself at multiple points throughout his life. I just remember hearing whispers and being concerned about him and not really understanding the concept of suicide, even though people talked about it on TV. Were his threats to kill himself some dramatic line he threw out to get help? Was it just performance, or did he really mean it? I didn't know. Was grandpa's mental illness and the whispers about it why I thought about suicide as a six-year-old?

Most kids I knew would say stuff like that when they fell on the playground or had something going on at home. "I should just kill myself," was thrown around like it was nothing. I don't think I ever acknowledged how disturbed my grandfather's mental state was until I was older and heard more stories about his life and his journey. Generational trauma says that somewhere in my genetic coding must have been the instinct to end one's own life because my first thoughts of suicide came when I was barely past being a toddler. Later in life, as I legitimately was considering killing myself, I probably could have benefited from my grandfather's input and perspective.

Grandpa Bill went from being violently mentally ill, divorcing my grandmother, and arrived, ultimately at a place of being a respected deacon in his church, happily remarried and seemingly healthy. How did he make that transition? Once he was diagnosed with bipolar disorder and put on the proper medication to manage it, his extreme manic phases were greatly reduced. He seemed content. He found hobbies like whittling wood that was connected with what he enjoyed most in life, what he shared with me, nature. I find myself inspired by his story while also feeling sad that he had to wait until he was sixty years old or so to find proper mental health treatment.

I'm grateful to Grandpa Bill for teaching me about nature, but also for teaching me that people change. That someone can change with hard work. He put a lot of hard work into changing when he realized his life was not going well. He created a beautiful life for himself in the end.

I always think about how lucky I am that I was able to have a second chance at life once I got sober and came out and accepted who I am.

As I swiped grandpa's stick like a web warrior along the creek, the sun came blasting out from behind the clouds and caused a breathtaking reflection on the water. If I didn't stop and really look at it, it would be just a creek passing by like any other day. But the way the sun hit the water in that particular moment made the creek shimmer. It seemed like there were sparkles everywhere. Was Grandpa Bill sending me a message to let me know he was still there with me, helping guide me through my journey?

Grandpa Bill brought me on my first creek walk, and my local creek these days is an extension of that very same creek. There was a time I would've been snorting pain pills and rolling blunts to numb myself and escape, and yet, eight years later, I find myself walking beside this familiar creek in the middle of nowhere, seeing life differently. God gave me this opportunity to have a second life, to have a new chance to create something beautiful, and I'm going to make sure I make the most of it. I'm learning my lessons from watching others and listening to my instincts. I'm not going to wait until I'm as old as my Papaw was to become the best me.

MESSAGE FROM BEYOND

I was in my car on my way home from somewhere about a week after Grandpa Bill passed away when I had this intense message come into me, and I suddenly started crying in my car. I had cried for his passing before and assumed these sudden tears were just a piece of the continued grieving process, but I felt I was getting this message from God. Perhaps Grandpa Bill was sending me a message. Maybe it was a combination of both. I pulled over and let it wash over me, trying to understand the meaning.

The inspirational message was that I should be proud of myself for accomplishing what took him sixty years to achieve. The message reminded me that when I was twenty-seven, I was already able to get to a place where I found God again and was mentally healthy for myself and my child. Then it went into how my grandfather had overcome his bipolar disorder through his relationship with God and a healthy lifestyle, meditating, and praying.

Note:

To be clear, I don't advise people to believe that because they found God, they are suddenly mentally healthy. Everyone's journey is different, and some people need to seek therapy on a consistent basis. Some people need medication. Some people need a combination of both. Some people can just be guided spiritually to get through those things, and luckily, I was able to do that with really hard work and determination and, honestly, with God's help.

God is the focal point for my journey. Without God, my day-to-day would be pointless. I'd go on a hike, and then I'd go to work, and I'd come home and eat dinner and go to bed. I got up for this memorable creek walk that day even though I could have gone back to bed. This hike I took was a wonderful experience because reminiscing about my Papaw was beautiful. I miss him a lot, and thinking about when I was a little kid reminds me of how much this type of memory probably means to my child.

My goal is to build up my daughter's self-esteem and confidence. I want her to have a storage bank of good, positive, loving memories of experiences and feelings that will stay with her. I'm going to keep spending time with her and filling up her memory bank.

GOLDEN RULE WITH A CAVEAT

We're all taught as children (or at least most of us) to treat others as we'd want to be treated, right? I think we always want to go to those principles that our parents taught us. I was taught this golden rule mantra growing up.

You actually find some version of The Golden Rule in every world religion. Kindergarten teachers use that as a lesson when children try to take things from another or interrupt each other. I wasn't too well-versed in the universality of that message until I did my undergrad internship at a place called Grailville, an all-organic farming community that held retreats in Ohio.

Grailville had a little gift shop that featured a wall filled with writings about almost every world religion I had ever heard of (Taoism, Christianity, Buddhism, Hinduism, Humanism, Judaism, Atheism, etc.). They also had every world view and philosophy, including indigenous Native American belief systems. Each religion basically paraphrased the Golden Rule in the way they uniquely presented it. In every one of those groups, the same message was shared about doing unto others as you would do unto yourself, treat others how you want to be treated, treat thy neighbor as thyself, and so on. These messages appeared on assorted styles of wall hangings and magnets to take home and post somewhere that would keep you perpetually inspired. Seeing them displayed all together was a great reminder of the many commonalities between religions across the board. I think when you get to the pure root of most religions (or maybe all of them), they're all rooted around love.

The problem with The Golden Rule lies in an assumption; most people want to be treated nicely and with respect. There's a caveat to the idea of treating others how you want to be treated because you must believe that you are **deserving** of being treated well, kindly, respectfully, etc. in order to treat others that way. Those aren't inevitable things. If you don't want those things for yourself and begin treating other people how you want or expect to be treated, what shows up for them?

If you don't want to be treated with love, kindness, acceptance, respect, etc., then you're treating people from a basis of fear. You begin looking at people with judgment, hate, condemnation, or whatever you feel about yourself. If you berate yourself with constant criticism and self-loathing, and if you live in fear of people really knowing/understanding you, it makes sense that this becomes how you're going to treat other people. Thus, you can only treat people as well as you treat yourself.

If the idea of living with intention brings what you intend, then having negative thoughts brings negativity. If I am greedy and want more, then I assume everyone else is the same, so I function in the world from a place of never-enough, and thus, everyone I come in contact with can be seen as potentially taking something from me or keeping me from getting more. How could that generate treating others with generosity, or even kindness and respect?

Current social media gurus, spiritual teachers, and philosophers say that you have to love yourself first. Even RuPaul on *RuPaul's Drag Race* stands up and finishes her evening saying, "If you don't love yourself, how the Hell you gonna love somebody else?" You have to love yourself first.

When I was younger, I questioned my life, wondering how was I ever supposed to be the change I wanted to see in the world when I was living in such a place of crippling fear and anxiety? How was I supposed to be the one to stand up and help make a change when I couldn't even change my reality? I was in perpetual fear of being outed and felt unwanted by my father. Until I dealt with my own self-loathing, I was unable to bring love and goodness into the world around me.

We all battle with things. We all struggle with past traumas and hurts. But if we don't look in the mirror first, nothing's going to change on the outside. The change starts within us; that's why there's a saying, "*Be the Change.*"

It's not necessarily saying that you have to change the world. It's saying change starts with you. You have to start with internal change for your own life, and from there, you can become a change agent for others.

I'd seen that quote many times and thought, *okay. Well, I have to start. I have to be the one to help change things.* And that's great, but if you aren't changing yourself and making yourself blossom, what are you really doing? Because then you're only trying to change the world to be as good as you can be in that moment. You can't change the world for its best when you're only half at your best.

And we're all on a journey, so there's no reason to feel inferior at any point. Nor should you feel superior. That's not what life's about. That's something that society has taught us, right? To place people on stages, on pedestals, on rooftops, or to push them to the floor, lock them up, and hide them away—neither is the goal in life. The goal is to hold our heads high and know that we have worth and value and that we are loved and worthy of that love.

It's important that you treat yourself with love so you can treat others as you want to be treated. If not, then the whole Golden Rule concept needs to be thrown out. That doesn't create a world that I want to live in; that helps perpetuate the world I lived in miserably and dangerously for many years.

PART V

THE WORK

*Bringing the lessons and messages
I've been entrusted with out into the world.*

32

MULTI-FAITH

During Pride month 2019, *Love Must Win* was asked to help coordinate a multi-faith service with local congregations. The organizing committee intentionally chose to call it multi-faith rather than inter-faith because inter-faith suggests that faiths had to all connect and be intertwined instead of multi-faith, which was meant to celebrate all religions (and belief systems) joining together in prayer. Multi-faith allowed for there to be a unifying piece around love regardless of your faith. The motto for the evening was *We Are Stronger Together When United For Love.*

Historically, it was the first time all three regional Prides (Cincinnati, Northern Kentucky, and Lawrenceburg) came together to do one big event. We included content and/or people representing many religions (Christianity, Judaism, Wiccan, Pagan, Humanists, Atheists, different denominations of Christianity, Islam, Buddhism, and Hindus) into the program.

The participating faith leaders each shared a two or three-sentence description of their belief system and philosophy with the audience. Then, together we participated in responsive reading, a litany of call-and-repeat for important sharing. This type of service is common in a lot of houses of worship. I am happy to have sown the seed for future shared events and cooperation as so many people commented on how much they enjoyed the program. The evening was deemed the largest multi-faith event that Cincinnati ever had for a Pride celebration. There were about 130 people in attendance.

At one point, as emcee for the evening, after our final keynote speaker concluded, I felt compelled to share about thirty seconds of my story. I essentially said that I could relate to what the keynote speaker had shared because I'd been on my own challenging journey. People who didn't know me may not know that I'm a recovering addict but that I'd been completely sober for almost six years. I'd survived attempted suicide and overcame self-hatred, and finally gotten to a place where I was/am able to help spread love. Finally, I told the audience that I consciously and deliberately remind myself every day that I love myself and that God loves me just the way I am. That was pretty much all I said. Then I thanked everyone for being there.

Some people approached me afterward to offer a comment or two about how the evening correlated so well with my non-profit, **Love Must Win**. A couple of people thanked me for sharing and told me how much my words and journey meant to them. I was humbled and welled up with tears.

The gay music director of one of the local churches in the community and his partner helped set up the sound for the evening. He came up to me at the end and shared that his brother struggled a lot with drugs, alcohol, and suicide and was a survivor. He thanked me for sharing my authentic experiences and said that having observed my life from the outside, seeing me as a community leader, he had no idea that I had ever faced any struggles.

Hearing the music director's impression of me encouraged me at that moment to always be authentic and share my story when I can. But beyond that is a reminder to be kind to people because you never know what they're going through. It didn't cost anything for him to reach out to me and tell me that story. Whether he shared for himself or maybe for me, or for us both, it was a kind thing. Kindness is free and something we can spread freely.

In the moment at the multi-faith service when I shared my story spontaneously, with authenticity, it was more powerful than something written and prepared earlier that I may have created. Anyone can make a speech and read it, but connecting with people in the moment can have more of an impact. I'm excited that I had that opportunity to do that to be there to spread love and light with people.

Hearing all these people share their gratitude for learning my story was a reminder that words are powerful, and thus, we have to be cognizant of the impact of the words we select and how we share them. The feedback substantiated my belief that words are sometimes exactly what we need to hear; words of affirmation, kindness, love, support, encouragement—big message.

As I drove home, I contemplated that if everyone in the world just shifted our mindset away from always wondering what we can get from people and related to others as real and treated each other in kindness, what an impact that would make! The whole world would instantly shift if we could find it in our hearts and minds to do that regularly.

33

PULSE!

When I was a child, I visited Orlando with my family. Other than that, I had no real connection to the city in Florida. When I heard about the shooting at Pulse Nightclub in June 2016, I couldn't stop crying and sat in shocked stillness. I didn't know anybody at Pulse, nor had I ever been there, but there are some nightclubs and venues that gay people know of by reputation. I was heartbroken for the hundred-plus people who were killed and injured (most of them Hispanic) by an Islamic terrorist declaring holy war against the sin of being gay (which Islamic extremists claim goes against Allah) and the United States' involvement in the Middle East. I found myself weeping randomly for days afterward.

The Pulse shooting was considered the deadliest mass shooting by a single gunman until the Las Vegas shooting a year later. As I write this, it is still the deadliest incident of violence against the LGBTQ+ community in modern

U.S. history. The Pulse tragedy is also considered the deadliest foreign terrorist attack in the United States since the September 11 attacks in 2001.

A year after the shooting, a memorial event commemorating the forty-nine lost lives at Pulse was scheduled to be held in Orlando as part of Orlando United Day: A Day of Love and Kindness. Jeremy, our Vice President at *Love Must Win* (LMW), knew one of the victims of the Pulse shooting. A group of volunteers in my organization were looking to do some work on Pride events, so we decided to go to Pulse to offer our support.

Love Must Win was one of the two non-profits from our state that were selected to participate. We were assigned to work on one of forty-nine community service projects for Orlando. A piece of the healing process is giving back and being of service and not feeling victimized.

Love Must Win has a core project called **Hearts & Hugs**. Essentially, we collect handwritten hearts filled out from all over the United States. Then we go to places where there have been heinous acts of hate, senseless acts of violence, hurricanes, natural disasters, and other types of traumatic or drastic events that happen in the world, and we deliver these hearts to the victims and community at large. We prefer to appear in person and actually give physical hugs and a handwritten heart. There are deep psychological benefits derived from a physical hug, especially if it lasts longer than twenty seconds. We have a way of providing these free hugs that keep the process safe, comforting, and without becoming too intimate or crossing professional lines.

For Pulse, we collected 10,000 handwritten hearts from all over the Midwest and decided to bring six of our team members to Orlando to deliver them personally. This trip was underwritten through our own personal funds. The six of us intended to hand out these thousands of handwritten hearts and offer hugs to anyone who needed or wanted one.

We completed an Orlando service project during the day on June 12, 2017. That evening we went to Lake Eola, where a memorial service was held. News reports said thousands of people attended that memorial; we thought there were hundreds of thousands there! We had recruited on-site about forty to fifty volunteers in addition to our six volunteers from Cincinnati who were just hugging people and handing out these hearts within the community. It was *Love Must Win* in action!

On a personal level, I've had a hard time sharing my own emotional experiences about this trip. I'll start with the first day when we arrived. It was later in the evening when we finally got settled in at our hotel. We went to the Pulse site for the first time. I didn't know what to expect. I guess, in my mind, I expected a huge club since it was known all over.

It wasn't that large a space, but the experience of being there was life-changing and heart-shattering. I wanted to give Jeremy space to process the loss of his friend but also be there if he needed support. I would periodically walk by and give him a quick hug or put my hand on his back or shoulder, just to let him know that I was there if he needed me. No words were necessary. I didn't want to interrupt his contemplations.

The club itself was more of a shrine than anything else. Jeremy and I were separately walking around and reading the messages people had left on the wall of the club as we absorbed the energy. I noticed a petite girl, with a cute bob, somewhere in her late twenties or early thirties, dressed casually in jeans, doing the same thing as we were, on her own. I was overcome with the certainty that she needed a hug. I walked up to her, delivered a big smile, and offered my arms to her. After I explained that I wasn't some stalker guy but was there representing **Love Must Win**, she accepted my invitation.

When Erica pulled back from the hug, she was curious for more details about what inspired us to come from Cincinnati to participate in the Orlando project and Pulse tragedy anniversary. I explained that Jeremy was an Orlando native who had moved away after finishing school. He knew many people who went to Pulse regularly, and what happened was just unspeakable; unthinkable. Jeremy had known someone who died, so we were there to honor the fallen.

Erica shared that she, too, had lost a few friends. I could have been a crazy person just going out hugging people, but she started sharing her story, and I was happy to listen. Trying to define how you feel after something like this is draining. This type of thing is not like a regular sad but perhaps understandable, explainable loss. It's much deeper than that when there's a loss that comes from a hateful action that targets a specific group of people. It's like hate on steroids.

I told Erica about the LMW mission and shared details about our **Hearts & Hugs** project that we would be sharing for the anniversary event.

This private visit to Pulse, I explained, was mostly personal for some members of our organization.

In sharing hugs, you learn that when people don't want to let go, you don't. You just keep hugging as they process their thoughts and emotions. If they speak, you allow it because it's part of what they're going through; whatever they need, as this is meant to be for their healing. It's not about consoling; it's more saying "it's going to be okay" through the hug. Mostly you don't say a word unless it's divinely guided. It's not easy to watch the mourning process. Not that mourning is ever easy, but I'd never felt such a depth of despair before that day. I'd been to funerals for family and friends before, but this was different. This was something that I couldn't wrap my head or my heart around. I just had to sit with it and sit with Erica and listen.

Ultimately, Erica turned out to be one of the most amazing people I've ever met. To this day, I still love her and care about her, and I see such value in the person she is. Her story touches my heart to its core, but it's not my story to tell. What I can share is how her story impacted me. Her story is what made me see that these five solo people who came with me from Cincinnati could make a much bigger impact than they would ever realize. We traveled twelve hours, each with a personal mission to reach at least one person we could touch and help. It was worth the money, time, effort, and love we put into it. Time and time again, people we had hugged and built relationships with shared from their hearts that words couldn't even express what the experience meant to them.

After talking to Erica, I introduced her to Jeremy, and they bonded over their losses and shared grieving. Yet, as transformational as it was to witness, it was also tough to observe their pain, hurt, and survivor guilt.

The next day was the culmination of the forty-nine community service projects that took place around Orlando. While the whole experience was significantly difficult, it was also uplifting. It was incredible to be able to interact with all these different people at this fragile time.

We displayed our Free Hug signs discreetly. If you needed a hug, we were there to give you a hug and be supportive and loving. We also distributed our handwritten hearts.

The positive experience that brought me to meeting Erica gave me the confidence to walk up to strangers who I could sense were hurting and ask if they wanted a hug. If they said no, they would be given a heart and encouraging message to help on their journey of grieving and healing.

I approached a crying young man. He didn't tell me his name. I asked him if he wanted a hug. He grabbed onto me and hugged me. His indescribable pain leaked from his body into mine at all the points we connected, and I could feel everything he was going through. He started heaving and shaking as he released the deep blueness of his energy into me; he let it all go. I'd never experienced someone actually sobbing before. I held him as he confided bits and pieces of his story and the healing journey he had been on. He told me he had plans to be at the club that evening and ultimately didn't go because he couldn't shake off some deep anxiety that made him feel like he didn't want to go out. He lost two friends and knew a few others who were injured; this boy was feeling big-time survivor guilt that it should have been him. He was carrying this huge burden in his heart.

I continued to hug him for more than fifteen minutes while he randomly shared words and thoughts between sobs. Eventually, he got to a place where he admitted, "I don't want to be here anymore. I have to leave this world." I knew what he was feeling, and luckily right then, one of our staff therapists (who also happens to be my mother) walked over and embraced both of us. I slipped out because I was more than a little overwhelmed and left my mom to guide the young man to a safe space. My mom (therapist, volunteer, and LMW board member) was able to get that boy some help. We gave him general resources and got him in touch with some people to help there on the ground in Orlando.

In an odd way, the whole experience felt like I was watching this boy's story play out in a movie. I felt his pain and yet could not fathom that he spent so much time wondering, *why couldn't it have been me instead?* My role wasn't, at that moment, about consoling him or telling him that this is what you have to do to get better. We witnessed the grieving process taking place all around the gutted club, and all my team and I could do was be there to give love. Advice and love aren't interchangeable.

When I walked from the side to the front of the club, I felt a breeze hit my skin. I looked down and saw that my shirt was literally drenched. I'm truly not exaggerating! From my shoulder, down was sopping wet with this boy's tears. Seeing his physical tears on me opened the gates, and I began crying.

I reminded myself that my tears were for him. I sort of scolded myself, *It's okay to be sad for him, but you have to be strong for him so he can have his healing and growth. You're here to show unconditional love and support. You're not here to break down yourself.* It was time for me to step back for a minute.

It's been a few years since that trip, and this story doesn't get any easier to share. I have to continue to share this because it is life-changing, and it's important to my journey of who I've become as a person. It's essential for **Love Must Win** in the work we've done and continue to do, and it's important to Jeremy. It's important to the Pulse patrons who were taken before their time, and it's vital to many other people with whom we share stories (even when they're complex) because it's not about staying in our comfort zone. It's about staying in a place of love and light all the time.

HEARTS & HUGS IN ORLANDO

The next morning, we did our **Hearts & Hugs** project at the tourist information center. For our project, we set up tables and snacks and encouraged people to fill out hearts that were going to be passed out that evening at a concert at Lake Eola. Our volunteers witnessed masses of people getting creative and healing through art. That was one of the most encouraging and rewarding things that happened toward community healing. That alone was powerful.

Later that day, we were about to have lunch, when the mayor's office called. The mayor's assistant said, "Hey, you've been requested to come to the private family service. Nobody else is allowed. It's by invite only. It's limited to family and close friends." Jeremy, my mother, and I participated.

We entered the church with our small, unobtrusive, "Free Hug" signs, as that is why we were invited. We were requested to be there by multiple people in different families who asked the organizers if the Hearts & Hugs people would be there. The families clearly felt they could really use us. They needed and wanted some love and support. We were honored to be invited to this private ceremony. We listened and paid our respects.

At the end of the ceremony, we stood on the side with our signs subtly visible for anyone looking for us, but we weren't broadcasting them. We feel that there needs to be immense love to heal hate, and we were there representing.

People would ask us where we were from and hug us. We told the story over and over again about why we were there, how we felt compelled to help, and that we felt called to be where there are acts of immense hate to fight it with love. The most common reaction was, "That's amazing, and we're grateful."

If there were more love in this world, hopefully, there would be no more need for events like this. That's where people sometimes misconstrue what we do as an organization. We do much for love and acceptance and kindness, but we're primarily trying to help advocate for those on the other side—on the prevention side—for mental health, for addictions, for suicide. To help alleviate those higher hurdles that the LGBTQ+ community faces.

After the family prayer service, we went from the visitors center straight over to Lake Eola to set up our LMW tent. We had recruited about forty on-site volunteers that were to join us. Some of the local hotels came specifically with their employees to volunteer. Hotel management encouraged their employees to help with our project, which had simple instructions: we would distribute thousands of handwritten hearts collected from all over the Midwest, which were supplemented by the ones written in Orlando earlier in the day. In addition, my LMW crew and any willing volunteers would provide hugs.

We set up two lines of official hugger volunteers on either side of the entrance walking path. One of the first ladies who gave me a hug (a sharp woman just under eighty) whispered in my ear that she had a secret. "One of the few things in life that gives and receives equally is giving hugs. Make sure that you're giving something, but you're also receiving something." I took that to heart but wasn't completely sure I necessarily knew what she meant. Later, after reflecting a lot about her "secret," I determined it to mean that sometimes you may be giving love and receiving love, or you may be giving love and receiving pain. Either is okay because we were there to be of service—mind, body, heart, spirit. We were of service for this work.

I stood there for six hours without a break giving hugs. At one point, it was pouring rain, and my Cincinnati team was holding umbrellas over the other volunteers so hugs would continue to be offered to the crowd that did not stop coming! It was hot. It was wet. I would eventually take a little break, come back, and give more hugs. Even when most people at other organizations dismantled their tables and were watching the highly anticipated concert, I was just standing there. I had a disheveled person say, "No one's hugged me in three years because I'm homeless and dirty." Kids came up to me and hugged me without restraint or embarrassment. Whole groups of people team hugged me!

Nancy came into my open arms and told me she was a survivor of Pulse and also 9/11! She said, "I needed to see you. I needed this hug." And then she pointed up to a mural on the wall and said the image painted was her. I have remained connected to Nancy and the amazing work she does to advocate for love and kindness in Florida. She's one of the most inspirational survivors I've ever met from anything I've done. When I think about how she survived two such crazy, huge things, I am impressed by how much inner strength she must have.

I randomly ran into a boy named Biff in a wheelchair three different times over the days we were in Orlando. We both had to acknowledge it was odd by the third time we crossed paths. He said, "You've given me three random hugs at three random events! Where do you live?" When he found out that I live in Cincinnati, he started crying, and he asked me how I knew what was going on in Orlando? Biff was not even out. He was at the only three gay events he'd ever been to, and I was there to hug him each time. Later on, he messaged me, and we connected on social media. We agreed that this was more than a coincidence. I was honored to help this sweet and kind young person come out to his family.

I've been sober since July 2013. I have a child who requires parenting and discipline, which is definitely difficult. I've gone through heartbreaks, and I've been through deaths. But I will tell you this Pulse event was literally the hardest thing I've ever had to do. It was also the most rewarding. I could share thousands of stories from the brief time we were there in Orlando.

The day we were leaving, I asked to make one stop that wasn't on our itinerary on the way to the airport. We stopped at Pulse again. There was a woman sitting in her parked car. She told us, "I'm a musician and singer, and I was supposed to be there at Pulse that night singing, and something happened. I canceled my performance and wasn't there. I haven't been able to come back since because it's been traumatic. I haven't been able to sing again. I see your signs for free hugs, and I could really use a hug today." I gave her a hug. And then one of our bolder volunteers asked her, "Would you sing us something?" She sang the most transformative "Amazing Grace" song I've ever heard in my life. We videotaped it. Maybe someday I'll post it.

When she finished, all choked up, the singer said that it was a healing experience to sing in a place that she never thought she could ever even go to again because she had much guilt around not being there that night. The singer then said she felt something released from her and felt that she would now be able to sing again. The stories like this are endless.

Since then, I've given free hugs everywhere. When you follow the guidance of love, and you follow your true heart, you can never be led astray. Your path will always lead you right to where you are supposed to be. The next time that you're in a place of not feeling connected or not feeling able to be yourself or when you're going down a road you shouldn't go down, connect back with your heart. Connect back to that place where you know what's right from wrong and figure out what feels right to you and allow that to guide you. Love is the guiding force.

This world can be ugly, but I will tell you this world can also be beautiful. I choose to look at the beauty even as I acknowledge the ugly. I recognize that love will conquer the ugly. It's not about the ugly taking control. It's about the acknowledgment that love swallows that up like nothing hateful or ugly ever existed.

Regardless of anything going on in your life, you are worthy of love. You're worthy of love from yourself and from others in the world. You're worthy of healing. You're worthy of anything you put your heart to. I honor you, and I hope that you can connect with your heart and realize how incredible you truly are, inside and out.

34

DR. ALLEN, I PRESUME

I had the idea of going back to school yet again and was guided by God to pursue my curiosity. I started looking into programs on divinity, specifically the Vanderbilt Master of Divinity. I really liked the program, but the school location just didn't make logistical sense. I had to have something closer to home. I couldn't leave Harper.

I started looking at local doctorate programs and happened to stumble across leadership studies coursework at Xavier University. They offered a Doctorate in Education. The program is set up to encompass the non-profit and for-profit sectors as well as the education sector. With me already doing so much non-profit work, I thought this degree and content would be helpful for my organization. I wanted to learn how to be a better leader. That resonated with me a hundred percent. Management was not my forte, but leadership was where I felt I would be most able to make an impact.

Entering the campus for my interview, centered and ready, thanks to my meditation, I saw the Xavier motto, which is, "All for one, one for all." The sign reminded me of why I was there; that we are all connected, and we are all one. I then knew I was at the perfect place. I guess they liked me enough between the written and verbal interview answers because they accepted me to the program.

Since then, I have delved into the coursework, and I've learned much about leadership theory. I've learned how I could help create more ethical organizations and how I can be more ethical in my practices. Mostly it's been a learning and growth process for me. I believe learning and growth are something we should engage in every single day until the day we die.

I think it's important to remember on our life journey to be mindful of with whom we spend our time. Stay away from people where every time you leave their presence, you feel less than worthy. If you feel drained or lacking any energy after spending time with someone, that person might not be good for your well-being.

I'm reading books and journals and writing papers on individuals that are draining. I'm also doing research-based learning. But as far as self-learning and growth, most of it is happening on an interpersonal level with how I view the materials. I mean, honestly, anybody can do that. We can all pick up a book and read and learn and grow from that experience.

I'm formally doing this coursework because it makes sense for my life. But there are a million other ways to get from point A to point B. Never pigeonhole yourself and think, "I just have a high school degree," or "I don't even have my GED," or "I only have an undergrad," or "I'm not as smart as this other person." That's not true one bit. I've met people with a fifth-grade education who are smarter than people who are doctors. Let's just be real about it. Intelligence and emotional intelligence (EQ) aren't dictated by ivy league education, and never ever devalue yourself because you're not as schooled as someone else. If anything, use the information as a catalyst to become more formally or informally educated. They are equally powerful.

35

BESTISM

There was a time when I wanted to go to therapy when I was a teenager. I was living with my dad and mentioned my desire to find a therapist. His dismissive response was that "Therapy is for wimps. You don't need therapy. Those people can't tell you anything that I couldn't tell you about what's going on."

Most teens would have just let it go. However, I knew that in general, I needed to talk, to express myself. I had deep psychological issues stemming from religion and family conflict (my parents were divorced, and there were stepparents and half-siblings in my life) and confusion about sexuality, drugs/alcohol, self-medicating, sex, etc. I tried to find a place where I could pay out of pocket. Sixty dollars was the least expensive place I could find, and at that time, I had bills to pay, and I was trying to get my drugs. Drugs came first, always. So, I wasn't able to go to therapy. How many teens do you know who actively seek out therapy? It strikes me now how self-aware I was to know what I needed to survive.

As a sober adult, I was able to go to a therapist. I went for several sessions and found the overall process helpful. Comparatively, I found therapy similar to the mentoring sessions I've had with a couple of mentors I see on a regular basis. Both of my mentors are gay men and leaders in their non-profits. One's the head pastor or minister of a church, and the other is a retired priest and is now the executive director of a non-profit. They both have a spiritual background, and I feel I get some spiritual guidance from them. Therapy was guidance but not of a spiritual nature.

I first started seeing a therapist because I was having problems with Will, the last guy I'd fallen in love with. I wanted to go for counseling because my romantic relationship was triggering some codependent behaviors. I wanted to make sure that I was taking care of that because when I find something that's not going well, my nature is to fix it. I don't sweep things under the rug. I don't ignore them. I find the issue and face it head-on.

I think about this a lot when I'm parenting Harper. I have days when I go to bed, and I believe I get an A+ for my parenting that day, and other days I go to bed, and I'm an F-. *Is that enough?* Because that's what I got today, and even on my F- day, I would argue it's not really an F. It's probably more like a B- but to me, a B- might as well be an F. This thinking was not really productive. I had to come up with a better way to assess my actions realistically.

I've identified that my real struggle is self-worth. I hold myself to extremely high standards because I expect to deliver what's asked of me, but like most people, the quality of my delivery can vary each day. I can have ten presentations lined up to deliver. Five of them go super great, two of them are good, three of them are just okay, but if I did my best in each presentation on ten different days, then that's the best I could do. I can't allow myself to be upset about the three times I didn't do *great* because I did my best on that day, at that moment.

I do analyze what went wrong. Maybe I was hungry or tired, or I didn't sleep well the night before. Perhaps I was stressed out because I had a big test on my mind. Whatever it may be, our best is different from day to day, and we need to be gentle with ourselves and remind ourselves that if we're trying our best, that's the best we can do. I call this bestism.

Bestism is about being your best in the moment. I'm hard on myself sometimes. I used to be hard on myself *all* the time. As part of my meditative practice, I try to evaluate my day as I'm lying in bed at the end of each day. I look at the things I did well, the things I did poorly over the course of the whole day, where I could do better, and the areas where I fell short. This process has helped me go to sleep at night because I used to stay awake with my mind wandering. I find this objective review gives me closure for the day. I don't dwell.

36

FIVE CONNECTIONS, FIVE LOVE LANGUAGES

I expect certain things of any potential partner, which include the five connections and five love languages. The work I've done to become the best me I can be has taught me that I don't have to seek out other people to assure me that I'm good enough. I don't have to find a man to let me know that I'm handsome or kind or sweet or smart or Godly or whatever. I want to be in a relationship with a partner who values me as I am. When we are able to find love for ourselves, we come to recognize when the connection sparks with someone who is a good fit. When we are engaged in self-destructive behaviors and always seeking affirmation from outside, from others, we can get stuck in harmful and destructive relationships. I've come up with what I believe are the most important things to share in healthy relationships. Each person will give different weight to each point, and the luckiest of us will find partners who match our values.

FIVE RELATIONSHIP CONNECTION POINTS

I always tell people I want five connections in a relationship. (1) spiritual, (2) physical, (3) sexual, (4) emotional, and (5) intellectual. Each of us will weigh the importance of each of these five points differently.

People have challenged my list, claiming that physical and sexual are the same. I believe physical and sexual are not the same. Sex is a part of most adult lives, at least at some point. Sex is a big piece of relationships, and we can't negate that. But sometimes I want to hold a man's hand, and he can kiss me all day, and I can cuddle with him; I may just love him to pieces, but as soon as anything sexual happens, I'm not into it. So, in that case, physically, I'm down, but sexually I'm not or vice versa.

I've had sex with people but then thought, *I really don't want you cuddling with me. I have to go now.* I don't know if it's an energetic thing, chemistry, or affection, but I've experienced both sides of the spectrum, and usually, a healthy relationship has both.

I feel there's a balance between these five connections I've listed. Spiritual is one of the top ones for me. Spirituality is such a huge piece of my life, and I end up talking about spirituality and God quite often. Everything in life is not a mere coincidence; to me, everything happens for a reason, and I'd correlate that back a lot to God.

Other people have prioritized intellectual conversation as more important than anything physical. And yet, I've dated people who didn't want to talk at all; their whole connection was based purely on physical chemistry.

I think all of these connections are super powerful. I deserve those five connections, I deserve to be happy, and I want to find that specific right person to fall in love with. Someone with whom I have a five-level connection.

FIVE LOVE LANGUAGES

The five love languages for fulfilling relationships are (1) words of affirmation, (2) acts of service, (3) physical touch, (4) time, and (5) gifts.

I need all of my love languages in a romantic relationship. You might only need one or two of them. Each of us is unique. Find what works for you and makes you feel satisfied.

My biggest love language, if I had to rate them, is definitely words of affirmation. I think it has to do with my whole life (since childhood) having feelings of not being good enough, not feeling wanted, feeling abandoned, etc. I need to know that being me is okay. In fact, that being me is awesome! That I'm great, just as I am. I'm not egotistical. I'm no better or worse than anybody. As a potential partner, I just need to know that you see me as good and understand that I'm a good-hearted person; that I'm a good, caring, kind person who is pretty both inside and outside.

The five love languages are all really important for me to know on a consistent basis. It's taken a long time to heal those wounds, and I'm still healing. I've done my forgiveness. Just because you forgive yourself, you can't move on if you don't forgive other people. If you forgive the people who hurt you, then you can move on, but you may still have wounds that need to heal. Some people's wounds heal faster than others, but some wounds may stay forever, becoming rough scars. With scars, someone can still pick at it and open the wound again.

A scar is simply a reminder of something that was a hard challenge and how you overcame that and persevered and grew and learned from that situation. I thought about that earlier today when I saw scars on my leg. I was sitting in the sun on a boat, and the light illuminated a big scar from the time I tried to kill myself when I was seventeen. Looking intensely at it, I also, though a bit fainter, could see the little scars. They were tiny scars all along my thigh as well. I just thought, *Wow. Thank God I don't have hundreds more of these or even one more. Thank God I was able to stop, to not continue doing that to myself.* I was able to find other ways to cope and deal. Some coping mechanisms were good, and some were bad, but I've gotten to where I am today. These scars now serve to remind me of my journey and how hard it was at times, and how I persevered and made it through.

I am just thankful that I am alive no matter what challenges I face each day. I have a roof over my head. I have clothes. I have a car. It's the blessings all around. I am able to feed my child. I am able to see my child. I am able to be a part of my child's life. My child is healthy. I have a loving mother and great brothers. We're in each other's lives as much as we can be. I'm healthy. I have a job. I've completed my education. I'm able to help people. I'm able to go to an event and help other people connect with love. Instead of looking at things as stressful moments, overwhelming challenges, I now look at things as these gifts, moments of recognition, that I'm able to do that. How wonderful is that? Thank God I'm alive.

UNCONDITIONAL LOVE

Over the years, my relationships have changed along with my personal and spiritual growth. When I was young, I was lost, angry, resentful, and had a lot of self-worth challenges. Thus, the people in my life with whom I interacted (family, friends, then romantic partners) were subjected to the whims and whirls of my needs and moods. This did not lead to anything good, I have to admit.

As my worldview expanded and awareness of my authentic being came to light, the kinds of people with whom I spent time and engaged became more of the supportive and enlightening type. The one person who rode this roller-coaster with me through it all has been my mother. I feel like my mother has been a part of my soul journey throughout many lifetimes, and she just happens to be my blood mother in this one. I think of her as my soul family.

A soul family is similar to a soul mate. We choose our soul family, or our soul family finds us, but regardless it's not always just our physical family.

I feel that we choose who our parents are before we come into this world. Great spiritual gurus across the globe have said similar. But I have come to know this as my truth—that I chose my parents before I came here.

The newest member of my soul family is Will. Remember Will from the chapter on me dating a married man? My faith in everything happening for a reason has come to fruition again. Will is back in my life, and we are a fully committed couple! I believe he is my soul mate. We have both grown and matured since our last attempt at a romantic relationship.

I have learned how to have healthy communication with my partner. I have been fully sober for years and have embraced fatherhood, dog parenthood, homeownership, and business success. I'm on an educational path that is stimulating and will lead me to help so many other people avoid all the pain I endured and inflicted. I am secure in myself and ready to partner in a healthy, mutually supportive way.

Will is ready for a long-term relationship, and, as of this writing, we are now sharing our families and lives with the goal of eventually getting married and spending the rest of our lives together. Like the famous Pointer Sister song says, "I'm so excited, and I just can't hide it, I'm about to lose control, and I think I like it!" It is possible to have a happy ending, I'm finding. When no one is watching, I dance around my home, shirtless, expressing my joy at being in this moment and place I now find myself. I wish this kind of joy for you, dear reader! When you have love in your life, you want to share love with everyone. The more love that's shared, the faster the Earth will heal, and unity will be the common language.

The foundation for the relationship I have with my mother has always been love. At times, we both created immense trauma for one another, but even during that time, there was love.

My mom always says I'm one of her greatest teachers; I often challenged her but ultimately led her to so much more love and light. I completely understand what she means because that's how I feel about her in return. And, as a father, I feel that my daughter is constantly teaching me.

On my spiritual journey, my mom has always been a guiding light for me. When I first found God again, she was the person who I knew would help connect me back to divinity; someone I could confide in. Someone I could talk to about what I was going through.

My mom has always been in the background of my life, lifting me up and holding me up even when I couldn't see. As if she carried me when I couldn't carry myself. Let's face it, hurt people hurt people, but those hurt people have to get healed in some way, shape, or form. I'm so lucky that I was able to use my spirituality and my focus on love, and my heart-centered approach to help heal myself and the relationship I have with my mother.

The love I have now with my mother is not the love I sought as a child from a place of desperation. It's not a love that I sought during my teenage years that was transactional; do what I want, and I will love you back. It isn't the love I sought as a young adult where I needed to be seen and heard and get attention. Our soul family love transcends all of that.

You know, I struggled writing about a mother's love more than anything else in this book. It was so difficult to say things that might not show her in the most favorable light. I worried about hurting the one person who had lifted me up and carried me through most of my life. My mother didn't want me to share my whole truth for fear that it would hurt me, that people would say horrible things about me once they knew how I was and what I'd done to myself and others. Yet, I had to stay authentic to my story and share the trauma I felt because it is important to show that even the worst of relationships can be mended when there's a foundation of love.

My message and the purpose of sharing the truth is to help lift up those going through a difficult time. Knowing that you can thrive after trauma and get to the other side of complex challenges enables you to keep putting one foot in front of the other until you reach that uplifting place.

My mother faced trauma from her parents, who also faced significant trauma around poverty and abuse. What I went through was mostly self-inflicted but no less traumatic. How we recover is what is important.

It had been two years since I had last seen or spoken to my father when I saw him at a wedding after I had come out publicly. My father gave my partner and me a hug. My dad and his wife were nice to us and accepting of our relationship. I don't think the reason why he doesn't talk to me is that I came out. Our relationship never mended after our physical confrontation and the words I said while high.

PART VI

NEXT GENERATION

When the student becomes the teacher.
What I've learned from those I lead.

37

LETTER TO THE READER FROM HARPER (AGE 10)

*W*hen *my dad told me that he was writing this book, I thought it is probably going to be amazingly awesome.*

While my dad is really connected to God, and that's important to him, I go to church with my mom every other week or so, and when I go, it makes me feel connected with Jesus and God.

Me and my dad like hiking and being outdoors together, where we talk about God and life and just goof around. We go to a climbing gym together to exercise and have fun. We go out afterward to talk about what's going on in our lives. My dad always wants to talk about what's important to me. And I like to know what's going on with him.

I feel safe and know that no matter what happens in my life, my family (mom, dad, grandmothers, etc.) are there to support me. I don't feel like I have to hide anything. I know that I can go to my dad to talk about anything. Sometimes he embarrasses me with how open he is to talking about ANYTHING, but it's all gravy. I know that isn't how my dad felt growing up.

The most important things I've learned from my dad and mom are to care for other people, to share what we have, to be honest and open, to always be respectful to everyone, and love EVERYONE no matter what.

A lot of the stories in this book I had never really understood before. Now that I know how much my family has gone through, I feel like I understand people who are different than me, and I hope that the readers will take some of these lessons and use them in their lives (and treat ALL people with LOVE).

When I have children or fur babies (I probably don't want kids as of right now, just massive amounts of fur babies), I want to teach them what I've learned from Mimi [my grandmother] and my dad…sharing and caring, to be respectful, be kind to your elders and ALL people, and treat people how you want to be treated (and treat yourself with love and little treats).

38

Healing Affirmation:
I am able to be authentic and present in all situations!

IS HELL REAL?

Harper and I go on an annual camping trip. A couple of years ago, we were hiking at Red River Gorge, and out of nowhere, Harper asked me if Hell was a bad word. I answered philosophically, "Well, it depends on what you are talking about. In church, we talk about Hell, or are you talking spiritually about it? Are you having a conversation, or are you telling someone to go to Hell? If you are saying that, it is mean and nasty, and we don't ever say stuff like that to people, ever. It's rude and wrong."

Harper said, "No, I just meant in general. Is the word Hell a cuss word?"

Stuttering along, trying to say the right thing, "I mean no, but you're not allowed to say it in a mean way."

She asked, "I can say it?"

I answered, "We can talk about Hell if you want."

Harper looked relieved and said, "At church, they were talking about it, and I don't know about Hell and how it goes."

I need to be honest with my daughter, so I tried to explain, "I honestly don't believe that there is a Hell. What do you think?"

My young protege inspired me with her answer. "Because God loves everyone, right? And God is loving. So why would God let there be a place like Hell?" So proud of my daughter! I thought to myself, *Damn girl! You are spiritually enlightened!* But really, how does a seven-year-old girl become aware that God would not need to have created "Hell"?

I do listen to a lot of Christian music while Harper's around, but I don't make her go to church with me. She goes to church with her mom and grandparents occasionally.

I said, "We can talk more about that. Tell me why you think God wouldn't create Hell?"

She said, "It doesn't make sense. God loves everyone you know. And everyone can be forgiven, and I just don't understand how my God who loves everyone, God who is *love*, would make people go to Hell because that place sounds really awful." I had struggled with this myself ever since I found God again as an adult, so I knew just what she meant.

I had a hard time with this discussion topic because I wasn't sure that I wanted to completely tell my daughter what I believed. Like many parents with younger children, on the one hand, I want to guide her, but on the other, I want to encourage her to make up her own mind about spirituality and God, theology, and philosophy in general. I wish for her to come from her own heart and not dogma and mandates. I believe that if people made decisions in this world from their heart, everything would immediately change. If we can raise our kids to think that way early on, I think ultimately the world would look very different.

I teach Harper to love God, and I pray with her. I let her sit with me in meditations if she wants to, but she's not too keen on that. Liz and I have talked about God, Jesus, stories from the Bible, and general life lessons as parents. But I never ever have gone to Harper and said Hell's not real, you shouldn't believe in Hell; you shouldn't believe what church tells you. My mama at four/five years old and my seven-year-old child both knew that what they were learning in church didn't align with what was in their hearts. To me, that is the power of the spirit.

Traditional Christians probably do not think or feel as I do. My view is not the "word." Our heart is where we're going to get every answer that is true. It's where we're going to understand the Bible. It's where we're going to be the best parent that we can be. It's where we're going to be the best executive or bricklayer or nurse. My truth is that the heart is where it all lives; everything good stems from the heart. Always.

UMBRELLA

Harper teaches me things every day. She is super feisty and one of the kindest human beings I've ever met. After I had a struggling-more-than-normal kind of day, I suggested we grab takeaway dinner en-route to soccer practice. Being the kind of parent I am, I suggested that we stop for the dessert first!

We were ten minutes from the practice field, dessert in hand, heading over to grab dinner when it started to sprinkle. I offhandedly mentioned how glad I was to have left a big umbrella in the back seat of the car. I was just thinking about how I would be safe and dry underneath this wonderful big umbrella when we passed a homeless guy on the side of the road, holding up a sign. We don't normally see individual homeless people on the roadside in rural northern Kentucky across the river from Cincinnati. His sign read something similar to, "help me if you can" or "I'll take any help I can get." Harper noticed the homeless person and said, "Hey, what can we do? Do we have any food in the car?" Oftentimes we have small homeless bags pre-made and stored in the trunk, or I have leftover snacks and stuff from events.

"We don't really have anything in the trunk, babe," I said. "We might have some sodas, but I feel bad to give him an eighty-five degree soda, and it's not nutritious in any way, shape, or form." In situations like this, we usually direct someone to a nearby church.

She said, "We have to give him our umbrella. It's starting to rain."

I tried to logic this out. "Well, babe, it's about to rain as you just said, and your practice is outdoors. What if it pours down rain? We don't have time to go grab another umbrella. We have to go get dinner and then head straight to the practice."

My young daughter reprimanded me! "Come on, Dad! That's selfish. You need to give him your umbrella now." She unbuckled her seatbelt, wiggled up into the front of the car, and pushed the emergency signal flashers. (Harper knows that's our protocol when we're delivering meals or doing other community support programs, as we're always about safety first and so no one runs into us, hopefully.)

I brought the car to a stop. The man with the sign was standing on the passenger side of the car. Harper jumped out, handed him our umbrella, and said, "We wanted to give you this, so you don't get wet today." And then she jumped back into the back seat of the car.

As soon as she dropped her foot on the road outside of the car, it had gone from misty sprinkling to actual hard rain. The look on this man's face was like he had just won the lottery. It was the most beautiful thing to see and then to watch Harper's face light up. Well, it's my favorite thing (as of this writing) that my daughter has ever done!

I always find it difficult to hold back my tears when I tell anybody this umbrella story. My daughter has this way of lighting up people's lives even when I can't see it or be the love and light I would wish to see in the world. She's able to do that and pull it out of me. I'll never forget that man's face, nor my daughter's.

I held Harper's hand for a minute as I started to tear up, and she had big tears in her eyes too. She's not usually a child who cries. She can fall and bust her knee wide open and have blood dripping down her leg, and she won't even tell me she fell, let alone cry. I mean, it's super rare. I just looked at her and said, "Thank you."

She asked, "Thank you for what?"

"Thank you for giving me a reminder that no matter what is going on in our lives day-to-day, we always have something to give." She gave me a super large grin followed by the stop-you're-embarrassing-me-look-away and shrug.

That $20 umbrella we just gave away was probably worth $200 or more to that homeless man. It's super cliche, and people say it all the time, but it's something I truly believe to my core that in giving, we receive. Saint Francis of Assisi said it a long, long time ago. It was valid then and is relevant now. At times when we don't feel we have anything left to give, we can still give a hug or a handshake or a hello. We can force a smile, which can be powerful to the recipient. We can give our time to help someone who needs a break. We can listen to someone who needs to talk or vent or work something out in their mind. I never want to forget that lesson because my eight-year-old daughter was showing me how to live it! *Hey, dude, you're stingy, and I need to call you on it!*

As it happens, I had a towel for Harper in the trunk that day because I was smart enough to know I don't want her muddy cleats in my car. That towel was fairly clean, but I didn't bring myself an extra clean one because I had an umbrella and planned on being dry! Now I would need this towel for myself.

The coolest part about this whole story is that we went to her soccer practice, and it sprinkled a tiny bit but never actually rained enough to be uncomfortable for the players or those of us in the stand. We were being watched over from above.

When your heart aligns with your intuition, you definitely need to follow whatever message you're getting in the moment. Harper did that, and I was honored to witness and be part of it. If obstacles and objections filter in, check to see if they're fear-based. What if I don't have enough? What if it pours down rain and I get wet, and I don't have a towel? What if, this or that, fears and doubts, worries and concerns? Those don't matter. Those are irrelevant. When you get a negative thought coming from your head, it needs to be acknowledged and then cleared—disintegrated into the universe—because it's not helpful. It's not important, and it's not going to help you on your journey at all.

If you really have a fear that needs to be followed for safety or security, that's a different feeling. I'm not saying fear can never be used as a catalyst for creating good, but check in on your gut instincts when making your decisions before acting.

Some skeptics might presume the man would use the umbrella and toss it away, and my full hour of wages spent on the umbrella would have gone to waste. Harper and I passed the same man about a week later on the side of the road again, not at a stoplight or anything. We just drove by him, and guess what he had in his hand? He was carrying that umbrella. It was cool to see him still making use of our donation a week later. For all I know, he may still have it to this day. For however long, he used it to make his life less miserable and more comfortable; for that brief time, isn't it worth it?

I am so proud and amazed and thankful that the lessons I've taught my daughter are coming back as lessons she's teaching me now. That's priceless. I am honored to be her parent in this lifetime.

Harper has a mom who is giving and caring. Liz is a schoolteacher and volunteers for the Ronald McDonald House. She collects stuff at Christmas time for kids in school who don't have enough. She helps with homeless outreach with Harper and me through school-based events. Whatever else may be going on as individuals in our lives, together as parents, we've taught Harper that giving is important. Spreading kindness is something that isn't just nice of you; it's mandatory for humans to be kind and generous. Harper has embraced this philosophy in all areas of her life, from school lunchtime to playground time to classes, and even to side of the road umbrella distribution!

Alternately, we can inadvertently teach our children the opposite of kindness if we are not conscious and present in the moment to realize our little ones are watching and learning all the time. Not just what we say, but what we do. The next time you are thinking about giving something or doing something kind, and you hesitate, remember Harper and the umbrella because if an eight-year-old can do it, I can do it, and you can do it too.

LETTER TO READER FROM WILL

I was basically raised in the church. I was brought to the church at six weeks old, and my parents, who had undergone church counseling before getting married, had committed to raising the family in the church. Wednesdays and Sundays for my entire youth were church days. My dad was a deacon. And from day one, anything beyond the teachings of the church was simply wrong. It's how we lived.

At two years old, I knew I was different. I couldn't name why—I just felt it. To fit in and try to hide my difference, I escalated my own church involvement. When I started school, my life was busy serving the church as an active volunteer. I played in the church band and attended services; wherever I could hide and repress everything in me with my busy schedule. I wanted my parents to be proud of me.

I found respite from the rigid rules of the church and my family by visiting my grandmother. When I arrived, I would go to the closet and pull out my special bag. Inside was a custom-made costume my grandmother had gifted me. I would slip into my Maria von Trapp apron and sing along with Liesl in the Sound of Music gazebo in Austria, "I am 16 going on 17." We'd watch this movie over and over again. I bounded across the couch, danced around the floor, spinning and spinning in my apron while grandma sat and laughed with me or did chores around the house and left me on my own.

I wore grandma's rings and jewelry around her house. Grandma bought me a pair of purple platform shoes that hid well under my long pants. I could take *on a new persona at grandma's. Someone freer and more like the real me that my church family would never want to see.*

One day I brought my costume home with me and danced around on my bed in my bedroom, with the door closed, singing in my head. I wasn't disturbing anyone. I wasn't revealing myself to the world. My mother knocked and didn't wait for my response; she just entered the room and found me standing frozen on my bed, wearing jewelry with the dress on. My mother was horrified and made me take off the costume and watch her as she threw it away. I secretly went back and retrieved it, put it in a bag, hid it in a shoebox, and kept it. But the feelings of that moment being discovered, how small I felt, how wrong I felt, stayed with me for a long time.

I didn't feel loved at home. I knew who I was but couldn't be open about it if I wanted to live with my family. At sixteen, I took a job at a restaurant to get out of the house and be around non-church people. I needed to earn my own money. I worked with people older who were more experienced in life than I. Soon, like Ryan, I could be "me" if I was drunk or high and at a party where everyone was free and giggly and absent of inhibitions. The relationship with my parents became strained because I was rebelling.

I knew I needed to take a bigger step. I was pulling away from my parents and lying to them about my activities with my restaurant friends but still being home by curfew. I was prepping to separate before I actually came out publicly. I had even taken to posting the fights with my parents on Twitter which, I later found out, my parents were monitoring through fake accounts hosted by other church friends. I drifted away from the church and more toward the party crowd.

At seventeen, I met an active-duty serviceman, much older (twenty-three or twenty-four), not a partier, with straitlaced friends who were in the military. I did not want to be silent any longer. I wanted to know what being with a man would be like. That first night with him, at his apartment, which was forty-five minutes from where I lived, I was so drunk and scared, a virgin, this man took advantage of me. I wanted to be loved. I wanted someone to want me. I had no confidence, no self-esteem at all. I took what I could get. We went on to have a relationship, but that first night was probably pretty typical for young gays. Ryan had a similar "first-time" experience. We share that. Ryan's mom, Cathy, a straight, white woman, had a similar experience with an older, more experienced man. Sexual trauma transcends all classifications.

Even with all that, in the shame of that first night, being with this man seemed like a healthier choice than continuing to go down the drugs and alcohol path. He was showing me a mature gay lifestyle. So, at seventeen, my new "I-don't-care" persona actualizing, I came out to everyone.

My parents immediately scheduled a meeting with the pastor for counseling. This raised a red flag for me. Couldn't my parents even talk to me? They needed to bring in a third party to change me and give me Christian things to do to make me not gay. I felt like I was being bashed, even though no physical violence transpired. Religious trauma as a child became worse as a maturing young man.

In that first meeting, I told the pastor that I didn't know the purpose of the meeting since he wasn't going to be able to pray the gay away and that I wasn't going to change to make anyone else happy. He saw my determination, felt the power of my words, and turned to my parents and said, "There's nothing I can do about it then." He told my parents they needed to figure this out. They looked at each other, lost, and said, "What do we do now?"

I was no longer going to be held back by religion or try to look good for anyone/everyone else. Coming out was not fun. Being gay was not a choice I made. It was a part of me, and my parents obviously did not want to recognize that key essence of who I was.

In the car on the way back from that meeting, I felt at first like I was drowning. Then, recognizing that I had just stood up for myself for the first time, I felt like I was a helium-filled balloon on a string, and I was finally rising up into the air and too far away for my parents to pull me back down to Earth. I was free! By the time the car pulled up in front of our home, I had realized that I had summited the mountain I had been sliding down over and over again all my life. I was going to plant my flag and celebrate and then move on with my life. This was going to happen with or without my parents' support.

Sitting on the floor of my closet, reading his text, this first boyfriend broke up with me and told me that he was going back to his ex. This finished the job to destroy my self-worth. I dated a bit. And then I started hitting the gym to deal with my frustrations and ultimately lost a hundred pounds to "show him" what he was missing. (Another experience Ryan and I shared.) I needed to find self-respect.

When I met someone, who treated me with kindness and showed me great affection, I jumped into an early marriage. He and I were such good friends. I wanted a happy home, family, love, the things many humans share. But, like

Cathy, a marriage created by a need to "escape" is not destined for long-term success. Like Ryan with his daughter's mother, sometimes even a friendship or a child cannot make a relationship work.

I met Ryan as I was going through a divorce. I was alone, just reaching out for comfort, and did not expect to be so powerfully connected to someone. I was in pain. Lost. I was smart enough to know I needed to heal from being broken (life, marriage, family, church) before going into another relationship. Even though we stopped seeing each other, our connection was magical, and I couldn't stop thinking about Ryan.

I worked to get myself together, heal, finish dissolving my broken marriage, find a career, and become a more complete person who loved himself so I could love Ryan (if he was still available).

When Ryan and I reconnected, he kept his cool. I don't blame him. He didn't want to be hurt again. But he was more together too. Ryan had spent our time apart learning how to communicate his needs and thoughts in a healthy way. In his doctoral program, he was involved in coaching others, running several non-profits, still sober, getting closer with his mother, being a great dad; so much to admire. He helped me learn to communicate better because he was able to point out when something didn't work for him.

An example: For Valentine's Day, we were heading to a restaurant and had reservations. We were given a twenty-minute wait time, so Ryan wanted to run over to the supermarket and pick up some stuff he needed. The restaurant kept calling us, probably to say that our table was ready, and Ryan wouldn't answer. I urged Ryan to leave the store. He was lackadaisical and said the restaurant could wait. I pushed. He shut down and became silent. So—two minds here. I have been a restaurant manager; it's Valentine's Day, and I know that people are waiting. I was feeling pressured like it was my restaurant, and I was annoyed that Ryan wasn't moving his butt along because no doubt the restaurant hostess was being questioned by other people waiting as to why they couldn't sit at the empty table. Ryan, however, felt that I was being aggressive, which sent him into a mini-PTSD moment from previous relationships where people were forceful and aggressive to him. I had triggered him. He and I were able to talk it through. I now know that my tone and mood are as important as the words I say, and he knows my stress in a situation like that from feeling empathy for the staff. It could have been a miserable Valentine's Day, but it was a growing experience instead, and we ended up having a great holiday. You can only have this kind of awareness and communication sharing if you are both open to it.

It makes sense that Ryan and I fit together so well. Like Cathy and Ryan, my life started with religion and feeling repressed by the inflexibility of allowing for individuality. We all left religion behind at some point. And, like Cathy and Ryan, I've found a way to reconnect to the spiritual side and the goodness that religion is meant to be about. That is an integral part of my feelings of belonging to this universe, soul, God, community.

Like Cathy and Ryan, I strive to move beyond familial trauma and create a safe and welcoming family, working together to heal what can only benefit all the others around us as well. Becoming someone in Harper's life is not only exciting but extremely intimidating. As I have gotten to know Harper, her spark of life brings so much joy and brightness into my world, and being able to help shape the next generation is something that is the highest honor. I hope to always have a beautiful relationship, full of laughs and tears, and everything in between with her as she grows and becomes an amazingly caring, loving, beautiful human being.

Does this mean that I live in a happy, musical Sound of Music castle in the mountains? No. I live in reality, and that takes work, but the work feels good and when one communicates, shares, and makes decisions from a place holding love and affirmations for self and partners and family, etc., waking up each day is joyous and full of light.

Unlike Ryan and Cathy, I never went to traditional therapy, but I went to energy healers, including Cathy. I dug down to find my trauma points. Meditations, like Ryan, are incorporated into my life. I worked on the traumas of my childhood, the sexual trauma of young adulthood, and coming out at seventeen. I imagined myself as an adult talking to younger me and forgiving and loving that younger person. So now, in a relationship with Ryan, I have done the work, he's done the work, we can now walk forward together.

I reached out to my parents with a ten-page handwritten letter expressing all of my thoughts and ending with my hopes for how we could be in each other's lives. I had in my mind a timeline, expectations, if you will, of when I wanted them to come around and address the many things that I touched on in my letter. One thing that I learned through the process of healing and setting healthy boundaries is also that, in that same regard, you can't set expectations for others in their healing and growth. My family has started to open up and has begun to invest more time, real-time, that I have craved for so many years. The growth has started small, but when you plant the first seed and water it, you have to allow it to grow—a very simple analogy for a very complex situation. They have always loved me, and now I'm truly starting to feel their love as they show up for me in my life how I always needed them to do. In return, I'm blessed to be able to show up for them more too.

Love wins! Love of self, love of a partner, love of family (however that looks) all lead to love of nature, community, God/spirit, and that just helps to heal the universe. When love of authentic self overflows into the outside world, all benefit.

EPILOGUE—TRAUMA IMPACT ON RELATIONSHIPS

W ill and I recently bought a home together. Our paths to get to this place may have taken different routes, but here we are, merged, going forward. Overcoming the various challenges, traumas, and bumps in the road along the way has made us who we are, and those experiences give us the strength to deal with anything that comes up in the future. They gave us the wisdom to navigate our relationship back to smooth sailing whenever we hit roiling waters.

Will and I growing up, both felt traumatized by the church and the verses in the Bible that depict being gay as wrong and religious leaders who promised us we would go to Hell. My mother felt the same thing about church in general; that it was preaching hate instead of love. At seven years old, my daughter questioned whether Hell was a construct that God would really have created.

Will and I both faced challenges with family and questioned ourselves about what would happen if we shared our truth with them. In my case, my mother sort of knew already and just accepted it. My elder relatives only appreciated me as they reached their more senior years. In Will's case, he had to share his thoughts in a letter that essentially told his parents that if they couldn't accept him as he is without continuing to hurt him, they wouldn't be welcome in his life any longer.

Liz, my child's mother, brandished my status as a member of the LGBTQ+ community as a weapon to threaten my career, peace of mind, and relationships with family. Whenever she let her family traumas come to the surface, when she didn't get her way in decision-making discussions/arguments, she threatened. She believed that you win the fight by being nastier than your opponent, that you bludgeon them with words and threats.

The willingness to move beyond the things we absorbed as children, the threats and punishments we endured marks Will and me as healthier individuals. We learn to disagree, compromise, and negotiate instead of lashing out and recoiling into hurtful or self-harm behaviors when we don't automatically agree.

It is our hope that, just as Harper said, you take the lessons in this book that resonate with you and let them permeate into your life and your heart and inevitably ripple out to others around you.

If you find yourself in a situation questioning your next step, first, check in with your body (and surroundings) and make sure you're safe. Then check in with your heart and make sure your emotional body and feelings are safe. Take a few deep breaths. Focus on one task that you can accomplish at a time in that moment. Then ultimately, ask for help when you need it!

Find help in your community. YOU ARE NOT ALONE! Recognize that there are people, professionals, groups, and organizations out there to help! Find affirming churches/spiritual centers in your area or other faith-based organizations, non-profit organizations, support groups, meetup groups, peer support, mentor programs, or seek help via online national resources.

Consider that everyone has their own trauma and has faced their own challenges, and that's what they're bringing to the relationship and any discussions. If everyone brought this recognition to every interaction, think of how kind people might begin to be to each other. Love Wins. Kindness Wins. Peace Wins.

LOVE MUST WIN

I encourage you to find a way to support people in your community around causes that mean something to you. *Love must win* is a philosophy of life. I dream of a world where all global citizens embody *love must win* as their personal mantra and the end goal whenever conflict arises, where people support others unlike themselves simply because they're human. In this day and age, unity is imperative before we divide so much that we won't be able to coexist.

I found a way to help and connect in my community through the creation of ***Love Must Win***. I'd like to tell you a bit about what we do and what it means to me and my midwestern region. I hope you find inspiration to make your mission come to fruition.

During the first semester of my doctorate studies, one of our assignments (it wasn't graded) was to come into class with an organization name and an object to use as a metaphor to describe the organization. I chose ***Love Must Win*** and a rainbow, not for our LGBTQ+ affiliations but more for what we do as an organization. "***Love Must Win*** is a rainbow maker."

Love Must Win takes people's darkness, their clouds, the rain, the storms, and we unite it with light, with love, with sunshine. And we help create rainbows from that. The rainbow can't be made without the darkness that people bring into the moment from the trauma they have endured through their life. The depression, the anxiety, the suicide attempts, the drugs, the

alcohol, the promiscuity, the sex, the mental health issues, the eating disorders, the self-mutilation, the whatever else—fill in the blank. Guilt, shame,
suffering. They have to have that coming into the experience, which is sad
because that's why we're trying to help create a world that doesn't have any
of those traumas and any of that negativity. But in this world, the way it is
right now, we all have darkness, and what we provide at *Love Must Win* is the
light. We provide the sunshine, the healing, the opportunity for education, a
way to get involved and be on the side of prevention.

If you were walking down the street and you had never seen a rainbow
before, and you saw one for the first time, that could be life-changing, to
some degree. That's how I think of *Love Must Win*—as a rainbow maker. We
can't create the rainbow for you and give it to you. It's something that you
have to do. Something that the participant has to do. You have to come to our
events. You have to come to our meetings. You have to listen to our messages.
You have to accept the light. Because that's the only way that a rainbow is
made; when darkness collides with the light, it creates a rainbow.

I know that we've impacted many people in the short time that the *Love
Must Win* organization has been here on this Earth. I've heard countless stories, and I am grateful for every single one because it makes me feel that the
light side is winning this battle.

I think there's a large battle on this Earth between light and dark. Dark
thinks it's going to win, but that's funny because the light will always win ten
times, a hundred times, a thousand times, a million times. It wins regardless
if it is just by a milli-percent; it wins.

But does it mean that the darkness isn't there? It doesn't mean that the
darkness doesn't try us, doesn't tempt us, doesn't lead us astray. When I was
growing up, my mom would jokingly say (we were a big geeky family where
Star Wars-related comments were an everyday reference point for us), "Ryan,
choose the light side. You have a battle of light and dark in you. Choose the
light side," and then we'd make Luke Skywalker fighting sounds.

My family would say, "Don't turn into Darth Vader!" For a time in my
life, I definitely turned into Darth Vader and a half. I was a lie-cheat-or-steal
addict. I'm not ashamed of it anymore. I've learned to use my story as a
catalyst to help other people, but it was a time of my life when I just wasn't
myself. I was hiding who I was because I didn't want anybody to know I was

gay (or bisexual or pansexual or whatever I am). I identify as pansexual[7], by the way, but, growing up, I didn't know what that was. I never even heard the term pansexual. I battled that darkness for years, and when God came into my life, it was the light I needed. Then from there, many other things and people and situations came into my life to turn my life 180 degrees from where it was. And it wouldn't have happened without people who cared. Without God.

The soul of *Love Must Win* is here to be that light. Our staff and volunteers choose to be those people who care for whatever you've got going on. Regardless of what it is, if it's something you're struggling with, we want to be there to help you through it. Our organization started right on the cusp of marriage equality. We started in the LGBTQ+ realm, and then we expanded from there to make sure we were hyper-inclusive of everyone.

Look for an organization that speaks to your identity in your community.

To make sure that kids have a voice and a special, safe place to go, we developed an LGBTQ+ program under the auspices of our *Love Must Win* organization called Ohio River Valley Pride (ORVP). ORVP works within the rural communities in our Cincinnati area to make sure that LGBTQ+ individuals have gay, straight, transgender alliances. Some people label them as gender, sexuality, and transgender alliances (GSTA).

Love Must Win holds a Pride parade and festival in rural Lawrenceburg, Indiana (about 30 minutes west of Cincinnati, Ohio). About 1,500 people have been attending. Considering how small the city is, that's a triumph and a win in our minds. If we were able to help even one young person not commit suicide, then we accomplished our mission.

We were all hyper-stressed about our first event partially because we went over budget because the KKK threatened on social media to show up and disrupt. We had to increase our security and pay extra fees for services to ensure everyone's safety. Thankfully, the KKK didn't show up.

To be honest, just knowing that an organization like that could come created a dark cloud for a lot of us that loomed over the event for the organizing committee. Hopefully, other people didn't see it. All we wanted was to hold

---

[7] Pansexual: Not limited in sexual choice with regard to biological sex, gender, or gender identity.

this event so that the youth in the community felt visible, knew they weren't alone, and knew we were there for them and that they mattered.

When we got home that night, I received a message from someone on our Facebook page, a young kid, who said, "Thank you for today ... it's the only time my whole life I was ever able to be myself." I cry every time I talk about that. I can't imagine what that child has had to go through. But maybe I can! And isn't that the point? To get people together who *do* understand.

I correlated his challenges with my story because I wonder what would have happened, who would I be, what would I have gone through differently, if I would have known where to find that support growing up? I had my nuclear family being supportive, but my extended family wasn't.

How many other kids were impacted by that day? How many people were helped? How many kids' lives might have been saved? Reading that Facebook message just reminded me that every bit of stress, every single dime spent for that event, was worth it. We gave this kid a safe place to go.

Love Must Win does school, business, corporate, and non-profit presentations around many topics, ranging from suicide prevention to awareness and education to LGBTQ+ literacy to cultural competency.

We recently held an event for the service industry in Cincinnati. It was particularly on LGBTQ+ education, but we had a member who is a professor at a local university come to share some trans education with the group. She's been out and trans for a few years and is inspiring to so many.

In addition to community events and education, we provide life coaching and mentorship. These programs are mostly available online via our social media.

We offer an annual Martin Luther King Jr. event called A Day of Giving Back. The event is a one-stop-shop for giving back to the community where we pull in multiple community organizations, and volunteers and guests can come to one central place and give back in multiple ways. Participants can make bags for the homeless, donate clothing for a clothing drive, and create hearts and write handwritten messages for sexual assault victims for our *Heart & Hugs* project.

We do a Safe Haven event every month at the Children's Home of Northern Kentucky, which overlooks the city of Cincinnati. It is such a beautiful space. They are one of our biggest allies in the community. We're honored to partner with them on a lot of our endeavors.

We helped spearhead a new non-profit entity called Building Bridges. It's a community collaborative with hopes of opening a community center for the LGBTQ+ community. It's meant to be an all-inclusive space.

Our mission is to be an umbrella of Love. We are doing a lot of work in the advocacy realm but also providing education and working on the prevention piece—love and acceptance on one side, prevention and education on the other. Advocacy and healing are always included as we need to work on both ends of the spectrum to prevent but also help heal.

Our hope is that we create a better world by helping people become healthier versions of themselves. We hope that we help create healthier people who don't have to have as much trauma as they would have had if they weren't healthy. Ultimately, the goal is to achieve lower suicide rates, lower drug and alcohol addiction rates, lower sexual assault and domestic abuse rates, anything bad across the board. And this is trackable and quantifiable to show the media and community the value of what is contributed and what is still needed ahead.

We're volunteer-based. I don't think some people understand how much work, time, and effort the whole team puts in. Our board members and volunteers include therapists, a medical doctor, health professionals, a human relations specialist, religious leaders, and community members from all kinds of professions and backgrounds.

I can't say enough how ***Love Must Win*** truly changed my life on so many levels. I think the name speaks for itself.

ACKNOWLEDGMENTS

My beautiful mother: Cathy Goulet

My spectacular child: Harper

My infinitely adorable lover: William Robert Dawson

My brilliant manuscript strategist: Fern Pessin

My amazing publishing strategist: Jenn T. Grace

My earth angel and editor mastermind: Stacy Flanary

My copyeditor turned lifelong friend: Gina Sartirana

My dear friend who pushed me to get started: Brett Stover

My supporters: those who provided comfort and help—mentally, financially, and spiritually!

Suicide Hotlines:
National Suicide Prevention Hotline
Toll-free 1-800-273-TALK (8255)

Trans Lifeline
Translifeline.org
Toll-free 877-565-8860

Hope Line
Hopeline.org
Toll-free 800-442-HOPE (4673)

Trevor Lifeline
Thetrevorproject.org
Toll-free 1-866-488-7386

Resources:
Love Must Win, Inc:
Lovemustwin.org/resources

Recovery/Addiction Resources:
National Help Line for Substance Abuse
800-262-2463

Addiction Recovery
Recovery.org
Toll-free 888-554-0054

Substance Abuse and Mental Health Services Administration (SAMHSA)
SAMHSA.gov
800-662-HELP (4357)

LGBTQ+ Resources:
It Gets Better
Itgetsbetter.org

Born This Way Foundation
Bornthisway.foundation

STOMP Out Bullying
Stompoutbullying.org

Kind Campaign
Kindcampaign.com

Love is Louder
Toll-free 1-866-488-7386
Or text START to 741-741

Domestic/Emotional/Psychological Abuse Resources:
Domestic Violence
National Domestic Violence Hotline
800-799-SAFE (7233)

Domestic Violence Hotline
800-829-1122

SafeQuest Crisis Line
866-4UR-SAFE (487-7233)

STAND Against Domestic Violence Crisis Hotline
888-215-5555

National Association of Anorexia Nervosa & Associated Disorders (ANAD)
847-831-3438 (Long Distance)

National Mental Health Association
800-969-6642

Kentucky Abuse Hotline
877-KYSAFE1 (597-2331)

National Child Abuse Hotline
800-25-ABUSE (22873)

Child Abuse Hotline
800-342-3720

ChildHelp USA National Child Abuse Hotline
800-2-A-CHILD (800-422-4453)

A Voice for the Innocent
Avoicefortheinnocent.org

National Teen Dating Helpline
Loveisrespect.org
866-331-9474

National Sexual Assault Hotline
Rainn.org
800-656-4673

Additional Resources:
National AIDS Hotline
800-342-AIDS (2437)

Shoplifters Anonymous
800-848-9595

National Safe Haven Alliance Crisis Hotline for Surrendering Infants
888-510-BABY (2229)

ABOUT THE AUTHOR

From the time I was very young, four years old or so, I knew I was different. I was different than my brother and my male friends. I tended to feel things so deeply. At the age of six was the first time I had thought about ending my life. Within a few years, I realized that I fell within the LGBTQ+ community.

By my teenage years, I was engulfed in self-destructive behaviors: self-mutilation, body dysmorphia, drug and alcohol use, and an ever-growing sense of self-loathing. Nevertheless, I survived suicide multiple times. As I entered college, I was in full addiction and spiraling out of control until my drug dealer and I talked about God one night. She simply was sharing her story with me about her connection with God. After our conversation, I went to the bathroom and fell to my knees, asking God to save my life. I knew if I continued on the same path, I would surely end up dead. From that moment, everything shifted and changed—some things little by little and others astronomically.

Eventually, I was able to get off hard drugs and become sober at the age of twenty-three. I was able to be the type of father to my daughter that my father wasn't to me. I was able to finish my undergraduate degrees, eventually a master's degree. Now I'm completing the dissertation process in my doctorate around leadership studies and spirituality at the age of thirty-two.

I helped form a non-profit organization around love and acceptance. When we founded the organization, we knew we needed to do something for those kids, teenagers, and adults, like me, who had felt a void of love and acceptance for themselves throughout their life. Through this work, I've had countless souls touch my heart and impact my story.

Within each story we share with others, we help break down walls and barriers that so often divide us. Storytelling creates hope! My dream is that by sharing my story, I will inspire others to share their stories authentically, with passion, and ultimately with love.

Ryan Joseph Allen's contact info:

Ryan.allen@lovemustwin.org

859.835.2764

Ryanjosephallen.org

Mydrugdealerbroughtmetogod.org

Social media (links on the website):
Facebook:

https://m.facebook.com/RyanJosephAllen

Instagram:

https://www.instagram.com/ryanjosephallen

(@Ryanjosephallen)

LinkedIn:

https://www.linkedin.com/company/my-drug-dealer-brought-me-to-god

(http://linkedin.com/in/ryan-joseph-allen)

YouTube:

https://youtube.com/channel/UCLGUzopA8wXzlQggBgeBKuQ

TikTok:

www.tiktok.com/@ryanjosephallen

(@ryanjosephallen)

Twitter:

https://twitter.com/rallen1507?lang=en

(@rallen1507)

HIRE RYAN TO SPEAK

Ryan Joseph Allen is an author, transformational and spiritual coach, and speaker sharing his life experiences, vast non-profit expertise, and ultimately leading leaders.

Ryan shares his story to inspire others to share their stories because he believes that when we show up hyper-authentically, we help change those around us simply by being ourselves.

Ryan has navigated the non-profit sector by co-founding, founding, and acting as the Executive Director for various non-profit organizations. His goal is to LEAD the LEADERS and show others how to impact the community and world through kindness, acceptance, and love!

Ryan wraps up his dissertation for his doctorate in education (Ed.D) in spring 2022, bridging the gap between leadership and spirituality. His focus is on post-traumatic growth after lived or perceived religious trauma within the LGBTQ+ community.

ABOUT LOVE MUST WIN

Where there is darkness, Love Must Win will be there to provide light. When there are acts of violence, Love Must Win will be there to provide kindness, love, and hope. We are combating hate, one hug and one heart at a time.

Love Must Win, Inc is a 501(c)3 non-profit organization based in the Cincinnati, Ohio area. Some of our programming includes:

Love Must Win Community Program: Safe Haven events, Hearts & Hugs project, Gempath-HIV peer support and community engagement (Gempath.org), school programs and workshops, and community building. Visit Love Must Win, Inc's website for more info: Lovemustwin.org.

Arts Must Win: Arts-based programming with an emphasis on healing through art, youth artistic development, and collaboration between Love Must Win and other existing arts-based community programs.

Ohio River Valley Pride: This program deals specifically with our LGBTQ+ community and LGBTQ+ youth programming. There are programming opportunities in Ohio, Kentucky, and Indiana (current program locations include: Corbin, Kentucky; Lawrenceburg, Indiana; and Defiance, Ohio). This program focuses on rural communities creating more inclusive and safe spaces for all. We also host Lawrenceburg's Pride parade and festival!

GLAST (Gays and Lesbians Achieving Sobriety Together): GLAST has multiple peer support groups in the region, sober events, community assistance programming, and community-building programs. Please visit the GLAST website for more information: GLAST.org

Safe Haven: This program works with university students to help create chapters of Love Must Win on college campuses called Safe Havens. The student-run groups reach out to various minority groups on campus to unify and unite underserved or marginalized populations of students and community members.

S.A.F.E. (Spiritual Acceptance For Everyone): This program unifies various spiritual and faith backgrounds by initiating and facilitating conversations, peer support groups, workshops, and other spiritually based programs. We work alongside churches, synagogues, and other faith-based organizations.

In the end, **Love Must Win**!

MY DRUG DEALER
BROUGHT ME TO
GOD

WORKBOOK

RYAN JOSEPH ALLEN

Download the printable workbook
version via: Ryanjosephallen.com/
workbook or by scanning the
QR CODE

HEALING REFLECTIONS, EXERCISES, AND AFFIRMATIONS FOR SELF-GROWTH AND AWARENESS

My journey from awareness to recovery to wellness was a bit like how I imagine the early American gold rush settlers made their way across the plains and mountains of the Midwest back in the day. To reach the gold was not a smooth ride. There were mountains to climb up and then avoid sliding down without destroying your wagon or depleting your horses; water to cross in the form of rivers, lakes, and streams; straight plains to cross with danger from wild animals, poisonous plants, droughts, and other hungry gold rushers. The prospect of getting the gold and finding a place to call home was attractive enough to keep people making the trek.

Trying to eliminate all my addictions went up with successes and down with backslides. There were times I felt I was drowning. There were times people tried to sabotage me for their own poisonous needs. There were many triumphs and regrets. There were times I felt alone and lost and wished I had some guidance. I chose not to reach out for help when I should have, and when I did ask for help, my request was rejected because I was told therapy appeared unmanly.

Ultimately, I pieced together my own path and found the strength within me through my relationship with a higher power. Had I been given the resources I now use, and if I was guided by someone who knew what I was going through, I would have avoided a lot of turmoil and pain for myself and my family.

My mission is to help people find the support they need to be their best selves. I start with sharing my own story. Here in this workbook section, I offer some tools that I find helpful to keep me moving forward in a positive direction. Addiction is a process, and we fight for stability and clarity every time the road gets bumpier than we'd like.

This workbook can be used to experience my memoir as a hybrid between a story and a self-help book. It can be utilized simply as a journal for reflection to help create learning and growth on your journey or path. Additionally, it can be used within a family or friend group or even more formally in peer support groups or other group therapies.

These exercises and reflections aid in personal learning and growth and can help you to understand why and who you truly are. When we know this, it's often easier to share our stories with others. My hope is that you share your story, which helps, in turn, make the world a closer and more connected place by displaying different perceptions or perspectives and ultimately allowing us to be a more peaceful and harmonious world.

Feel free to reread the sections that correspond with the reflection or exercise, or simply do the exercises and reflections in order straight through the workbook. Skip around, go in order, start from the back and go forward; whatever feels good for you. There's no right or wrong way to experience self-learning and self-growth.

Share with your friends, family members, and support systems and ask them the reflection questions or have them do the exercises with you. As we grow and expand, we create movement in our spaces, not only for ourselves but also for those around us!

If something challenges you or pushes a button, reach out. There are resources in your community or the next town over or on the internet with those of us who have gone through our own journeys and want to be there to help you! Truly! If the first person you reach out to isn't your cup of tea, search again. You'll find the right fit just when you're meant to. The right fit could be the stranger you meet on an airplane who instinctively "gets" you, or it could be a therapist; it could be a religious leader or a yoga teacher; it might be a classmate, a neighbor, or your local barista.

May you find the answers that lighten your load and lift you up.

May you find the people who will make your journey lighter/easier.

REFLECTIONS
& EXERCISES

REFLECTIONS

Chapter 4   Six Years Old—Chains
- *Are there things from your childhood that you enjoyed doing that others around you didn't enjoy?*
- *Were there activities or things you enjoyed that made you feel different, out of place, or not "normal"?*
- *Did you seem to fit in or always stand out or somewhere in the middle?*

Chapter 5   Be Careful What You Say
- *What are things you tell yourself on a daily basis that are part of your self-talk?*
- *Are they deliberate? Are they positive, negative, or neutral?*
- *How could you augment them to serve you and your life better?*
- *How do the same patterns when you were a child show up today in your self-talk or mindset about yourself? Paralleled, completely different, or somewhere in the middle?*

Chapter 6   13 Years Old—A Cut for Help
- *Are there current triggers that can be traced back to childhood trauma for you? What are those triggers?*
- *Have you ever had to hide who you were on a consistent basis or hide something about your life from a certain group of people? What toll did that take on you?*

- *Have you done the work of tracing that trauma back as far as you can into your young life?*
- *What growth have you made to heal the past trauma?*

Chapter 7   The Birds and Bees

- *Is there anyone in your life who would benefit from knowing that you are open to listening and helping without judgment about whatever challenges they have?*
- *Have you ever presumed you knew the whole story about a situation, person, or group of people and then later found out you were a little bit (or a lot) wrong?*
- *Did you make amends?*
- *Did you educate and teach yourself how to do better in the future?*
- *Did you self-regulate so, in the future, you can notice those thoughts and patterns emerging and potentially steer them in a different direction?*

Chapter 8   13 Going on Addict

- *Are some of your childhood or young behaviors still being mirrored in your current day-to-day life?*
- *What are patterns that were created throughout childhood that still take a hold of you?*
- *What addictions did you form when you were younger that you still haven't shaken off, grown out of, worked hard to release, or obliterated?*
- *Are these addictions based on showcased behavior from friends and family, from TV or media, or simply original situations that turned addictive as a coping mechanism or self-medicating?*

Chapter 9   Bad Influence

- *Have you ever had friends (or even family members) in your life who steered you in the wrong direction when you knew it was wrong, but you love them so much you veered off your path to join them on their path?*
- *Or maybe you've been the person leading people astray?*

Chapter 10   Free to Be Me

- *What do you do to escape from challenges and overwhelming situations?*
- *Did you use these same coping mechanisms while you were growing up? Or did you develop them along the way?*
- *Are there things that you noticed your parents or family members did growing up that now you do?*
  - *Belief systems they held that you now hold?*
  - *Patterns, behaviors, prejudices, beliefs?*

The Letter

- *Does journaling or writing down your thoughts sometimes help shift your current energy?*
- *What kind of artistic expression did you use when you were younger?*
- *What materials or medium could be brought back into your life as an adult to provide comfort, support, and growth? Perhaps sharing words, art, music, dance, or other forms of self-expression?*

Coming Out for The First Time

- *Have you ever told someone something and instantly felt the weight of the world lift off your shoulders?*
- *Or quite the opposite: Have you shared something and then felt the doom and gloom of oppression and obligation?*
- *Has someone ever shared something with you that was hard to hear and it was challenging to provide support to them?*

Embracing the Fiend

- *Have you ever done something knowing that it was harmful to yourself or someone else but still made the conscious decision to do it? Or perhaps felt you had little or no control to stop it?*
- *In what ways have you self-medicated through various aspects or parts of your life?*
- *What coping strategies have you developed to get through the complications of life?*

Sewing Shears

- *Is there a time that you needed help and didn't ask for it?*
  - *Or asked for it and didn't receive it?*
  - *Or asked for it and then received it?*
- *Are there patterns in your adult relationships or friendships that are molded by triggers from the past around acquiring help?*
- *In which areas do you currently recognize that you could benefit from support/help?*
  - *Physically*
  - *Spiritually*
  - *Mentally*
  - *Psychologically*
  - *Emotionally*

Chapter 11   Mother Issues

- *Have you ever tried your absolute best in a situation and still felt like you didn't meet the needs of the other party?*
- *Have you ever felt like the whole world was against you? Or that you were against the whole world?*
- *Are there times when you felt like the other person in a relationship (family, work, school, romance, etc.) was trying really hard to do the right thing but completely missed the mark, and you still harbored resentments toward them either in your childhood or adulthood?*

Chapter 12   Confrontation Reaps Turmoil

- *Have you ever felt so minuscule based on something you couldn't change about yourself? (Something as simple as having too many freckles? Having too thin or too thick hair? The wrong color eyes? The wrong body type? The wrong kind of clothes or style?)*
- *Have you ever made anyone else feel small for not being like you?*
- *Did you make amends and do your best to reconcile the situation or do healing with that person/group of people? Have you done spiritual or energetic work around that situation?*

All Boys, All the Time

- *Have you ever had that one friend who was able to help you through a really hard time?*
- *Do you ever wonder if that person knows how much they helped you?*
- *Have you reached out or told them?*

Birthday Trouble

- *Have you ever had a situation that you couldn't control that felt absolutely unfair, unjust, or wrong and had no way to voice your concerns?*
- *Did that make you feel trapped, or were you able to learn mechanisms for releasing that and flying free like a bird that's let out of its cage? Or...*
  - *Did you stay stuck in that cage? How did that make you feel?*
  - *Are there patterns from your childhood around hopelessness or feeling loss that you still carry today in certain situations that arise?*

Pain Rises to the Surface

- *Have you ever done something that you didn't share with anyone for an extended period of time?*
- *How did holding on to that secret make you feel? (Did you feel heavy, dark, closed off, or living in fear that someone might find out?)*
- *Have you recognized that the more secretive you were, the more you thought other people might be secretive and hiding things from you?*
- *Did the secrets eat away at you until eventually you let them out, or did they no longer have a hold on you, thus enabling you to release them?*
- *How do you deal with secrets that other people share with you? Do they put a heaviness onto your shoulders or onto your heart?*
- *Do you ever have an "odd feeling" like things happened that you don't remember or that other people know things you don't know? Like there might be secrets buried in your subconscious that your family hasn't shared with you, but that might be impacting how you interact with the world day-to-day?*

Chapter 13   Living with Dad

- *Do you ever assume you know what someone's thinking without asking them?*
- *Do you presume that simply by someone's actions, or lack of actions, it means something about you or who you are as a person?*
- *Did/have you questioned them or tried to create a conversation around it?*
- *Have you ever been unable to express how you truly feel in a situation, and someone has misread or misinterpreted your intention?*
- *Were there things your parents didn't do for you growing up that would have been beneficial to you as an adult?*
- *Were your parents able to show up for you not just in the physical sense but also emotionally and build a connection with you about your emotions and feelings?*
- *How did your relationship with your father or father figure in your life sculpt your current relationships with males or other men in your life?*
- *How did your relationship with your mother or mother figure in your life sculpt your current relationships with females or other women in your life?*

Nashville, Tennessee

- *When you were little, did you ever wish for something so badly and then finally get it and be disappointed or end up feeling not as good as you thought you would?*
- *As an adult, have you ever received one of your dreams from when you were a child and realized it fell short of what you truly wanted as a kid or even as an adult? Did it not align with the vision of how you saw it coming to be?*
- *Did you have to do things you weren't proud of to achieve or obtain that dream? How do you feel about that now?*
- *Are you excited to have envisioned and had a dream come to fruition in your adult life?*
- *What dreams do you still have that you can bring to fruition?*
- *What do you hope achieving that dream will help you to feel?*

Consequences—More First Times

- *Are there areas in your life (currently or when you were young) where your thoughts and feelings don't/didn't align with societal norms?*
- *How did your first sexual experiences impact sexual orientation and behaviors as you reached adulthood and beyond?*

Freedom on Wheels

- *What in your life sculpted who you look up to and why you look up to them?*
- *What kind of influence do you believe you have on other people?*
- *Who influences you these days?*
- *Does likeability come into play when you feel influenced or are influencing others?*
- *How do you differentiate between control and influence?*

Work & Wheels

- *Has there ever been a person who has come into your life and lifted you up but at the same time brought you into experiences that tore you down?*
- *Have you been the person in someone's life who helped lift them out of the darkness only to somehow find yourself wrapped up in a whirlwind of negativity with that person?*
- *How do you differentiate between positive and negative relationships now?*

Intention

- *Growing up, did you ever get blamed for things you didn't do?*
- *If so, how do those situations play out now in your life when someone accuses you of something that you didn't do? How do you react?*
- *Are you quick to accuse other people of wrongdoings even if they haven't done anything wrong?*
- *How do you differentiate intuition from past traumas and triggers?*
- *Who has been an advocate for you at critical times in your life?*
- *Have you been an advocate for anyone to help them through a tough time?*

Chapter 14   The Pink Bath

- *What scars do you have on your body? How did they happen?*
- *What scars do you have on your heart? How did they happen?*
- *Have you done enough work to mend the emotional scars/trauma and heal them to prevent adulthood-triggered behaviors stemming from what happened in childhood?*
- *How do you acknowledge and prevent reactions to the past from creating a bigger scar or reopening old wounds?*

God's Adult Bookstore Message

- *Have you ever received a message at a time or place when you feel like you shouldn't have received the message?*
- *Have you ever had an unexpected gut feeling to go somewhere, say something, or show up in a certain way? Do you believe you were divinely guided there?*

Emancipation

- *Have you ever said or done anything that you can't take back but wish you could?*
- *How did you work through it? Who did you turn to for advice or help?*
- *Were you able to admit to yourself that you made a mistake immediately, or did it take a while to realize that mistakes were made on your part?*
- *How do you respond when someone else says or does something that you know they don't mean? Do you give them the benefit of the doubt, make up stories about why they might have said it, ask them directly and have a conversation, or use other techniques to break free from the entrapment of what other people say and do that hurts you?*

Chapter 15   The Airport

- *Have you ever had two family members or friends who didn't get along, and you were put in the middle of that situation?*
- *Maybe you are that friend or family member who didn't get along with another friend or family member, and there was a third party who was affected by it. How did that feel?*

- *How have you learned how to have healthier relationships and not triangulate situations as a control mechanism?*
- *When you were a child, did you ever see triangulation in your family or with groups of friends, and how is that played out in your adult life? Do you see those patterns arise when significantly triggered or upset with yourself, your spouse, or your friends or family?*

Jagged Edge

- *Two wrongs don't make a right, and two unhappy people don't make a happy relationship. Have you ever been in a relationship where both parties were unhappy? How did that transpire?*
- *What did you learn from that situation?*
- *How did you (will you) go from that unhealthy and unhappy relationship to a healthy and happy relationship?*

Big News

- *Did you see abusive types of relationships growing up with family or friends or your parents?*
- *Have you ever been in an addictive, abusive cycle?*
  - *If so, how did you get out of it?*
  - *How many cycles did you go through before you were able to break free? Why did you stay as long as you did?*
- *As an adult, if you notice that one of your friends or family members is in an abusive situation, do you call it out and help them get out of it? Do you ignore it?*

Mommy, I'm Gay or Bisexual or Whatever

- *Normal…?*
  - *What are social norms growing up that didn't feel good to you?*
  - *Gender norms that didn't feel good?*
  - *Religious norms that didn't feel good to you?*
  - *Just norms, in general, that didn't feel like they resonated with your heart or soul?*
- *As adults, how do we free ourselves from these societal norms and break free into our own essence?*

- *How do we express our own individuality in a positive way while still being welcomed into society?*

Chapter 16   I'm Coming Out Again

- *Answer this in a virtual or physical journal: If someone gave you an assignment to share your truth, what would you share?*
- *With whom do you need to share this?*
- *How would it make you feel if you didn't keep this to yourself anymore?*

Need to Know for Sure

- *When do people push your buttons now? How do you react? Do you call them out? Do you simply sit back and not say anything and keep your cool?*
- *If you notice you're pushing people's buttons, how do you work through that to get to a healthy place where both people in the relationship feel good about it?*
- *Have you ever been friends with someone or dated someone who you knew wasn't good for you? Did you stay because you didn't want to be alone?*
- *Have you seen these behaviors in those around you? Either growing up or currently?*
- *How does codependency take form in your life?*
  - *With people?*
  - *With food?*
  - *With substances?*
  - *Within situations?*

Chapter 17   Here We Go Again

- *When you find yourself in a deep hole, how do you dig yourself out?*
  - *Do you ask for help?*
  - *Do you expect other people to intuitively know to pull you out?*
  - *Do you lay in the ditch and cry?*
  - *When do you decide to try to climb up the side of it, digging your fingernails into the dirt and mud?*

- *How do you know when to help others when you can see that they are struggling?*
- *How do you lend them a hand without doing all the work for them?*
  - *Or do you swoop in like a superhero and do everything?*
- *Where have you seen all these behaviors modeled in your life?*

Out of Control

- *Have you ever been wildly out of control?*
- *How did you reign it in? How did you regain control of your life?*
- *Have you seen other people around you spiral out of control?*
  - *Did you step in and intervene?*
  - *Did they ask for help?*
  - *Did they ever get the help they needed?*
  - *Do they talk about it openly and with authenticity? Or keep it hidden?*
- *Do you share stories about your struggles and spirals?*

EXERCISES

Chapter 18   To Heroin or Not to Heroin

Write down four things you saw as struggles (negative, caused hardship) but turned out to be blessings.

- What did you learn?
- What pain did you avoid in the future because of something that happened earlier?
- What person did you meet or skill did you learn that turned out to be helpful later on?
- What revelations did you have by coming through a challenge that helped you teach others or bring more blessings on you and your family ultimately?

Going forward, using a journal or any pad of paper, write down your struggles as they come up and leave room to go back and re-evaluate them in regular increments (30 days, 60 days, each quarter, each year.)

- How many of your challenges have you later determined were there as messages/blessings/gifts?
- What lessons did you learn that you can now use to inspire, lead, teach, and help others?

Chapter 19   Trippin' and Rippin'

If you'd like to start understanding your body's connection to the energy of the Earth and open yourself to clearing out any negative energy that may be causing distress or illness in your body, you may consider beginning a meditation practice. I have several free meditations and links to various resources on my website at www.ryanjosephallen.com or www.mydrugdealerbrought metogod.com.

Included is a page for you to write down your experiences that may seem other-worldly, godly, angel-like, messages from loved ones, etc. Once these visions and messages start being collected in one place, you will find yourself at peace knowing that we are all part of a much bigger picture, and everything and everyone has a purpose.

Include your thoughts; what you know to be true in your heart.

_____

_____

_____

_____

What would you do if none of the voices of judgment were in your head?

_____

_____

_____

_____

If money wasn't an obstacle, what would you want to accomplish, create?

_____

_____

_____

_____

What does your intuition tell you about what you were meant to do and be here on Earth?

_____

_____

_____

_____

Chapter 20   Evanescence

A few lined pages and questions follow. These are meant for you to combat your past by writing the actions you have taken that have created an energetic toll on your body, mind, and spirit, as well as on the people around you. Once you've put them into writing, you can examine them and begin healing. You can even rip them right of this workbook (or print them off) and burn them outside to fully release them.

Write about the things you do to make yourself sick or abuse your own body or mind.

_____

_____

_____

_____

Make a list of the things you regret doing because other people persuaded you to. Especially note down if this action went against your better instincts/gut.

_____

_____

_____

_____

What is blocking you from achieving everything you could ever want? Why can't you let it go?

_____

_____

_____

_____

Some people feel that they can better express themselves through artistic immersion. If so, perhaps you can make a list of what songs, movies, podcasts, or writings move you. What expresses who you are/how you feel?

_____

_____

_____

_____

If you could write (or film) a song/poem/story what would you include? Why?

_____

_____

_____

_____

If someone was going to write your life story or a memoir about a significant part of your life, what would they include? What would they possibly learn from that set of experiences?

_____

_____

_____

_____

Chapter 21 Rebooting

Mother Mary Healing Meditation

Use this worksheet to write down affirmations you would like to repeat to keep your energy focused on what you want to welcome into your life. Examples: I love myself. I am perfect, just the way I am. I choose to put healthy, life-sustaining foods into my body. God loves me. I am full of love and light. I am a beacon of the divine's love. I am strong mentally and physically. I am beautiful just the way I am. I AM, I AM.

_____

_____

_____

_____

Chapter 22 Getting Back on the Right Path

When is the last time you checked in with yourself? What is your motivation for wanting to change your life or habits?

_____

_____

_____

_____

How will you set up a routine or reminder to check in with yourself regularly? Write your commitment to do so here.

_____

_____

_____

_____

What signs have you witnessed in your life that led to good decision-making?

_____

_____

_____

_____

What signs have you missed or ignored that led to negative situations?

_____

_____

_____

_____

What negative habits do you have that make you feel shame after indulging?

_____

_____

_____

_____

Do any single habits lead to a pattern of troublesome behaviors?

_____

_____

_____

_____

What healthy resources do you have in your life to get you back on your intentional path? Social, physical, emotional, spiritual, financial, educational, etc. Write those contacts here:

_____

_____

_____

_____

Chapter 23   School of Metaphysics

When have you found yourself someplace that you felt compelled to go despite everything else going on around you, and it turned out to be a significant experience in your life?

_____

_____

_____

_____

Why was it significant? Was it someone you met? Something you learned? Something you received, saw, or heard that was used to help you achieve your mission in life?

_____

_____

_____

_____

Will you take what you learned and share it with other people? If so, how and when? And it may help you to include a list of who you want to share with as well.

_____

_____

_____

_____

Chapter 24   Joey

What are your life priorities? Do the people you care about know and recognize/honor them?

_____

_____

_____

_____

How do you include self-care into those priorities?

_____

_____

_____

_____

What have you learned from the significant relationships in your life? What have they taught you about trust, boundaries, past triggers, and current triggers?

_____

_____

_____

_____

Chapter 25   Education/Cultivating My Own Style

Who do you think would benefit from hearing your story? Are there lessons you've learned or cautionary advice you can offer that could help others? How might you go about doing that?

_____

_____

_____

_____

Chapter 26   Recovery from Addiction

What can you not live without in your day-to-day life? If you were heading for a castle on your own island for a year, what would you insist be included in the supply list? Are the items on that list good for you? Healthy for your mind and body? If not, can you begin a program to reduce the need for these things in your life?

_____

_____

_____

For fun, make a list of what you would bring in your single suitcase for one year and why. Then review the list every six months or so and evaluate if those same things are still important to you.

_____

_____

_____

_____

_____

What do you struggle with?

- What would your life be like if you didn't struggle with that anymore?
- Do you have a plan to control this? Who could help you?
- Have you identified enablers that facilitate your indulgences?

_____

_____

_____

_____

Chapter 27   Perfectly Imperfect

A) Pick one area for self-improvement and make a list of five steps you can take in the next 30-60 days to reach your goal(s).

B) Reread this list every day and, when you finally reach your goals, rework your list and continue.

To help you start your list:

What are you already pretty good at?

_____

_____

_____

_____

What area of your life would you like to improve upon?

_____

_____

_____

_____

What does "being the best" in that area realistically look like for you?

_____

_____

_____

_____

Chapter 28   Safe Haven 2015

I have found that there is nothing that makes me feel better about my purpose on Earth than knowing I've made a difference. Here are some small ways to make a big difference in your community, family, and life. These are just meant to inspire your thinking process. Feel free to expand as much as you like!

_____

_____

_____

_____

What in your life brings you down? Is there a perspective shift that can make you think of that in a different way to bring you a more positive outlook?

_____

_____

_____

_____

What program or event has impacted you in a meaningful way?

_____

_____

_____

_____

Did you thank the person/people who put that together and/or brought it to you?

_____

_____

_____

_____

Make a list of people you may want to thank for the positive impact they've had on your life. Doing so will improve their lives immeasurably.

_____

_____

_____

_____

Thank a sponsor of an event and patronize their business in some way so they will be inclined to continue offering support for the organizations that mean something to the people in your community.

_____

_____

_____

_____

Who have you supported or listened to this week? Ask yourself that question each week.

_____

_____

_____

_____

Who listened to or supported you? Did you remember to say thank you and show your appreciation?

_____

_____

_____

_____

Chapter 30   Falling for a Married Man

What do you feel you need to do or learn before you can be fully present in a relationship? If you're not there yet, perhaps you want to make a checklist here of things you plan to achieve/accomplish so you are ready when love shows up for you.

_____

_____

_____

_____

Chapter 31   Intention of Beliefs

How can you expand your understanding of other people? How can you help others understand you?

Make a commitment to try something new with someone not in your regular circle within the next sixty days or so. And then invite a new face to join you for your family customs and celebrations.

Suggestions:

- Attend an event from a different culture or religion, perhaps a Jewish Seder or Hanukkah menorah lighting or an Indian wedding or a Native American sweat lodge or French Bastille Days or Mexican Day of the Dead, a Brazilian or New Orleans Mardi Gras/Carnevale or Italian Feast of San Gennaro, etc.

- Volunteer at an event at a group home for Down syndrome adults or Alzheimer's/dementia residents in memory care or homeless veterans.
- Attend a festival that celebrates a culture or heritage other than your own. Pride festivals, Chinese New Year, Puerto Rican Culture Celebration, Juneteenth, etc.

_____

_____

_____

_____

Message from Beyond

What memories are you contributing to your loved ones' memory banks?

_____

_____

_____

_____

What small pleasures do you find in your day-to-day life? Do you take the time to appreciate them and add them to your memory bank?

_____

_____

_____

_____

What can you add to your plans to increase the number of positive memories for yourself and your family and loved ones?

_____

_____

_____

_____

Learning from Each Experience
- What have you learned from your last or most recent relationship?
- What do you think you have taught people in your life?
- What would you like people to say about you after they've gotten to know you?
- Do your current behaviors reflect that?
- If you're not sure, ask three people who know you to describe you in three sentences. What have you learned from their answers?

_____

_____

_____

_____

Golden Rule with a Caveat
Make of list something you will do to treat yourself well, give yourself respect and love, every week for the next twelve weeks. I've started with some things my friends said they do and hope that you will add your own to the list.

Suggestions:
- Take twenty minutes to meditate in the morning
- Turn off media, phone, and family for thirty minutes to enjoy a warm beverage and look at a pleasant view/pictures
- Take a run or walk in nature
- Go to a flower market and just stand there, breathe in and smell, and look at all the glorious selections. If you're feeling generous, buy yourself a flower or two. If you're broke, wait until the market ends and look for someone who wants to give away what they didn't sell!
- Get a snorkel mask and go for a swim and listen to the sounds of your heart

- Bake or cook something you love
- Call a friend you miss talking to
- Take a drive to a peaceful spot and just sit and be still
- Pamper yourself with something good for you that you don't often allow yourself (massage, facial, manicure/pedicure, wax, hot shave)
- Record a journal entry on your phone
- Write a letter or card to someone
- Confess your darkest secret onto a page and then burn it
- Ask a friend if you can take their dog for a walk
- Eat a treat/snack you loved as a child
- Tell someone you forgive them
- Tell someone you're sorry

Your list?

_____

_____

_____

_____

_____

_____

Chapter 32   Multi-faith

What part of your story might help someone else to make a decision, learn something new, change perspective? We all have a story to tell. Where will you share yours? Make a plan to share your story sometime before the end of the year. Write down the story points here and the lessons you think people will get, and then come back to write how you felt after the experience of sharing.

_____

_____

_____

_____

_____

_____

Chapter 33   Hearts & Hugs in Orlando

One of the greatest gifts we can offer to people that costs us nothing but time and attention is to listen and let someone unburden. You don't have to agree with them. You don't have to offer help. Make a commitment to help someone by listening. Maybe just once, maybe once a week, maybe once a day, or more often if you find it lifts your spirits and makes you feel great too.

Using supportive statements when listening to someone who needs to share is a great way to help your community and family. Supportive statements don't offer advice, critique the problem/person, nor put anyone down. They let someone know you care and that your opinion of them hasn't changed just because of the challenge ahead.

Offering to listen, empathizing that a problem sounds challenging or hard to handle or you can understand why they would be upset, and affirming that you see why this seems like a problem is being supportive.

Then you can talk about how it would make you feel in the same situation. Is the situation one that you would struggle with as well? Would it make you angry or sad or scared? Does it seem like a difficult situation that would challenge anyone in a similar place?

Even something as simple as recognizing and empathizing that you're sorry that they are going through this, and thanking them for trusting you with the information is vital in healing and being heard. Then offering support in a way that you can healthily offer. Let them know that you admire them.

Chapter 34   Dr. Allen, I Presume

Commit to including educational experiences into your life to enhance your mind, reduce the risk of dementia, feel stimulated, and get your happy on.

- I challenge you, especially if books aren't your thing, to watch an informative TEDTalk. They are highly impactful, short in duration, and helpful videos and podcasts. You can find tens of thousands of them on YouTube, TED app, and through your favorite search engine.

- Maybe go to a museum.
- Write a story or paint a picture or play an instrument.
- Learn to sail or drive a race car or ride a horse.
- Make your own fishing lure.
- Plant a tabletop or herb garden.
- Go outside and explore a park or waterway.
- Learn how to build a campfire like you've always wanted.
- Learn how to camp and go on an adventure.
- Learn to make something you've always wanted to make.

Make a commitment to stimulate your brain by learning something new. Write a list of things you'd like to learn about, things that inspire your curiosity, and then set a goal for when you might start exploring one or two of them.

_____

_____

_____

_____

Write here how you feel about what you have learned and how it has impacted your life. When you finish with one area, set a goal to complete another! Or revisit areas after some time goes by to see what has possibly changed since the initial learning opportunity?

_____

_____

_____

_____

Chapter 37   Next Generation

What "You Must…" rules have you questioned? Are your questions coming from your heart and innate sense of right and wrong, or does your questioning come from lack or perhaps a desire for more—money, things, time?

Write down the things you question and listen to your heart for the answers.

_____

_____

_____

_____

Tenfold Return Challenge

"I ask and receive a tenfold return on this _____ for the goodness of all concerned."

Day	First Day: ___/___/___ Making this contribution makes me feel…	Name: I received/noticed the following…
1		
2		
3		
4		
5		
6		
7		
8		
9		
10		
11		
12		
13		
14		
15		
16		
17		
18		
19		
20		

21		
22		
23		
24		
25		
26		
27		
28		
29		
30		
31		

NOTES AND COMMITMENTS:

_____

_____

_____

_____

_____

_____

_____

_____

_____

_____

_____

_____

_____

_____

_____

_____

_____

_____

_____

Closing Healing Affirmation:
I am constantly and consistently learning and growing from
the vast experiences in my life. My journey is full of gratitude,
grace, forgiveness, hope, faith, and ultimately love.
I am LOVE!